PRAISE FOR *BEING PRIME MINISTER*

Each of the remarkable people who have occupied Canada's highest office are brought vividly to life on the pages of this immensely readable book. A super fun and worthwhile read.

— *Senator Linda Frum*

With lively anecdotes and thoughtful insights, Stewart reminds us that there are human beings behind the headlines. This absorbing and original book explores aspects of political life that are too often ignored.

— *Charlotte Gray,*
author of The Promise of Canada

Bursts with details and anecdotes on the daily lives of the very human men and woman who have led us. A trove of trivia treasures.

— *John Ibbitson,*
Globe and Mail *journalist and author of* Stephen Harper

A valuable and insightful look at the triumphs, trials, and tribulations of the people who have held the highest office in the land. A must read for anyone who wants a better understanding of what it takes to lead our country.

— *Don Newman,*
retired senior parliamentary editor for CBC Television

A fun and fascinating book that reminds us that prime ministers are human, each with unique strengths, quirks, and foibles. Well researched, crisply written, and refreshingly non-partisan, it is immensely enjoyable, gossipy, heartwarming.

— *John Boyko,*
author of Cold Fire

BEING PRIME MINISTER

BEING
PRIME
MINISTER

J.D.M. STEWART

DUNDURN
TORONTO

Cover design: Laura Boyle
Cover image: istock.com/CSA-Printstock
Printer: Webcom

Library and Archives Canada Cataloguing in Publication

Stewart, J. D. M., author
    Being prime minister / J.D.M. Stewart.

Includes bibliographical references and index.
Issued in print and electronic formats.
ISBN 978-1-4597-3848-5 (softcover).--ISBN 978-1-4597-3849-2 (PDF).--
ISBN 978-1-4597-3850-8 (EPUB)

    1. Prime ministers--Canada--Biography. 2. Prime ministers--
Canada. I. Title.

FC26.P7S74 2018   971.05092'2   C2018-901298-6
                                              C2018-901299-4

1 2 3 4 5   22 21 20 19 18

We acknowledge the support of the **Canada Council for the Arts**, which last year invested $153 million to bring the arts to Canadians throughout the country, and the **Ontario Arts Council** for our publishing program. We also acknowledge the financial support of the **Government of Ontario**, through the **Ontario Book Publishing Tax Credit** and the **Ontario Media Development Corporation**, and the **Government of Canada**.

Nous remercions le **Conseil des arts du Canada** de son soutien. L'an dernier, le Conseil a investi 153 millions de dollars pour mettre de l'art dans la vie des Canadiennes et des Canadiens de tout le pays.

Care has been taken to trace the ownership of copyright material used in this book. The author and the publisher welcome any information enabling them to rectify any references or credits in subsequent editions.
— *J. Kirk Howard, President*

The publisher is not responsible for websites or their content unless they are owned by the publisher.

Printed and bound in Canada.

VISIT US AT

dundurn.com | @dundurnpress | dundurnpress | dundurnpress

Dundurn
3 Church Street, Suite 500
Toronto, Ontario, Canada
M5E 1M2

For my students, past, present, and future

CONTENTS

The Prime Ministers
of Canada

PRIME MINISTER	POLITICAL PARTY	DATES IN OFFICE
Sir John A. Macdonald	Conservative	1867–73; 1878–91
Alexander Mackenzie	Liberal	1873–78
Sir John J.C. Abbott	Conservative	1891–92
Sir John S.D. Thompson	Conservative	1892–94
Sir Mackenzie Bowell	Conservative	1894–96
Sir Charles Tupper	Conservative	1896
Sir Wilfrid Laurier	Liberal	1896–1911
Sir Robert L. Borden	Conservative/Union	1911–20
Arthur Meighen	Conservative	1920–21; 1926
W.L.M. King	Liberal	1921–26; 1926–30; 1935–48
R.B. Bennett	Conservative	1930–35
Louis St. Laurent	Liberal	1948–57
John Diefenbaker	Progressive Conservative	1957–63
Lester B. Pearson	Liberal	1963–68
Pierre Trudeau	Liberal	1968–79; 1980–84
Joe Clark	Progressive Conservative	1979–80
John Turner	Liberal	1984
Brian Mulroney	Progressive Conservative	1984–93
Kim Campbell	Progressive Conservative	1993
Jean Chrétien	Liberal	1993–2003
Paul Martin	Liberal	2003–6
Stephen Harper	Conservative	2006–15
Justin Trudeau	Liberal	2015–

INTRODUCTION

Who is the prime minister of Canada? Politically, he or she is a member of Parliament and leader of the Government of Canada. In the past, the occupant of this position has been described as "first among equals" in relation to the Cabinet he leads, but in practice the PM is, by far, the most powerful figure in Canadian politics. This is despite the fact that the prime minister has no formal constitutional power. As the late political scientist and McGill University professor J.R. Mallory noted in his 1984 book, *The Structure of Canadian Government*: "The office of prime minister, the most important single office in the government, is, while not unknown to the law, entirely lacking in a legal definition of its powers."

Unlike the president of the United States, whose powers are specifically spelled out in that country's Constitution, the prime minister has no clearly defined constitutional authority; and yet the PM has enormous control over the government in Canada. He appoints and directs the Cabinet, which is at the heart of the executive branch; leads the direction of the government in the House of Commons (the legislative branch) and outside of it; and appoints justices to the court system, including the Supreme Court (Stephen Harper appointed eight), part of the judicial branch. He also effectively appoints the governor general, senators, heads of the military, deputy ministers, and ambassadors; the prime minister is also the country's leader in its foreign relations, notably with the United States, and also represents the country at numerous international summits and organizations such as NATO or the U.N. He or she is the national and global face of the government and country, and as such is the single most important figure in Canadian politics. In addition to all of that, the PM leads a national political party. As Brian Mulroney once noted, "The traditional definition of the prime minister's role as *primus inter pares* is, in reality, on a daily basis significantly understated."[1]

But how well do we know our prime ministers? How well do we understand the nature of the job? "It's never easy to be prime minister," Jean Chrétien once wrote, years before he took the keys to 24 Sussex Drive. "He has to hurt the feelings of a lot of people on a regular basis; he has to operate in the public eye with MPs who fret and bureaucrats who gossip and colleagues who disagree." The prime minister may have to do more than hurt people's feelings. He may send troops to war or make policy decisions that hurt some people economically. His decisions are always bound to upset someone.

As the head of the government and the biggest star on our political stage, the prime minister is always in the spotlight. He has the power to lead the country where he wants. "You can make a difference in what is happening," Jean Chrétien told me.

"When you're prime minister you can make a decision that does more good in five minutes — something that would take you five months to work on when you're not in government," reflected Paul Martin on the abilities a PM has to effect change.[2] When Louis St. Laurent was asked about what pleasures he took from the job, he struck a similar note: "I suppose the principal compensation is the illusion, perhaps, but nevertheless the satisfaction of feeling that he has been useful."

Clearly, the prime minister is an instrument of power. But what else is there to the country's highest position of leadership, and what do we know about the people who have served in that role? That is the question that this book attempts to answer. Bruce Hutchison, the venerated Canadian journalist, put it well in his 1965 book, *Mr. Prime Minister*, a survey of the country's leaders. In pondering the future of Canada, Hutchison suggests that former and future Canadian prime ministers "must see that the great imponderable is not economic, financial, or legislative but emotional, psychic, human. It therefore centres in the prime minister not as a constitutional instrument but as a human being."

Focusing also on that human dimension — and perhaps the exigencies of the job — Lester Pearson remarked, "Prime ministers require the hide of a rhinoceros, the morals of St. Francis, the patience of Job, the wisdom of Solomon, the strength of Hercules, the leadership of Napoleon, the magnetism of a Beatle and the subtlety of Machiavelli."

Being Prime Minister peels back the curtain to allow the reader to see our former leaders in ways that no single book has before. How did they travel? What pets did they have? How did they treat others? What was life like at home? What were their pastimes?

Those who love history often love it because of the small anecdotes that entertain or reveal character. This was something historian Barbara Tuchman called "history by the ounce" — little stories that illuminate. Through anecdotes about the lives of prime ministers while in office, readers will see these twenty-two men and one woman in a new light. They will see them as humorous and hard-working, vain and vulnerable, riled and relaxed. They will see not only what animated Canada's prime ministers when they were not sunk in briefing books, but also how the office of prime minister has changed by exploring it through lenses such as security, travel, and daily routines. Readers will see how our PMs worked, as well as the toll exacted by the stress of being the leader of Canada.

Canadians have always had an interest in the lives of their country's prime ministers. Magazines and newspapers have regularly run features and rankings about them. Books — and there have been many — whether they chronicle all PMs, such as Jack Granatstein and Norman Hillmer's 1999 book, *Prime Ministers: Ranking Canada's Leaders*, or focus on a single prime minister, such as John Ibbitson's 2015 biography of Stephen Harper, are bestsellers. National conversation fixates on the PM. What is more, in an age where increasing attention is paid to celebrities, it is little wonder that the most important political figure in the country receives more scrutiny than ever — something leveraged well by the current prime minister, Justin Trudeau.

The office of prime minister has changed, and the experiences of those who occupy it have also changed since 1867, when Sir John A. Macdonald became Canada's first PM. He handled his own correspondence, he had no security detail, and did not have to deal much with a prying media or the demands of thirty-six million Canadians. His travel was limited, and he made just one cross-country trip. Justin Trudeau, 150 years later, has a small army of people working for him to allow him to execute the powers of his office; travels on almost a weekly basis, visiting places across Canada and around the world; and has numerous files to track in a Cabinet of more than thirty ministries (Macdonald had fifteen). Indeed, the PM of our time suffers from an "overload" problem because of the amount of work and attention demanded by the job.

Despite differences in historical contexts, our prime ministers are all linked by the nature of the office. The former prime ministers still living (and I interviewed six of the seven) are well aware of those who came before them. In 1999 Jean Chrétien told me he often thought about how Wilfrid Laurier might handle one situation or another. Brian Mulroney wrote in his memoirs that "sometimes in Cabinet, when I'm having a particularly difficult time of it, I glance at the painting of Sir John A. that faces me and wonder what that wise old head would suggest I do. Sir John and all his successors as prime minister have known moments of great sadness and personal defeat." Mulroney's comments hint at the emotional, personal side that Hutchison spoke of.

Canadians are quick to criticize a prime minister for his policies and often conflate the political with the personal. That's politics. But when you go behind the scenes of this most important job, you see that there is a fascinating and human element to being prime minister. You see individuals with an incredible capacity for work, a deep sense of commitment to making Canada a better place, and varying aptitudes for managing people and circumstances. You also realize that when you strip away the trappings of power and get to the people, under the cloak of authority is a familiar humanity. "We're human, we're families," Joe Clark told me. This book chronicles some of the personal and private aspects of the lives of prime ministers as well as the nature of the position. "It's not a perfect job," Pierre Trudeau once said of being prime minister, "but it sure beats working."

Chapter 1

"Keep a Cheerful Mind": A Day in the Life of a Prime Minister

> The in-tray of a prime minister is never empty and phones are never silent.
>
> — Brian Mulroney, *Memoirs*

MORNING
6:30 a.m. — 24 Sussex Drive, Ottawa

Prime Minister Brian Mulroney wakes up at 6:30 a.m. and heads to his dressing room to scan the day's headlines. After a quick look at newspapers from both English and French Canada, he heads to the shower to get ready for another day leading the country. Although there is an agenda for the prime minister, exactly how the day will unfold is anyone's guess. As Mulroney notes, "There is no such thing as a 'typical day' in the life of the prime minister." One thing is certain: There will be no minute unaccounted for and the day will be long.

By 7:15 a.m. the prime minister's children are up and join him for the usual family breakfast featuring a level of chaos any working family in Canada would know well. Mulroney has four children and they all need to get to school and, because it is winter and this is Ottawa, there is a "scramble for school books and mittens." Once they safely depart, the prime minister makes a quick call to Paul Tellier, the Clerk of the Privy Council, the government's top civil servant, or Stanley Hartt, his chief of staff, or, possibly, to Donald Mazankowski, the deputy prime minister and Mulroney's trusted confidant. It's cold outside, but things are just warming up for the PM.

By 8:50 a.m. Mulroney says goodbye to his wife, Mila, and heads out the door of 24 Sussex Drive to the waiting motorcade. Escorted by a convoy of three cars driven by his RCMP security detail, the prime minister makes the short trip from his official residence to his third-floor office in the Centre Block of Canada's Parliament Buildings. In Room 311-S the business of running the country will begin in earnest.

What is a day like in the life of a prime minister? As Mulroney recalled, there is no typical day. But themes do emerge. The hours are long but rarely dull; the work is hard but satisfying; the demands on the PM's time are endless but necessarily come to a conclusion; and there are a great number of people whose job it is to help the country's leader manage it all.

At least, that is the case now. In the early days of Canada's prime ministers there was no such thing as an entourage or even an official Prime Minister's Office. As Canada changed and grew, both in population and geography, the job of the prime minister became more complex. Think about it: when Sir John A. Macdonald became prime minister in 1867, the Dominion of Canada, as it was called, consisted of four small provinces and 3.4 million people. Justin Trudeau, in 2018, is the PM for ten provinces, three territories, and thirty-six million citizens. Despite the differences between 1867 and today, the job has always been a busy one, and Canadians have always wanted to feel close to their prime minister.

This chapter will explore how the country's leaders have structured their days, from the importance of handling their correspondence — a huge part of their day, particularly for earlier prime ministers — to attending Parliament and greeting guests. This is their life in Ottawa, where the PM is at the centre of all political activity and the focus of media scrutiny.

Sir John A. Macdonald's day shared only a few similarities with that of Brian Mulroney or that of Justin Trudeau. Canada's first prime minister awoke around 9:00 a.m. at Earnscliffe, his home overlooking the Ottawa River — a house located just a few doors down from 24 Sussex Drive, now the residence for the British high commissioner — and had a cup of tea. He got dressed and headed downstairs to his office, which he referred to as his "workshop." The only person permitted to enter there without being announced was his secretary. Macdonald even had a secret door installed so he could evade any unwanted visitors.

As with all prime ministers who followed him, Macdonald spent time each morning reading the morning newspapers, but rather than head off to his office in the East Block of Parliament, he continued to work from home and began to tackle his correspondence. It is here that we see a significant difference between his habits and those of our more modern PMs: while today's prime ministers have a large staff dedicated to dealing with the voluminous amounts of correspondence that is received daily, John A. Macdonald, like a number of his successors, handled his letters on his own. He answered virtually all of his letters by himself and by hand (by the late 1880s Macdonald would allow the typewriter for routine correspondence and more letters were dictated). Most of this correspondence dealt with policy, patronage (i.e., political appointments), or other political matters.[1] Ordinary Canadians also wrote to him.

Compare all of that to today. Millions of Canadians take the time to write to the prime minister, either by letter or email. In fact, in 2005–2006, prime ministers Paul Martin and Stephen Harper received more than two million pieces of correspondence. This number has only grown as more and more people have email. But the chances that any of this gets

During Sir John A. Macdonald's time, the prime minister dealt with his correspondence on his own and sittings of the House of Commons often lasted until late into
the evening. Macdonald had a Cabinet of fifteen while Justin Trudeau's Cabinet has
thirty members.

read by the PM are slim to none. Unlike the mail of VIPs, ordinary correspondence from average Canadians gets handled by the Correspondence
Office of the Prime Minister and a form letter is sent out. Even those letters with a wonderful signature from the prime minister in bold blue ink
are unlikely to have been signed by the PM; the signature is more likely
to be the product of an automated machine — known as "PM2." This
machine actually holds a real pen to sign his name and is kept under lock
and key. But your letters are rarely, if ever, read by the PM.[2]

All of this is so different from the quaint Canada of Sir John A.
Macdonald, who routinely fielded correspondence from citizens writing about strangers in their town or even about mathematical problems. But Canada was a much smaller place then and, as Richard Gwyn
writes in his 2012 biography of Macdonald, "in a country where the
people across its expanse had little in common, Macdonald belonged
to everyone. He was both their leader and their friend."

Correspondence was similar for Wilfrid Laurier, who received more
than his share of unusual letters, in addition to those about the serious
matters of politics and patronage. A number of young people who had
the same first name as the prime minister wrote to him to remind
him of that treasured association. If the prime minister responded, the
letter would be duly noted in the local newspaper, which would only
encourage more people to write to Laurier in the hopes of receiving a
response. "The first citizen of a great country like Canada cannot spend
hours answering all the letters which come to him from juveniles who
happen to boast of the name of 'Wilfrid,'" noted a 1909 magazine article. "He would have no time left for the affairs of state."[3]

A detailed 1946 article from *Maclean's* magazine tells us just how
important correspondence was when times were different and volume
made it more manageable. For Prime Minister William Lyon Mackenzie
King and his office, letters consumed a sizeable chunk of time. It was
the first order of business in his working day. King received about one
thousand letters a week: mail of all sorts from a range of people across the
country. And the rule in King's office was that each letter must receive a

reply within twenty-four hours of its reception.* Much like the way people feel about sending emails today, King said, "Nothing annoys people more than not knowing whether their letter has arrived." Letters or postcards that came as a part of an obvious awareness campaign were exempt from this rule. "But the ordinary mail is all answered, and it covers an amazing amount of territory — pleas for jobs, favours, permits, priorities, and, of course, any amount of free advice." The tone of letters ranged from complimentary to nasty. One correspondent with King kept writing the "kind of letter Frank Sinatra gets from his bobby-sox admirers."

Rather than using the PM2 — the autopen — King's secretaries signed 90 percent of these letters, while he would receive a report on the topics about which people were writing to him. The one hundred or so letters that did make it through to the PM were from VIPs such as provincial premiers, Cabinet ministers, or communications of a private nature from friends or family. These always went to the prime minister unopened. The correspondence clerks got so adept at their job that they were able to sort through all of King's mail, pulling the personal and VIP letters without having to open them first.

Some mail may have been better left unopened, at least for R.B. Bennett, King's successor and prime minister during the first half of the Great Depression. Like most of the other PMs before him, he was an early riser — his days usually began about 7:00 a.m. and often lasted well past midnight. And he was a prolific correspondent. As the leader of the country during its worst economic times, Bennett, who was independently wealthy, received letters from many people seeking help. And the letters were heartbreaking:

CANTAL SASK
Aug 15/35

Mr. Bennett I am a mother left with a little girl 1 year old, and I have nothing, and I am badly in need and unable to work

And as Winter is coming on, and my baby needs

---

* King received thousands of birthday cards and he always insisted that each of those were answered, driving his small staff just a little crazy.

everything, I have no warm cloths either, but I think of my baby first.

I was told you would help, so I thought I would write for babys sake. Mr. Bennett I'd be very grateful if you could send me some money

Yours Very Truly
Ellen Field

Bennett sent $5 in his reply, as he often did to letters of this type.

Another letter came from an eight-year-old boy who wrote to the prime minister to say he "wanted a little red wagon to hich my dog to for so many years, but daddy has no money. Please Mr. Bennett would you send me enuff money to buy my wagon. Thank you so much."

Bennett replied with a contribution and received a letter of thanks from the boy with the postscript that he was "going to vote for you when I get to be a big boy."

Other letters were less cordial:

May 20/31

Mr. Bennette

Since you have been elected, work has been impossible to get. We have decided that in a month from this date, if thing's are the same, We'll skin you alive, the first chance we get

Sudbury Starving Unemployed

The letter does not appear to have received a response.

John Diefenbaker was also deluged with correspondence. "After lagging behind singer Paul Anka for a while, Prime Minister John Diefenbaker is now firmly in the lead as Canada's No. 1 pen pal and target for autograph seekers," wrote Klaus Neumann in *Maclean's* in 1958.

The Chief received up to nine hundred letters per week, many asking for signed pictures. Diefenbaker loved children, and after young people visited his office he would instruct his personal secretary to write to them and send along photographs. But there were numerous other requests, some on the strange side. One letter came from three women in Togo (then called Togoland) asking for training as midwives. One Indigenous woman wrote to Diefenbaker and continually sent him homemade candy. Before he went on a worldwide trip in 1958, she sent him a collection of Indigenous remedies and herbs to take along with him.[4]

Dief loved these epistolary relationships and was dictating — rather than writing his own as Macdonald and Laurier did for many of their letters — up to sixty replies a day. Not everything got his undivided attention, though.* Marjorie (Bunny) Pound, his secretary, wrote letters on his behalf to his mother and brother. The PM just signed them without reading their contents.

Lester Pearson, Diefenbaker's successor, loved his mail, too. He was very interested in his correspondence and wanted to know what Canadians thought. He often brought mail with him to caucus meetings in support of a point he was trying to make. As Liberal MP John Ross Matheson wrote, Pearson's "humanity was so apparent and so real that large segments of the Canadian population felt that they could communicate directly with him. The masses of letters that were received by him in Parliament confirmed how generally accessible citizens and even outsiders believed him to be."

In one example, Stuart MacKay, an eleven-year-old Nova Scotia boy, wrote to the prime minister on April 11, 1965, to take issue with Pearson's opinion of a couple of NHL hockey players, as expressed on the previous night's televised game. "It said that you thought Red Kelly**

---

* Diefenbaker was notorious for losing important papers, including an invitation from Winston Churchill and a letter from Dwight Eisenhower, the former later found under his bed.

** Leonard Patrick "Red" Kelly also served as the York West Liberal MP from 1962 to 1965, defeating Alan Eagleson in the 1963 campaign. A member of the Hockey Hall of Fame, he played with both the Detroit Red Wings and the Toronto Maple Leafs. As a member of these teams, he won the greatest number of Stanley Cups (eight) ever won by a player who never played for the Montreal Canadiens.

was just as good a hockey player as Gordie Howe. I knew something was going on all the time. You should give them a going over for making such a boob," he wrote, with what appears to be a reference to the broadcasters who related Pearson's opinion. "Just because you are for Toronto, that doesn't mean that Red Kelly is the greatest. Gordie Howe has a quicker and faster shot than Kelly. Howe is a very fast skater but Kelly is slow and dreary."[5] The prime minister's response — handled by his secretary, Jules Pelletier, was equally charming. "As hockey fans yourselves [a "Sandy" was included in the response, perhaps Stuart's brother], you know that everyone is entitled to his personal opinion, which is what Mr. Pearson was expressing at that time. That you should have written to the prime minister is appreciated and he extends to you best wishes for your studies at school this year." Written over top of the letter in Pearson's handwriting was his suggestion: "Why not explain what I did say which wasn't that Kelly was a better player!"[6]

This does not mean the prime minister was reading every single letter, but it does reveal that, even in Pearson's time, correspondence

Wilfrid Laurier's desk in the East Block of Parliament. Sir Wilfrid received many letters, including some from young Canadians writing about the fact they shared the same name as the prime minister. If he answered all such letters, "He would have no time left for the affairs of state," wrote one magazine.

from ordinary Canadians was taken more seriously than it is today. Pearson at least appears to have read a healthy sampling of his letters and, according to Matheson, they helped to enlarge "his sympathetic understanding of the country. It augmented his personal resolve, and frequently in caucus Pearson would startle his supporters with some telling and apt reference to a letter he had 'just received,' from some angry person, some child, or perhaps from an acknowledged authority."[7]

Email has changed everything. That, along with a growing population, has led to an explosion of correspondence to Canada's prime ministers. Paul Martin received close to three thousand emails per day and needed a staff of thirty-five (compared to three for Diefenbaker) to handle correspondence, which ranged from lengthy, thoughtful, and detailed letters to those addressed to "Paul" or, in one case, to "Mr. Dithers." As with the messages sent to all of Canada's prime ministers, the tone in them ranged, but one might assume that Laurier never had to deal with missives such as this one to Martin that came in an email: "If you want to get re-elected you better do something to get in touch with real Canadians and I don't mean kissing babies; if I was one I would throw up all over you!" Another told him, "You are in my mind a waste of hair and skin."[8]

As the country has grown, so, too, has the distance between the people and the prime minister. No longer will a PM sit down and read his mail from ordinary Canadians and dash off a reply. The volume is simply too great, the country too large. But from the days of John A. Macdonald to the present, Canadians have continued to write to the prime minister as though the PM is their next-door neighbour, or an uncle who lives in the next town. They write to him about all manner of things: to ask for jobs, tickets to events, to get information, for photographs and signatures, for endorsements of causes, to offer goods and services for free or for sale; or to send their poetry or interesting news clippings. Rarely today will they even get an answer from the person who actually read the letter, let alone a response from the prime minister.

One idea for the PM might be to adopt former U.S. president Barack Obama's practice of receiving a curated package of ten representative letters from Americans to which he makes a personal response. For Obama, it was his way of escaping the presidential bubble. Fiona Reeves, his director of presidential correspondence, told the *New York Times* the letters are the most genuine information he gets. "If you work at the White House and write something for the president, a lot of people review it to make sure it's thorough or accurate, or that it's ready for the president to see it. If you write to the president, you go through this pretty low-filter channel of our volunteers and staff and straight to his desk."[9]

But back to the mornings. The beginning of the workday has varied for Canada's prime ministers. Brian Mulroney rising at 6:30 a.m. made him something of an early bird, especially when compared to John A. Macdonald or Wilfrid Laurier, both of whom started their day at the rather leisurely hour of 8:00 or 9:00 a.m. Laurier read the *Ottawa Citizen* with his breakfast, which sometimes consisted of oatmeal eaten in what was known as the true Scottish fashion — with salt. Otherwise, Laurier enjoyed a poached egg, baked apple, plain bread, and some tea. Occasionally, he might venture to have toast, but mostly Laurier kept his meals simple.[10] After that, he went up to his home office at his residence in the Sandy Hill area of Ottawa (his home was later to be known as "Laurier House") to deal with his correspondence. Perhaps we can forgive the later starts of Macdonald and Laurier; their days were often longer than those of present-day PMs since sittings of the House of Commons routinely lasted well into the evenings during their times.

Like Macdonald and Laurier, Mackenzie King was a late riser. He was usually up by 9:00 a.m. as well, but rather than a quick look at the newspapers, King liked to begin his morning by reading a passage from the Bible and from *Daily Strength for Daily Needs*, a book of encouraging quotations about the benefits of leading a morally upright life. King continued his working morning by reviewing correspondence at Laurier House, which served as both his residence and office for much of his time as prime minister. Only one modern prime minister shared the late-rising habits of Laurier and King: Pierre Trudeau. He was notorious for hating early mornings. He was not at his best "until I have my coffee in my bloodstream."

R.B. Bennett, John Diefenbaker, Jean Chrétien, and Stephen Harper were all up early. Chrétien ("I get a jump on all those sleepy-heads out there," he would say) liked to quickly down a glass of juice, followed by some toast, Raisin Bran, and a cup of coffee before, perhaps, a swim for twenty to twenty-five minutes in the pool at 24 Sussex Drive. He then enjoyed a coffee with his wife, Aline, in the sunroom of the residence. Chrétien might subsequently spend an hour reading briefing books or signing letters.[11]

Harper typically began his day by watching French-language television news on TVA or Radio-Canada in order to keep his French sharp. Harper, notes his biographer, John Ibbitson, also paid close attention to the *Ottawa Citizen* because it was the local paper, while his wife, Laureen, spent a lot more time with the papers, noting articles to which her husband should pay particular attention. Like Mulroney, Harper was the father of a young family while PM, so time was spent with his children before getting them off to school. After that, the real work of being prime minister could begin.

9:15 a.m. — Parliament Hill

After his breakfast of juice, cereal, bacon, and one egg, Prime Minister Louis St. Laurent completes the short, ten-minute walk from his home in the prestigious Roxborough Apartments on Elgin Street to his office in the East Block of Parliament Hill. Along his route to work, a number of Canadians say hello and the gentlemanly prime minister with the nickname "Uncle Louis" politely doffs his hat in reply. He has already read the *Gazette* from Montreal, and he is ready for the first business of the day: a meeting with his senior secretary, Pierre Asselin. The mail is on his desk — the same one Wilfrid Laurier used — with the most important correspondence on top. There are numerous diplomatic memos and departmental briefings that need the attention of the PM. Each has a short note briefly summarizing the contents. St. Laurent is working in his tie and suit jacket as he does every day unless it is extremely hot. The unwritten rule in the office is that other staff members will only remove their jackets if the prime minister does.[12]

For the prime minister, the agenda gets rolling upon arrival at the Parliament Hill office in the morning. "My working day was tightly organized," wrote Brian Mulroney in his memoirs as he detailed his day. "It always began with a meeting with the Clerk and my chief of staff to preview the day: the decisions, communications with world leaders, domestic challenges, parliamentary activities, and, occasionally, important appointments for party matters that were on the agenda." The PM has so many balls in the air to juggle that he relies on his staff to help prepare him for his numerous responsibilities. It is a big operation.

These important meetings with staff in the prime minister's Parliament Hill office or in that of the Clerk of the Privy Council have been a staple in the daily schedule of the PM since Pierre Trudeau gave the PMO the modern organization it has today. When he came to office in 1968, Trudeau revamped the PMO, giving it a clearer organization and authority while doubling its size from the forty who worked for his predecessor, Lester B. Pearson, to about eighty. Even Pearson recognized changes were needed when he noted how small his staff was and wished he "would not have had to work quite so hard on matters of detail."

The key is to have the PM's day well-organized. The demands on the time of the prime minister and the number of things to which his attention must be devoted is a common theme running through the history of being prime minister. Here is how Eddie Goldenberg, chief advisor to Prime Minister Jean Chrétien, summarized it:

> The demands of the time of a prime minister are almost infinite: Cabinet, caucus, the House of Commons, meetings about government issues, delivery of speeches, foreign trips, receiving foreign visitors, meeting provincial premiers, spending evenings at partisan political events, as well as just staying home to read and think. This makes the time of a prime minister one of the most

precious commodities of any government and it should be used as sparingly as possible. Managing a prime minister's time and the flow of thousands of documents a year to him is a twenty-four-hour-a-day job.

Time. There is not enough of it for a prime minister. This has been the case since the days of John A. Macdonald. "Occupied with the thousand and one cares that make up the life of a prime minister, it is difficult to understand how Sir John Macdonald found time to fulfill those manifold duties of a departmental character which demanded his attention," wrote Joseph Pope of the country's first PM, who also happened to hold the titles of minister of justice and attorney general of Canada. Almost 150 years later, Prime Minister Justin Trudeau agreed. When asked soon after he took office in 2015 if anything surprised him about the job, his answer was unequivocal:

> The pace. The limit of hours in the day. And the extent to which I need to be really ruthless about ensuring that I do have time with my family, time with Sophie, and time to decompress at the same time as I'm going full out. If I'm left to my own devices, I'll work all the time and go home with briefing books and go through them all the time and Sophie says "no, no, no" you have to spend time with the kids so that you can make sense of everything else that you do.[13]

Political scientist Donald Savoie wrote a landmark book in 1999 about the exercise of power from the centre of government — in other words, the prime minister. In *Governing from the Centre* he looked at the 1974 schedule of Prime Minister Pierre Trudeau and noted that

- in the average month Trudeau worked 250 hours or sixty-plus per week;
- 36 percent of Trudeau's time was spent on government business including Cabinet and committee meetings;
- 20 percent of his hours were spent on political activities,

including meeting with ministers, MPs, senators, and party officials;

- twelve and a half hours — or 5 percent of his time — was spent on press conferences or other interactions with the media;
- he spent thirty hours or 12 percent of his time with staff in the PMO or Privy Council Office; and
- Trudeau used 67.2 hours or just over a quarter of his time on paperwork, telephone calls, and correspondence. "On a typical day," wrote Savoie, "his activities as prime minister have spanned eleven hours."

It is no wonder, then, that the prime minister needs a hard-working, dedicated, and efficient staff to manage his affairs. There are more requests for the PM's time than can be accommodated, and as one PMO official said during the Chrétien era, the staff need to "squeeze forty-eight hours out of the prime minister's average day."

This sentiment was perfectly captured in a 1931 article by Grattan O'Leary, writing about R.B. Bennett:

> Mr. Bennett works thirteen to fourteen hours a day, seems to crowd at least one hundred minutes into every hour, sees countless callers, hears numerous deputations, receives a deluge of mail. Mr. Bennett's private secretary works one hour longer or later than Mr. Bennett, sees more callers, meets more deputations, receives infinitely more mail.[14]

As a result of the insatiable demands on the PM's time, he has come to rely on his staff to make it all work. Today, these people include a chief of staff, a director of communications, and a principal secretary, among many others. But behind the scenes is the all-important executive assistant. Think of Charlie from *The West Wing* television show of the late 1990s and early 2000s. The executive assistant to the prime minister is essentially the "gatekeeper" for access to him. In other eras he was referred to as the "private secretary." What does he do? A 1931 description of the job from *Maclean's* magazine gives some idea:

The private secretary of a prime minister must act as a bodyguard, a policeman, a doorman; must have patience, firmness, kindness, humour. He must be a philosopher and a politician all in one; must know which callers to admit and which not to admit; know who must not be offended; know also the precise cost of offending anyone. Anyone, that is, of the thousands who come to see the prime minister, of the thousands of others who write to the prime minister.[15]

How smoothly it all goes often depends on the person at the top. When Gowan Guest, a Vancouver lawyer, was recruited to work in John Diefenbaker's office he agreed to do so without knowing exactly what the job would entail. "I expect you to figure that out," the Chief told him. Guest "soon learned that the Chief's habit was to let things flow around him as he responded to crises and immediate enticements. Anyone within range, at any time, might be called upon for 'stuff' for speeches; anyone was a suitable audience for the prime minister's latest belly laugh."

At the other end of the spectrum was the tranquility of Brian Mulroney's office, described by Michael Valpy in a 1993 feature in the *Globe and Mail*:

Here is what an outsider sees: The prime minister operates in an oasis of calm. Much of the time he is alone at his desk — with one aide or another (most frequently Paul Smith) bringing in documents for him to review or sign. Everyone speaks in muted tones. A sense of formality is omnipresent. Mr. Mulroney is always addressed as prime minister.[16]

"The prime minister's day runs to a very definite, well-planned rhythm," Mulroney agreed in his memoirs.

10:00 a.m. – Cabinet Room, East Block

Cabinet meetings remain an integral part of a prime minister's duties, and while the Cabinet may not meet every day (it usually meets Tuesdays), such meetings are an important element of the schedule in the life of a PM. Given that, it may seem surprising that until the 1940s there was no formal Cabinet structure; in fact, meetings were quite informal, with no agenda and no one to record what transpired. In 1940, with the Second World War creating a huge complexity to governing, Mackenzie King agreed to have agendas and to record Cabinet decisions. The Clerk of the Privy Council became Secretary to the Cabinet — Arnold Heeney was the first to take on the position — tasked with developing and running a system of record keeping. Since King's tenure, the size and structure of Cabinets has varied from PM to PM, but, as part of the executive branch, it has always served as the essential decision-making body of the government. As such, its composition and functioning is a key responsibility of being prime minister.

The number of times a prime minister's Cabinet meets has depended on the inclinations of the person at the head of it. For example, Louis St. Laurent's Cabinet met ninety-one times in 1956, whereas the Cabinet of John Diefenbaker met 164 times in 1959 for a total of 826 meetings in its less than six years in office. To say the least, it was not very productive. In fact, St. Laurent and Diefenbaker could not have been more different in their administrative capacities. Let's compare. Here's Jack Pickersgill who worked in St. Laurent's PMO:

> As St. Laurent hated to waste time, Cabinet meetings were exceedingly business-like. He always read the Cabinet papers before meetings. I cannot remember a single occasion on which St. Laurent was not [as] well informed about any subject under discussion as the minster who presented it, and I can remember many times when he was much better informed. He was always attentive and rarely impatient.... More than any prime minister I have known, St. Laurent

dominated his Cabinet, not by imposing his authority, but by his sheer intellect, his wide knowledge, and
his unequalled persuasiveness.

Diefenbaker, on the other hand, was not skilled at managing his
Cabinet and left decisions unmade for too long. Cabinet meetings were
often tense, or fruitless, or both. "He came to the toughest job in the
country without having worked for anybody else in his life; he had never
hired or fired anyone, and never administered anything more complicated than a walk-up law office," wrote Peter C. Newman in 1963. "The
lifelong habits of a lone-wolf defence lawyer made it difficult for him to
delegate authority — an essential of Cabinet government."[17] Even the
Americans wondered about Dief's ability: "There is great skepticism as
to his ability to put together a truly effective Cabinet and administer it
with skill," said a report from the U.S. ambassador in 1957.

Running a Cabinet is an essential skill for a prime minister, a key
to success for his government, particularly in a minority situation when
a Cabinet usually needs to meet more often, or during a time of crisis,
such as a war. At the Cabinet table, the prime minister sits in the middle, or at the end, in a chair that is slightly higher than his colleagues',
evidence of his position as "first among equals," though, as noted, in
reality the PM is much more than that. He is the most powerful person
in government and his opinions will usually carry the day.

But this book is not about political science or executive power
per se; it is about what life is like for our prime ministers, so perhaps the anecdote about the side table in John A. Macdonald's East
Block Cabinet room is more apt. This table contained an array of
port, sherry, brandy, whisky, and beer. Today you are more likely to
see light snacks, water, or pop. Smoking has come and gone, but
as recently as Brian Mulroney's day the smokers (those still using
the "demon weed," as he called it) were permitted in the Cabinet
room, although they were shunted to one end of the room.* On the
other hand, there was no smoking permitted in Mackenzie King's

---

* "Nicorette gum was the order of the day for myself and the other recovering smokers. In those days we somehow believed that cigarette smoke wouldn't spread across a
table!" Mulroney wrote in his memoirs.

Cabinet room, an imposition on many members during an age when smoking was common.

As mentioned at the beginning of this section, presiding over Cabinet meetings remains an important part of the PM's job and how that is done is reflective of the person in charge. The status of the Cabinet has changed over time. Indeed, both the importance and size of it has ebbed and flowed. From John A. Macdonald to Pierre Trudeau, Cabinet meetings were held in the East Block. The growth in the size of Cabinets — Brian Mulroney appointed a record number of forty in 1984 — necessitated a move to a larger room in Parliament's Centre Block where it continues to meet to this day when in Ottawa.

AFTERNOON
12:30 p.m. — Laurier House, Ottawa

Mackenzie King walks down the stairs from the top floor of Laurier House, where his office is located. He has been working there since midmorning, filing through his correspondence and sorting through numerous briefings from the Department of External Affairs (today called Global Affairs Canada), for which he also serves as minister. The "blue sheets," from the Dominions Office in London, are essentially reports from various British consular agents in the empire; a pink sheet is a memo from Georges Vanier, the Canadian ambassador in Paris. He makes pencil marks on those that need further review: "Bring up later" or "Speak to me re," he writes. "All of these things, domestic and external, pour into Laurier House in a fairly steady stream. This does not, of course, mean that the prime minister is able to handle them all as they come. Like anybody else, he gets behind." Indeed, the papers pile up and King is unable to catch up. As a result he continues to put off tasks that he must attend to, such as drafting his next speech, a task he loathes to no end.

Few realize it, but King's office in his home at Laurier House is essentially the epicentre of the Canadian government. It is here where the prime minister completes the bulk of his work on most days. He sorts his work into four or five neat piles and prepares to head downstairs. Breakfast is substantial, consisting of a grapefruit, egg, toast, and coffee, but he's ready for a light meal now, followed by a half-hour nap.

As for most people across the country, lunch is an important part of the day, but our prime ministers seem to have made more of that time than most of us. They often took advantage of that moment in the day to truly get away from the office and have a meal. Sometimes they reconnected with their families; other times they met with parliamentary colleagues. Take John Diefenbaker for example. He had no children of his own, so returning to 24 Sussex Drive was not a priority for him. Instead, he enjoyed eating in the parliamentary restaurant, where he regaled a few Cabinet colleagues with jokes, stories, or other bits of small talk. Typically, Diefenbaker talked about sports or great historical figures. If you were eavesdropping, you might have heard him tell a story about Winston Churchill or discuss the fighting styles of boxers Joe Louis and Cassius Clay (Muhammad Ali).[18] When the Chief did not eat in the parliamentary restaurant, he often ate a home-cooked meal in his East Block office, delivered in a special box he had made just for this purpose.

Brian Mulroney and Louis St. Laurent were far more likely to head back to Sussex for their lunch. St. Laurent liked to head home at 1:15 p.m. for a light meal. When it was macaroni and cheese, he was very pleased.* He made the most of this time by taking correspondence home with him and by reading and working in the car during the travel time to and from Parliament Hill. Mulroney's habits were not terribly different. He would head back to the prime minister's official residence for lunch. He might meet with the Clerk of the Privy Council, his chief of staff, or other colleagues from Parliament. Over lunch, the discussion would include the coming Question Period. Once the meal was over, Mulroney would shave for a second time and put on a fresh shirt (Mulroney liked to change his shirts a lot).

There are some insights to be gained about prime ministerial style and personality by looking at how they took their lunch. It reflects who they were. Mulroney and Diefenbaker were social and enjoyed

---

* Joe Clark, apparently, was also a big fan of mac and cheese, as was Paul Martin, who admitted he was "no gourmet."

continuing the workday in a less formal manner over a meal. St. Laurent quietly and efficiently went about his business while heading home for his lunch. Mackenzie King, the loner, usually ate by himself. The same was true of Stephen Harper, who preferred to eat alone at his desk while poring over government documents. His lunch was simple: usually a sandwich and soup brought to the office from 24 Sussex. He ate directly out of the containers in which his lunch came and washed it down with a Diet Pepsi. A 2017 photograph of Justin Trudeau at lunch in his office showed a desk with a modest lunch container on it, as well.

While the lunches of most prime ministers take place offstage and allow the PM a moment to refuel and gain sustenance for the several hours of hard work that follow it, in today's social media world lunch can turn into a public event, as was the case when Prime Minister Justin Trudeau visited a McDonald's restaurant in 2016, in Whitby, Ontario. The unannounced visit created a stir online and in social media. But perhaps one McDonald's employee summed it up best when he told CBC News, "I guess he was just hungry."[19]

2:15 p.m. — House of Commons

It's 2:15 p.m. and the House of Commons is set to begin its daily exercise in political theatre. This will inevitably lead to television clips appearing on the evening news, so it is a moment in the parliamentary schedule for which the prime minister must be very well prepared. Stephen Harper has been getting ready for the session practically since his day began, with a morning meeting of his senior staff. They discuss what might come up in Question Period, or QP, as it is known. Even if the House is not sitting, the meeting of his staff "pretends that it is." After lunch, more preparation time is devoted to the forty-five-minute question-and-answer period that most Canadians have likened to a room full of misbehaving schoolchildren. And that's being polite.

The meeting is attended by Cabinet ministers and parliamentary secretaries who take turns preparing each other for the onslaught of questions that will come from the opposition parties. Sometime between 2:00 p.m., when Members' Statements begin, and 2:15 p.m., the prime minister heads down the famous set of stairs with the polished brass bannister. He walks into the House of Commons, brightly lit with klieg lights for television, and prepares to take a question from the leader of the Opposition.

Despite its lamentable reputation among the Canadian public — even Brian Mulroney called it a period "full of feigned outrage and unrequited indignation — in both official languages" — Question Period remains an important part of the parliamentary day. The prime minister and this House of Commons show are inextricably linked. As Richard S. Conley wrote in the *Canadian Parliamentary Review*:

> Prime ministerial activity in Question Period represents a fundamental component of democratic accountability that is crucial in parliamentary systems. In theory and in practice, opposition parties and individual MPs are able to hold the cabinet responsible for its policies and actions by posing questions to, and scrutinising the head of Government in an open forum. As such, Question Period — whatever its putative inefficiencies or frequently raucous nature — is vital in the maintenance of confidence in the Government by the legislature.

It is not surprising, then, that preparation for this parliamentary theatre takes up a significant portion of the prime minister's day. Most prime ministers seem to enjoy the cut and thrust of QP. Jean Chrétien had to stop himself from answering every question put to him. "I enjoyed Question Period too much and loved the challenge it provided," he wrote in his memoirs. "Far from being a dreaded burden, it had become an exciting part of my life: opposition members attacked me, I fought back. I won or lost or held them to a draw, and the next day we did it all over again." Brian Mulroney was well aware of the two sides of QP: "There were moments ... of genuine passion, real importance, even danger during these sessions, and these moments I treated with genuine concern. The rest was showtime." Indeed, it was. As Jim Coutts, the principal secretary to Pierre Trudeau, said of Trudeau and Question Period: "He's the best actor I've seen. He's got more moves than Bobby Orr."

The speeches and actions of some of the actors in Question Period — members of Parliament — can be awful. One example is the time in 1988 that Sheila Copps heckled Brian Mulroney, calling him a "slime-bag." And there was the famous 1971 exchange between Conservative MP John Lundrigan and Pierre Trudeau. The Newfoundland MP poked the bear with the preamble to his question: "Can I meekly, mildly, and gently approach the esteemed and honourable gentleman who is occupying the throne of Canada at the moment —" The Speaker admonished him to get on with his question in parliamentary fashion. As he started his query once more, Trudeau mouthed to him "fuck off." The House erupted. Outside the Commons, the prime minister said two MPs were "crying to mama and to television." Reporters asked him what he was thinking when he mouthed the words.

"What is the nature of your thoughts, gentlemen, when you say 'fuddle duddle' or something like that? God."

Attending Question Period is just one of the prime minister's responsibilities in Parliament, but it is, today, his most obvious and public one. For PMs who served earlier in Canadian history, the House of Commons played a much bigger role. John A. Macdonald, Wilfrid Laurier, Arthur Meighen, R.B. Bennett, and John Diefenbaker all built their reputations on their prodigious parliamentary performances. When a prime minister had something important to say it was always uttered in the House, never in a pre-scripted event built around a photo op. For example, after Diefenbaker's 1961 trip to see President Kennedy in Washington, the prime minister returned to the House of Commons and reported on the visit the *same day*, something unheard of now.

The Commons was the centre of the political universe, and prime ministers were among its many stars. They also spent a considerable amount of time there. Parliament routinely sat into the evening, with the prime minister usually in his seat. Sir Wilfrid Laurier was noted for his excellent attendance in the House and earned respect and accolades from colleagues for sitting through the speeches of even backbenchers, whom he often sat beside to listen to their issues. It was in the chamber that Laurier continued to hone his considerable language and orator-ical skills, occasionally asking a page to bring him a dictionary so that he might look up a new word. Louis St. Laurent often just sat in a back row in the corner of the Commons reading papers or working on files. "I think those many long hours that he spent in this house were not a waste of time," recalled fellow MP Hazen Argue. "They enabled him to conduct better the position of prime minister."

Diefenbaker took the House of Commons seriously but presaged some of the decline in the importance of the place we see today:

> When the House was sitting, I tried to be at my Commons desk as often as possible, although I did not manage this to the extent that Prime Minister St. Laurent had. I felt it important that, as prime minister, I should participate in the debates under our parliamentary system, but this requires a lot of effort if one is not content to have others prepare final drafts of his material. When I participate in debate, I do not recite or read scripts, I enter into the current of discussion. To me, this is what Parliament is all about.

This reverence for the House of Commons did not prevent Diefenbaker from having a listening device set up in his East Block office, allowing him to aurally follow the proceedings of the House without having actually to be there. He borrowed the idea from British PM Harold Macmillan.[20]

The situation is different today. The role of Parliament has diminished in the face of the growing power in the executive. The prime minister has become more of a focus than ever, while the House of Commons has become less important to the PM. There are more responsibilities and a much larger agenda than was the case during the days of Diefenbaker and St. Laurent. The PM has other avenues through which to reach out to Canadians, such as websites and social media. But as the parliamentary day has come to focus on Question Period, it has also intensified the spotlight on the PM and, as a result, the number of utterances has skyrocketed. Since the election of Prime Minister Jean Chrétien in 1993, the number of times a PM has participated in QP has increased by close to 700 percent.[21] Even though Stephen Harper cut his appearances at the daily spectacle down to three times per week, he took the vast majority of the questions, leaving his ministers little time in the spotlight. In 2017, Justin Trudeau tinkered with the idea of taking all questions during QP on a single day, as is the practice in the United Kingdom in what is known as "Prime Minister's Questions." The jury is still out on the success of that attempt. For good or ill, it is clear that preparing for this event has become a key piece of the PM's schedule when Parliament is sitting, while debating in the House has not.

3:15 p.m. — Centre Block

For a prime minister, the time after Question Period usually entails a variety of meetings. "The range was enormous," wrote Brian Mulroney:

> Frequently, there were groups of wide-eyed school-children visiting the Commons for the first time, and I would often try to see them in my office. Similarly, there were often premiers in town for discussions with the government, as well as mayors, religious leaders, university presidents and the like, many of whom were advancing a case, and all of whom were glad to go back and report that they had given the prime minister a piece of their mind.

These kinds of meetings can be fun and sometimes involve meeting a famous Canadian artist, Nobel laureate, or athlete who has accomplished something significant. They are not only an opportunity for a great photo op with a celebrity, but also a chance to meet ordinary Canadians and even those who can give the prime minister special insights into any topic. Meeting people is simply a big part of the job, though some PMs have loved it more than others. "I tried at all times to make myself easily accessible," wrote John Diefenbaker. "Incidentally, this applied to the man in the street as well as to those who were highly placed. There never was a time when I did not want to find out what the people were thinking."

The Chief loved meeting people so much that he often engaged in impromptu conversations with school groups passing through on tours of the Parliament Buildings. (Inevitably, all of the students on tours of Parliament are described as "wide-eyed," but I can assure you this is only the case if they are fortunate enough to run into the prime minister.) Occasionally the students touring Parliament in Diefenbaker's time ended up in the Chief's office to hear him hold court, telling any number of stories in an animated style that hooked so many Canadians. He was a staffer's nightmare, though, as these meetings threw a spanner into the works of his schedule. But contact with the public energized him.

Wilfrid Laurier evidently loved to receive guests in his office and was said to be easier to reach than a member of his Cabinet. There was no guard outside his office; a visitor simply announced his presence to his secretary, who would determine who got seen. Laurier was known to meet with up to one hundred people a day, from Cabinet ministers to ordinary citizens. Each person came away smiling, even if they did not get what they came for, such was the Laurier charm. "There [was] no stiffness or formality about his welcome," observed *Maclean's* magazine in 1909.[22]

William Lyon Mackenzie King was a man far less outgoing. Beyond his Cabinet, fewer than a half-dozen people interacted with him on an ordinary day. "On many occasions, even during normal working hours of the day, he would close the door to the library, which meant to us that he was meditating and he was not to be disturbed under any circumstances. This was, to me, the loneliness of a recluse," mused one close aide.

The importance of these meetings is not to be underestimated. Whether it is for a photograph with an MP whose constituents are visiting or a quick chat with a business leader, access to the PM is important and the visits can go a long way to making Canadians feel some form of connection to their prime minister. George Radwanski tells the story of following Pierre Trudeau after Question Period in 1977. In seven minutes he had met thirty-two people who "will long remember and recount their 'personal' chats with the prime minister of Canada." On the other hand, Trudeau had a button under his desk that he would press if any meeting in his office had gone on too long. Access and time has its limits.

EVENING

6:15 p.m. — Prime Minister's Office, Centre Block

Prime Minister Pierre Trudeau is already thinking about seeing his three boys. It has been another long day at Parliament Hill, including a stormy Question Period during which the Opposition, as is its job, tried to trip up the prime minister. It is not an aspect of being prime minister that Trudeau particularly enjoys, unlike a number of his predecessors and successors. Now, after signing a few more letters and other documents in his office and reviewing the schedule for the next day with his executive assistant, Trudeau heads down the two flights of stairs and out the front doors of Parliament to his waiting limousine. On the way home, he discusses longer-term scheduling and a few other minor issues that have not been addressed during the day. At the end of the three-kilometre drive, the prime minister gets out of the vehicle and heads into 24 Sussex Drive, the official residence. There he greets his wife, Margaret, and kisses each of his three boys, Justin, Sacha, and Michel. It is time to leave behind the pressures of being prime minister and reconnect with family.

Leaving the Hill and coming home to a family or a spouse has been an important part of the lives of many, but not all, prime ministers. Those with families had obvious motives for getting home. "I remember when I'd go home and play with my children," wrote Pierre Trudeau in his memoirs, "it was almost as if 'the Prime Minister' was someone other than me":

> "Those are the things he's doing, but I'm doing something else." I wouldn't spend a moment worrying about the silly mistakes I had made during the day, or the unfortunate incidents in Parliament, or the defeat or failure of this or that policy. I would start worrying about that only after breakfast the next morning, when I had woken up well-rested and had seen my kids off to school.

The dinner hour is a convenient and much-needed break in a prime minister's day, affording an opportunity for creating a "church and state" separation between work and relaxation. Trudeau tried to keep a "watertight seal" between his work as PM and his family life. His family kept to a routine when he came home. The kids would have already eaten by the time he arrived to see them. They were then whisked upstairs and dressed in bathrobes while the PM headed for the pool to get his exercise by swimming precisely forty-four lengths. The children were expected to arrive at the very moment he completed his swim for quality time with their father, which might include some swim training or just playing around. At eight o'clock it was time for Margaret and Pierre to sit down to their own dinner. Occasionally they might go out to a Lebanese or Japanese restaurant. Afterward, they might listen to music or look after some domestic minutiae. After about forty-five minutes, Trudeau would pull out his briefcase and his nightly work would begin.

Trudeau was not the only family man to be prime minister, and the others took a similar approach. Being in Ottawa certainly gave a more predictable schedule for the PM. Brian Mulroney was the father of four children while prime minister, including one, Nicolas, born while he was in office, making him the last PM to have such an experience.[*] Like Trudeau, Mulroney liked to get home for dinner and, if possible, attend one of his children's sporting or school events. On other nights he might join them in the pool for a swim. What is clear from these reports is just how important family is to a prime minister. As Mulroney wrote in his private journal in 1992, near the end of his time in office: "They have been my real inspiration, my shelter in the storm, my reason for persevering."

The routines for prime ministers with a family are remarkably similar. Stephen Harper was also the father of a young family while he was in office and he, too, usually returned to Sussex by 6:30 p.m., when the family would enjoy their dinner together. Afterward, as was the case with

---

[*] Mulroney told his caucus before Nicolas was born that anyone attacking the universality of the baby bonus "will have serious problems with me!"

the Mulroneys, Harper might head out to the hockey rink to watch his son play or to the gym to watch his daughter dance. Later on, there was perhaps some relaxation — watching a little television or ploughing through briefing books in the office. Between 11:00 p.m. and 12:00 a.m. it was time to turn in for the night.

More than a century earlier, John A. Macdonald also liked to get home in the evening to play with his daughter, Mary. A dinner with a glass of wine followed, and this time at home with family was restorative. "What most impressed those who saw Sir John Macdonald at home, was the faculty he had of divesting himself of the cares of State," recalled Joseph Pope. "One found it hard to realize that he was the same man who, a few hours before, had been harassed by the grave and perplexing problems which awaited him on the morrow."

Those prime ministers who were childless or had grown children still came home for dinner, all around six o'clock. Louis St. Laurent loved chicken or roast beef and might unwind by playing canasta (a rummy-like card game) with Mrs. St. Laurent. If there were family guests, the evening might include a game of bridge or Scrabble, though Mrs. St. Laurent was no fan of the latter. They didn't watch much television unless it was a hockey game.

St. Laurent, however, did have one important post-dinner ritual he liked to follow on days he had to return to the House of Commons for an evening session. His assistant, Mike Deacey, found out the hard way how important it was to him. After taking the prime minister's hat and coat, he turned to see St. Laurent at his desk with a newspaper, beginning to work.

The PM looked up: "Yes?" he inquired.

Deacey, who was actually filling in for another assistant who better knew St. Laurent's habits, told him there was a Quebec City MP and two others waiting to see him. "Don't forget, his mother was Irish and St. Laurent had an Irish temper which he showed on occasion," Deacey recounted when telling the tale. "This was one of those occasions."

When told about the requested meeting, the normally phlegmatic prime minister blew his stack. He didn't want to see the men under any circumstances, he roared. All they wanted was a patronage appointment. "He was really mad," Deacey recalled. But St. Laurent met with the men and dispatched with their requests in the gentlemanly manner for which he was known. Later, Deacey asked Pierre Asselin, the PM's usual assistant, why he thought the PM lost his cool.

"You know how Mr. St. Laurent comes back from dinner, you'll often notice he has a paper under his arm or it's right on his desk," Asselin told him. "Well, he does the bridge problem. He's quite a bridge player and don't bother him when he's trying to work out that bridge problem."

Mackenzie King returned to Laurier House for his meals, half of which were eaten alone. The other times King would entertain friends or have a few MPs over in order to get to know them better, but he did this much less in his final years in office. But he worked around the dinner hours and thought very little of anyone's family time. "A man may be in the very act of carving a roast before his guests when the phone rings," wrote Blair Fraser in *Maclean's* magazine. "If it's the office, he puts down his carving knife and departs. The busier of King's secretaries are accustomed to work three nights a week, and often work five."

While Kim Campbell was only briefly prime minister, she made some astute observations about how the life of a PM functions in Ottawa. "What is really helpful for the prime minister, and you see this with the American president living [in the White House] where his office is close," she said, "is that the geographical configuration of the prime minister's life in Ottawa is quite family friendly. You're not far from the office, you're not far from the Hill. You don't have long distances to go so there isn't a lot of wasted time in terms of getting from A to B."[23]

The job "makes you very aware of the work-life balance," intimated Justin Trudeau, who is in the unique position of having been the son of a prime minister and of being a father while serving as prime minister. "You have to be very, very deliberate about when you get moments actually to be together." Like society in general, contemporary politicians, especially those with families, try to pay more attention to creating this balance than did those in the past. This is true of unmarried prime ministers also; Kim Campbell was certainly as mindful of her private time as Mackenzie King, the last unmarried and childless prime minister of Canada before her. Who knows what hours another single PM may want to keep.

10:00 p.m. — Earnscliffe

It is late in Ottawa and Sir John A. Macdonald is ready for bed. The day has been a long one, since the House is sitting. He has had his customary late-night snack and is heading to bed now, but his evening is not over. As is his habit, Canada's first prime minister takes a stack of newspapers and magazines with him to bed for his nightly reading. In all likelihood, he will fall asleep reading them. Some people over the years have wondered how Macdonald appeared to be so well read and up to date on current events when they never saw him with books or papers at the office. The secret was his regimen of late-night reading.*

For a job as demanding as prime minister, it is no surprise that work drifts into the late evening, and many of our prime ministers have been, as a result, night owls, toiling away on some matter or another as the midnight oil burned away. That might have involved attending debates. It was not until 1982 that the House adopted a measure to fix sitting days and adjournment times. Now that the House no longer sits late into the evenings (there are exceptions, such as at the end of a session when hours may be extended), most prime ministers spend their late evening hours reviewing briefing binders or doing other reading.

As far as the night owls go, R.B. Bennett and Mackenzie King take the cake. "Perhaps no other prime minister worked as hard as Mr. Bennett did," the *Globe* once wrote. He sometimes kept a whole team of secretaries and stenographers working throughout the night as he attended to a number of details for his job, as well as treading on the boundaries of those in his Cabinet, whose responsibilities he often encroached upon. It was not unusual to see the lights in his East Block office flicker until 2:00 a.m. "He never knew when to quit," a newspaper wrote of him after he returned to work from having a heart

---

* His reading in bed nearly cost him his life in 1866 when his papers caught fire, sending his London hotel room up in flames. Macdonald narrowly escaped with his life.

attack in 1935. "Night after night the light shone from the window of his little room in the old, now-gone Parliament Buildings — just as it twinkled from behind the shades of the prime minister's offices in the East Block these last five years. Work has been this man's play."[24]

As a bachelor, Bennett was perhaps better able to indulge in such a lifestyle than other prime ministers, such as Stephen Harper or Justin Trudeau, have been. But it is interesting to note that Laurier, Borden, Bennett, and King — prime ministers of Canada from 1896 to 1948 (interspersed by very brief Arthur Meighen interludes) — were all childless. Borden, who was married, worked late into the night in his library, and when he finished around midnight he usually made some notes in his diary. Much like Macdonald, at night he enjoyed reading a number of the newspapers that were left beside his bed. Borden's bedtime reading might also have included a speech by Demosthenes or Cicero in the original Greek or Latin.

Mackenzie King worked long hours, too. He doggedly dictated letters and dealt with the nation's business after dinner and into the evening at his Laurier House office. The signal that the working day might be over was often the ten o'clock news on the radio, but if the PM was working on important matters it was not unusual for him to continue until at least midnight. After that, it was reading in bed, which more often than not would be a book with some sort of spiritual emphasis or a biography of an English statesman. Bruce Hutchison's famous biography *The Incredible Canadian* gives us a good idea of King's approach:

> After dinner the real work of the day began. Almost every evening secretaries and stenographers were summoned to Laurier House and infrequently left before midnight. Being a bachelor, King had no notion of other men's domestic arrangements, cared nothing for their inconvenience, worked them unconscionably, and was amazed when a secretary asked a night off to see a hockey game.... If the Prime Minister dined out he might summon an assistant from his bed in the middle of the night.

Making use of the late evening is something of a habit among prime ministers. The job necessitates it given the amount of documentation that must be read. One study estimated that a prime minister needs to read about three hundred pages of briefing notes per week, and that Pierre Trudeau, because of his larger Cabinet structure, was likely reading closer to one thousand pages. This has a strategic element. A well-briefed and knowledgeable prime minister is better able to make his influence felt around the Cabinet table. Most of our recent prime ministers repaired to the home office to do their reading or reflecting. Some, such as Brian Mulroney or Paul Martin, might make a late-evening call to the Clerk of the Privy Council or other trusted political confidants. Stephen Harper rarely made these types of calls.

An evening off had consequences, as Pierre Trudeau noted:

> I know every evening that I take off during the week, whether it be to go to the ballet or to spend a long dinner with friends, means that I have to work that much longer on the weekend catching up whatever I didn't do that particular night. This is not a line that I'm [not] a terribly hard worker, this is a line that there's so much work to do and … I'm always surprised to hear that, you know, Mackenzie King was always having people in to dinner and staying late and so on. Well, heck, I thought that would happen a little when I married Margaret, that it would get more active. But rather than she influence me, I ended up influencing her. We'd say, "Well, we've got to change that, see more people" — and we never would.

Though Trudeau seems to have been mistaken about the dining habits of Mackenzie King, he alludes to what is perhaps the great common thread running through the life of a prime minister: the workload and exigencies of the job. Today, it is not a job for an older man, so all the more credit to Jean Chrétien, who took office two and half months before his sixtieth birthday (some may argue that this is young — it depends on your perspective) and remained prime minister until he was a month shy of turning seventy. His successor, Paul Martin, was sixty-five when he moved into Sussex Drive. Since Lester B. Pearson, they remain the only people to assume office over the age of sixty. Stephen Harper was forty-six, Justin Trudeau, forty-three. The youngest person to take office as PM was Joe Clark, who was thirty-nine years old in 1979.

It is no surprise, then, that all prime ministers have noted the pressures of the office and the sheer demands of the job, but it seems to have been worse for those leaders whose style leaned toward the micromanagement of affairs, such as Bennett, King, Diefenbaker, and Harper. This is not to say that others did not register a note about the punishing hours, just that perhaps their perspectives were different. In one letter, John Diefenbaker wrote of the workload: "Today I should be getting ready for the Dominion Provincial Conference on Monday. I am really not ready for it at all and will have to put in many, many, hours of work. Unfortunately, I promised to go to Toronto to a Shrine meeting tonight and I am trying to get out of that because it is just impossible." In another letter he wrote of the constant demands placed by public engagements: "Olive and I are not taking any more social engagements than are absolutely necessary. I don't think I could do my job as prime minister if I were to accept 5 percent of the social engagements."

Nothing much has changed since then. Pierre Trudeau was always negotiating with his staff how often he would have to attend social functions and how long he would be required to stay. It got to the point that Bob Murdoch, his executive assistant from 1973 to 1978, had to devise a carefully calibrated system based on the number of minutes Trudeau would be required to do these types of events, and then Murdoch parcelled them out and tracked them on a weekly basis. "I think this system appealed to his logical and rational mind," he recalled.

There is always someone who wants a piece of the PM. Sign this. Call her. Meet him. Consider this. "The in-tray of prime minister is never empty and phones are never silent," Brian Mulroney wrote. "And people tend not to want to contact you when they feel that everything is going just fine. Problems, usually unanticipated ones, can be anticipated. Visitors — either distinguished arrivals from abroad or important Canadian figures — have to be accommodated, usually with photographs taken in the prime minister's office to commemorate the occasion."

Mackenzie King was very aware of how the demands of the job had an impact on him. He intensely disliked the encroachments on his personal time and did his best to limit it, much like Pierre Trudeau did. In 1938 he had some advice for incoming Conservative Party leader R.J. Manion, but in truth it is worthwhile counsel all prime ministers may want to consider. He told Manion, "Try not to see too many people. There is nothing more fatiguing. You must ration very carefully the number of people you see each day or you can't carry on as party leader."[25]

King may have been reflecting once more on his own perspective on the job, as he was not much of a retail politician. But his point is well taken. Prime ministers need time to recharge the batteries, connect with family, and reflect on the problems each is facing. Every moment of their day is full and the energy required is difficult to imagine. "It is always an absolute marvel how a man in your position can do one fiftieth of what you do. How do you manage it?" Hugh MacLennan once asked John Diefenbaker. "It's because I get lots [of] rest," he replied. "I was just reading about Mr. Pearson today. He sleeps with ease. Well, I sleep on the least provocation. I get between seven-and-a-half and eight hours' sleep at night, regardless of anything."[26]

Rest is essential. Both John Diefenbaker and Paul Martin were inveterate nappers. Exercise helps, though few prime ministers were able to maintain the habit of a daily fitness regimen and many have admitted that it was one of the first things to go once they took office (see chapter 5). But perhaps it is mental fitness that would be of most benefit to those who achieve the highest office in the land. While Arthur Meighen was not prime minister for long (briefly in 1920–21 and again in 1926), his sage advice in a letter to Senator Frederick Schaffner in 1920 is a fitting place to draw a conclusion on a day in the life of a prime minister:

> If there is one thing more than another which has impressed me since I took this office it is the necessity so strongly urged by you in this letter of keeping a

cheerful mind under all circumstances. If one is not able to do this to a fair extent anyway he would break under the load before very long. I want to assure you that this task and indeed the task of all Ministers for that matter, but of course the task of prime minister in particular, demands an intensive concentration hour by hour and moment by moment [that] it is hard for one who has not some experience in it to realize.

2:00 a.m. — Laurier House

"To bed about 2."
Mackenzie King's diary, July 2, 1927.

CHAPTER 2

"MACKENZIE KING WITHOUT A OUIJA BOARD": PORTRAITS OF THE PRIME MINISTERS AS OTHERS SAW THEM

> What is remarkable about the prime minister, at least before power changed him, is that he could have been the next door neighbour, anywhere in Canada. It is not just that he felt at home. Canadians feel at home with him, and that is a real and personal tribute.
> — Joe Clark, speaking about Prime Minister Jean Chrétien, House of Commons, November 6, 2003

It is August 1910 and Sir Wilfrid Laurier is on another stop in western Canada as part of a grand tour that will take him to four different provinces. When he gets back to Ottawa he will remark that he has returned "ten times more Canadian." At each stop he is presented with flowers and the prime minister dutifully gives each flower girl a paternal kiss. While Laurier has no children of his own, he is well known for his fondness of young people. On this trip, when Laurier is missing from breakfast, an MP travelling with the entourage assures everyone: "You'll find him outside somewhere playing with the youngsters."

One little girl in the crowd notices the attention given to flower girls and decides she would like some of the prime minister's sparkle dust for herself. She heads over to where some wildflowers are growing and plucks them for herself. Intent to give them to Laurier, she makes her way through a throng of men but is rebuffed by some trying to keep the PM moving along. Crestfallen, she begins to move away when Laurier spots her. "Were you good enough to mean these for me, little girl?" Laurier asks, tenderly. The youngster quickly puts her arm forward with the wildflowers and the prime minister takes them and gives her a kiss. He does not hand the flowers off to an aide but instead takes a sprig from the bunch and puts it in the lapel of his coat. Laurier then gets into his car and waves to the adoring crowd, leaving one child a story she will tell for the rest of her life. "The Laurier the child met," writes the *Globe*, "is the Laurier those who are travelling through the West with him are learning to know."[1]

The question people are perhaps most inclined to ask about those in power or about those whom they know only through books or television is "What is so-and-so really like?" There are a number of ways to answer the question. For prime ministers who have served during the age of television, it is, perhaps, easier to get a sense of what they are like. Their words, voice, physical expressions, and the look in their eyes are all there for the viewer to see. A clear impression is created. But there is a danger in simply relying on impressions left by television because they are only representations of the public prime minister.

To get a sense of our prime ministers, we can also read what others said about them, in particular those who worked for the country's leaders or observed them closely as journalists. When one goes behind the scenes to get accounts from those who saw a PM up close, we get a better sense of what they were like. A quick example from Stephen Harper illustrates the point.

Few people developed an affection for Harper, a result of his austere and stiff television personality. And so, many Canadians were surprised to hear that behind the scenes he was known to have a well-honed sense of humour, and that he had a large repertoire of impersonations he liked to do, among them Brian Mulroney and Paul Martin. "He worked very hard at these," noted former chief of staff Ian Brodie. But Brodie also shed light on the constraints facing a prime minister. "Mr. Harper was much more careful about the public nature of the job," he said, noting that "no sense of humour is safe in public for a politician. In private, [Harper] was much more free flowing."[2]

Through anecdotes and observations of those who knew Canada's leaders, we can get a sense of "what the prime minister was really like." How did they treat others? What did their Cabinet colleagues and others think of them? How were they thought of as their time in office came to a close? This chapter will not look at the successes or failures of prime ministers and their political initiatives, but, instead, will draw a portrait of each PM based mostly on the accounts of others. It will take you behind the scenes to discover what they were like as people. Necessarily, more time is devoted in these brief sketches to those prime ministers who served longer terms than to those who held office for just a couple of years, or less. Most prime ministers here are not presented in chronological order but, rather, by groupings, loosely based on their styles and attributes. Sketches of short-term PMs, however, are presented chronologically at the end of the chapter.

Part of being a successful prime minister is the ability to engender the loyalty of the Cabinet and caucus. At the same time, the PM wants to continue to have the support of the Canadian electorate, an electorate that, according to a 2006 poll, values the common touch more than anything else among qualities they want to see in a prime minister.[3] How many of our PMs fit that description? Wilfrid Laurier's gesture to the young girl in Saskatchewan was a small but powerful example that demonstrates something of Laurier's gift with people. It was part of the reason one of his MPs, Charles "Chubby" Power, said "he had the gift of being loved."[4]

THE CHARMERS: JOHN A. MACDONALD, WILFRID LAURIER, AND BRIAN MULRONEY

Macdonald

The country's first prime minister, Sir John A. Macdonald, also had the gift of being loved. Much has been written about Laurier's vaunted "sunny ways" but as Richard Gwyn wrote in *Nation Maker*, his biography of John A., "Macdonald was the first of that seductive political breed in Canada." He was witty, personable, adorable, incorrigible. "Ordinary people outright loved him," Gwyn wrote, "because he was funny, unstuffy, a natural showman, daring, treated all as equals, and was adept at putting down hecklers in a way that never humiliated them."

Indeed, humour was one of Macdonald's great weapons — one that his successors, such as Laurier, Pearson, and Mulroney, would all put to effective use. Some said he "usually joked with a serious purpose," and colleagues occasionally worried that Macdonald was making light during some of the most serious situations. "The more grave the situation appeared to them, and the more anxious their minds were, the more apt he was to break off in the midst of the discussion with some story or joke; and on these occasions — like Abra[ha]m Lincoln's jokes — they were not always relevant."

This whimsy was one of the keys to Macdonald's success. He was a man without pretense. Like Laurier, he was gifted with children and charming to women, who enjoyed being in his company. Hugh MacLennan once wrote that he was "this utterly masculine man with so much woman in him." He liked being around people and could forgive their mistakes. He drank too much, told off-colour stories, and could have a nasty temper at times. He enjoyed the exercise of power. E.B. Biggar wrote of him in *Anecdotal Life of John A. Macdonald*: "A friend and admirer of his considered that the two most marked features of his character were love of power and contempt of money."

Today his drinking problem gets a lot of attention; it's a flaw that makes him more human. But it is clear from the recollections of people who knew and worked for Macdonald that he was a person with an excess of charisma and charm, as well as a warm heart. He was an expert manager of men and exceptionally clever in his politics. His irreverent personality seemed at odds with the job he had. "He seemed to be made so incongruously for the task which he had taken up," wrote Donald Creighton in his biography of the man known as Old Tomorrow. "He wore the dignity of a prime minister much too gaily. Surely it was a mask and he an actor."[5]

Laurier

It is difficult to understand the charisma of Wilfrid Laurier from the standpoint of today. Was a Canadian prime minister really so revered? Journalist Bruce Hutchison wrote that Laurier had a "mystical power over other men" and that "his supreme achievement was himself." Indeed, it is a challenge not to be drawn in by the descriptions of Laurier by those who knew him — and many have been over the years, from Jean Chrétien to Justin Trudeau — so it is no wonder that today he remains in the pantheon of the country's most-loved prime ministers. John A. Macdonald is his only company.

What was Laurier's secret? Indeed, what was the secret of those prime ministers such as Laurier and Macdonald who elicited such admiration from their followers? Time, attention, egalitarianism, and authenticity come to mind. Laurier, like Macdonald before him and Mulroney after him, always made time for his caucus members. Charles "Chubby" Power, a Liberal MP from 1917 to 1955, crossed paths with Laurier when the former was a young, new MP.

> He was always ready, even anxious, to talk to any
> of his followers, no matter how trivial the subject.
> One of the things that endeared him to the younger
> members of the party was his habit of meeting us in
> the corridors, inviting us into his office to smoke a
> cigarette, and passing five or ten minutes in asking us

how Bill Jones was in such-and-such a village, how so-and-so was and how he was getting along, and inquiring about our own studies and interests. After ten minutes' talking we returned to the House ready and eager to do anything we possibly could for the leader with whom we were in such perfect communion of heart and mind.[6]

Laurier exhibited a sense of egalitarianism and authenticity that others noticed and admired. Whether he was making time for MPs on Parliament Hill or hosting them and their wives at his home — which he did regularly — Laurier's charisma touched everyone. He was equally at home among royalty, but everyone was treated the same. "Courtesy was not assumed as a mantle," said Canada's first female senator, Cairine Wilson, in a remembrance of Laurier. "For at Windsor Castle or in the humblest home Laurier was always the same and appeared to shed lustre on any surroundings."[7]

Hutchison's apt phrase describing Laurier as having a "mystical power over other men" is a theme that comes up consistently in what is written about the Liberal party's greatest icon. In Richard Clippingdale's 1979 biography, the author writes, "One word of warning may be appropriate for the uninitiated in Laurier land: Sir Wilfrid is awfully hard to resist once you get to know him at all. As that jaunty journalist Edward William Thomson said of him in 1911: 'He bamboozles me most sweetly, often. I know when he does it, and he knows I know. Still I am bamboozled, which is the main thing.'"[8]

Whether it was with his colleagues, royalty, or children, Laurier was gifted among Canadian prime ministers. He remains the avatar of the very best in our leaders, so it was not surprising that Prime Minister Justin Trudeau invoked Laurier's famous "sunny ways" in his acceptance speech after winning the 2015 election. When Laurier died in 1919, Prime Minister Robert Borden was in France taking part in the Versailles treaty negotiations. It was left to his minister of finance, Sir Thomas White, to praise a leader the *Globe* newspaper called "Canada's most distinguished son." He captured Laurier's indelible attributes:

He was endowed by nature with a singularly graceful, picturesque, and commanding personality, a stately bearing, a most gracious charm of disposition. He had high intellectual culture and much personal kindliness of heart. The combination made him a great gentleman, whose distinction and individuality wrought an indelible impression upon all with whom he was brought in contact. While conciliatory and always a believer in persuasion rather than in compulsion, he had a firm will and strong tenacity of his settled views, opinions, and policies. This gave him strength which always of itself attracts. He had in marked degree that mystic quality, that innate attribute, called personal magnetism or personality, which is really the totality of excellence, physical, mental, and moral, in its fortunate possessor.[9]

Sir Wilfrid Laurier had the human touch like few other prime ministers. In this photograph, taken in 1911, Laurier is holding the hand of Doris Harcourt, daughter of Viscount Harcourt, who was the minister in charge of the colonies at the time. Laurier's display of tenderness — extremely rare for the time — reveals his ability to connect with people of all ages, and the affection he held for people and they for him.

Mulroney

Sir John A. Macdonald and Sir Wilfrid Laurier are well known for their talents at managing men and holding loyalty. Their personalities, while different, still led to the same successful route as prime minister. While many Canadians might be loath to admit it, the same could be said about Brian Mulroney.

Unlike Macdonald and Laurier, who never experienced comparable drops in their approval ratings, Mulroney's popularity among Canadians reached historic lows in the early 1990s. While he enjoyed a 60 percent approval rating in March 1989, by the middle of 1991, in the aftermath of the failure of the Meech Lake Accord and challenging economic times, Mulroney's approval ratings dropped to a record low of 12 percent. Even during his first term in office his approval rating once dropped to 23 percent. And yet, throughout all of this turmoil, there was no caucus revolt asking for Mulroney to resign. Canadians may have wanted it, but not those who worked for the prime minister. Why?

As was the case with Macdonald and Laurier, Mulroney liked people and put the time in to cultivate relationships. Former senator Marjory LeBreton, who worked for four different Conservative party leaders, including as appointments secretary to Mulroney, observed:

> Even in the darkest days when we were low in the polls, the one thing the media or the public never really fathomed is how Brian Mulroney kept people working so closely with him in caucus, so loyal to him; there must have been something there. And there was. He didn't ask you to do anything he wasn't prepared to do himself. I had worked for four leaders, and far and away he was the most personable, the one I had the most fun with, the one who was the most considerate of my family, the one I could sit and talk to on the phone for hours. He was a genuinely interested, friendly, and nice person.[10]

Mulroney genuinely loved his caucus; in fact, he said it was one of the main things he would miss about being prime minister (the other being Harrington Lake). His use of the telephone was legendary, a tool he employed like no other PM before or since to keep in touch not only with his caucus but also the members of his bulging Rolodex. This communication was one of the reasons so many people appreciated Mulroney, but it was a side of him that took place far from public view.

Two quick examples: In 1989 when there was speculation Finance Minister Michael Wilson would be fired because of a budget leak, Mulroney personally telephoned Wilson's elderly father to assure him this was not the case. On another occasion, he called a journalist who had checked in to a detox centre and offered his support.[11] He reached out to people on their birthdays and other important moments. As LeBreton noted, "That's why people who have worked for him will say that he's the mirror opposite of what the public thought of him."[12]

Like Macdonald, and to a lesser extent Laurier, Mulroney had a sense of humour — though it was sometimes described as vulgar. And he loved to tell a good story. He had a large ego (all prime ministers do; it's just that some hide it better than others), which was often on display. When given a list of criticisms of his leadership in 1991, Mulroney responded, "That is exactly what they said about John A. Macdonald."[13] Mulroney often made comparisons to Canada's first PM. He told Peter C. Newman, as part of what became the 2006 book *The Secret Mulroney Tapes*, "By the time history is done looking at this and you look at my achievements as opposed to any others, certainly no one will ever be in Sir John A.'s league — but my nose will be a little ahead of most in terms of achievements."

Brian Mulroney had his detractors. There were many. Some found him too glib or too prone to hyperbole. Others described him as unctuous or vain — a 1991 *Maclean's* magazine profile said, "Mulroney too often seems to be the first and most effusive admirer of his own accomplishments." On more than one occasion he got himself into trouble for speaking a little too candidly or colourfully (some might appreciate such candour today). He could come across as "too hot" for television. And he could be his own worst enemy.

But in his interactions with others, you will have to look far and wide before you will find someone who will say something disparaging about his interpersonal skills and ability to manage a caucus, Cabinet, or party. Like Laurier, he knew how to flatter. (In my interviews with him for this book, he made me feel like an insider. He shared inside gossip with me and once asked my opinion of a speech he was working on after reading me an excerpt.) It must also be said, however, that he always took an interest in the lives of those around him. Like all prime ministers, he had considerable strengths married to undeniable flaws.

THE GENTLEMEN: LOUIS ST. LAURENT AND LESTER B. PEARSON

St. Laurent

Where Brian Mulroney was criticized for his vanity and hubris but revered for his behind-the-scenes ability to manage colleagues, two prime ministers stand above all others for their utter humanity and deft common touch: Louis St. Laurent and Lester B. Pearson.

Louis St. Laurent earned a reputation for his human touch, although he did not always exude the warmth that his successor as Liberal leader, Lester Pearson, did and was sometimes remote from his colleagues. In public, he was perceived as "Uncle Louis," a nickname he got during the 1949 election campaign. St. Laurent was suffering from laryngitis and the advice was that he should not give any speeches. "Just shake hands and give the impression of being benevolent, old Uncle Louis.[14] A reporter put the label on him and it stuck.

There were two sides to St. Laurent: the Uncle Louis side and the CEO side. "While he was invariably courteous and straightforward in his relations with persons who worked closely with him, and inspired in them a high degree of loyalty and devotion," noted Dale C. Thomson in his biography of him, "there was a lack of personal contact between him and his staff that was difficult to reconcile with his public image as 'Uncle Louis.'" One public servant from the St. Laurent years captured this duality, saying the PM was "a man who, in his time, was very, very highly regarded, indeed. I just had, as everybody did, the greatest respect for him. That having been said, he was, I think, a very remote man. He was not the kind of fellow you'd sit down with and have a drink with."[15]

Canadians saw both the avuncular and executive sides of St. Laurent. Running a government and a Cabinet, he was efficient, disciplined, and results oriented. "More than any prime minister I have known," wrote Jack Pickersgill, who was secretary to the Cabinet, "St. Laurent dominated his Cabinet, not by imposing his authority, but by his sheer intellect, his wide knowledge, and his unequalled persuasiveness." There was an old joke that used to be told around Ottawa that said St. Laurent made governing look so easy he made Canadians think anyone could do the job — so they then elected John Diefenbaker.

Around Parliament, his respect for the lives of others made an impression. One evening when the prime minister was leaving his office he asked the elevator operator why he was still at work. "I leave when you do," the operator told him. "From now on," St. Laurent replied, "you go home at the end of the day with everyone else. I can get myself down the elevator just fine."[16]

These are the types of anecdotes about St. Laurent that come up repeatedly in any accounts of those who spent time with him. Mike Deacey, who worked for four prime ministers as a personal assistant and regarded St. Laurent as a father figure, told of the time the PM asked him to accompany him and Mrs. St. Laurent to New York City. Deacey demurred, saying there were officials with higher seniority who should go. But the prime minister was adamant he come. In fact, St. Laurent had manufactured a reason to need to go to New York in the first place because he had discovered in conversation that Deacey had a sister who lived there. The trip would afford Deacey a chance to visit her. St. Laurent even insisted on meeting her, too, so he and Deacey made an impromptu visit for tea while in Manhattan.

It is rare to see a prime minister as highly regarded as St. Laurent. He was admired by those both inside and outside government. "Whether it be in public or private life," Conservative leader George Drew once told the House of Commons, "I trust and I am confident that the prime minister will at all times have in his heart a feeling of satisfaction knowing that, whatever our political opinions may be, we all respect him for the public service he has rendered."

St. Laurent's utter lack of ego seems so out of place when we consider our politicians today, but his disposition is worthy of emulating.

Prime Minister Louis St. Laurent got the nickname "Uncle Louis" because of his gentle and benevolent disposition. He is pictured here with two of his grandchildren in 1948. St. Laurent was one of Canada's most highly respected leaders.

Pickersgill put it well: "What I admired most was not his superb intelligence and his judgment, which rarely failed, but his genuine modesty, his lack of concern for his place in history, and his complete freedom from meanness [or] malice of any kind. To me, he was the greatest Canadian of our time."

Pearson

Even more than St. Laurent, Lester Pearson was genuinely liked. "He was the nicest guy you would ever meet," remembered Jean Chrétien, speaking of Pearson.[17] "Mike," as he was known, made the most of his folksy charm and self-deprecating wit. One story he loved to tell was about a phone call he took from his wife, Maryon, after he became Liberal party leader. She congratulated him and told him not to forget to pick up a pound of hamburger on the way home.

Before Pearson became prime minister he was a Nobel Prize–winning diplomat, winning the laureate in 1957 for his work at solving the Suez Crisis. The skills he honed as a diplomat never left him. In 1965, when he travelled to London for the funeral of former British prime minister Winston Churchill, there were a number of VIPs standing around waiting to get into Buckingham Palace. Stilted conversation and much discomfort among the idling guests ensued. That was until Pearson came forward to engage the Russians who were in the queue. Suddenly there was conversation, banter, and laughter. What had Pearson done?

"I couldn't think what on earth to say to them until I thought of hockey," the prime minister told a reporter. "Then they gave me a sort of ribbing about us losing and I told them that didn't mean much because we had all these better players that we couldn't play internationally," the prime minister continued. "Then Marshal Konev [a Soviet military commander during the Second World War and at the time inspector general of the Ministry of Defense] said he had figured I was up to some sort of manoeuvring when I brought up hockey in the first place. And I told him he hadn't been so bad at manoeuvring himself during the war."[18]

Canadians saw Pearson as approachable as a next-door neighbour. In 1964, after the Toronto Maple Leafs won the Stanley Cup, he went to the winning dressing room to congratulate the players. Pearson spoke to journeyman player Gerry Ehman:

"Congratulations, Mr. Ehman," the prime minister said.

"Put 'er there, Mike," was the player's reply as he stuck out his hand.[19]

The perception that Pearson had an easygoing manner was real. His long-time personal secretary, Mary Macdonald, said, "He never affected an imperial style."[20] Mike Deacey, who served as a secretary to him, remarked that Pearson "never changed" after he became prime minister. "Cheerful, charming, always had a smile and you could always firmly believe when he said something, he meant it."

Ironically, Pearson had this reputation despite the fact he wore homburg hats and bow ties, the latter something he regretted. "I got a little sick of being called a bow-tie boy," he mused in 1967. "I used to wear them because I liked them, but they became a kind of political symbol, and I became tired of that." Maybe, he reflected, he should have "picked on a pipe or something more manly as a trademark."[21]

THE LONERS: ALEXANDER MACKENZIE, ROBERT BORDEN, MACKENZIE KING, R.B. BENNETT, AND STEPHEN HARPER

Mackenzie

Not all prime ministers exuded great charisma or were adept at attracting followers with magnetic appeal. One such was a stonemason whose personality was not much different from the materials with which he worked before entering politics.

Of the prime ministers who won at least one election, Alexander Mackenzie (1873–78) is the least well known. He served only one term, sandwiched between the epic governments of Sir John A. Macdonald; his time in office was nearly 150 years ago; and his personality was rather taciturn. Indeed, he was the complete opposite of Macdonald.

"As men saw him, he was industrious, reliable, competent, and uninteresting," observed Bruce Hutchison, "a devout Baptist who prayed morning and night, never touched liquor, and spent all his spare time reading the classics, or his new discovery, the Toronto *Globe*." It's a challenge to live on in the history books when that is how others see you, but any Canadian prime minister would have been wise to try to emulate Mackenzie's decidedly ethical approach to governing. He was, after all, responsible for giving the country the secret ballot.

"He aimed to do what was right and just, be the consequences what they would," wrote the *Globe* upon Mackenzie's death in 1892. "Although it might seem to some [a] shortsighted and misguided policy in a political leader, he never swerved from it, and from it he derived much consolation after he retired from the more active duties of public life."

Alexander Mackenzie was Canada's second prime minister. He was not the most charismatic person to lead the country. As Bruce Hutchison wrote, "As men saw him, he was industrious, reliable, competent and uninteresting."

Borden

If you asked Canadians which former prime minister they would love to meet if they could travel back in time, no one responds by saying Robert Borden, a leader who barely registers at all on the index of well-known Canadians, despite the fact he led the country through the significant challenges of the First World War. He also spent decades as the face of the $100 bill, though plans were to remove him from the banknote as part of the shuffling of faces on the country's paper currency — a result of the Trudeau government's decision to put Viola Desmond on the $10 bill in 2018.

Borden's anonymity is mostly the result of the country's general historical amnesia, but it is also the product of the stolid persona of a United Empire Loyalist from Nova Scotia. Becoming prime minister after defeating Wilfrid Laurier in 1911, Borden naturally endured comparisons to his predecessor, a contest he was never going to win. Borden was as straightforward and modest as Laurier was eloquent and magnetic.

"In contrast with the brilliant Laurier … he was called cold and unappealing," wrote the *Globe and Mail* at the time of Borden's death in 1937. "He was not the type of politician usually sought to cast glamour over the electorate."

That is the portrait of Borden that prevails, and to some extent it is accurate. He had a serious and taciturn disposition. He, too, was capable of enormous amounts of work, often running himself down to the point of exhaustion. His speeches set no one on fire. A 1914 description of him could well have been written about Harper: "Borden does not try to melt or to move. If he did he would be unsuccessful. He addresses his argument solely and wholly to the reason. He is a great advocate, but he never relies on rhetoric, or sentiment, or emotion. He is practical, argumentative, logical, austere, and stern."[22]

In his Cabinet, Borden allowed for a full airing of views and sought consensus, but few saw him as an inspirational force. "He was deliberate and patient with his colleagues," wrote Robert Craig Brown in his biography of Borden. One Cabinet minister wrote of the prime minister after a meeting: "Undecided as usual."

There was another side to Robert Borden. He had a sense of humour and was said to enjoy a crude joke over a drink. Not only did he indulge in alcohol, Borden is also the only prime minister to chew tobacco (he also smoked a pipe), which he did only in private, keeping a small quid under his cheek.

There was a humanity to him that few saw, however — a tenderness that belied the stone face with large moustache that appeared on the banknote. He wrote constantly to his wife, Laura, when he was away on government business. Visiting wounded Canadian soldiers during the war was a priority for him — he stopped by fifty-two hospitals in one 1915 trip to Europe — and they struck an emotional chord with him. "It was the most deeply moving experience of all my life," he said.[23] "What splendid boys they are," he wrote to Laura after a 1917 visit. "It warms my heart to see them."

Intellectual, faithful, compelled to duty, stern, and even a tad boring, Borden was not the country's most compelling prime minister in terms of personality. Perhaps that is why so little has been written about him since his death in 1937. On the occasion, the *Globe and Mail* wrote, "At all times Sir Robert declined to be spectacular, and made no display of brilliance; but he was a statesman of unusual culture, and gave added dignity to whatever position he held. Of his greatness there can be no doubt."[24] Not such a bad epitaph.

King

Today, people still wonder how Mackenzie King was able to stay in power so long, especially given his lack of personal appeal. He was also notorious for being terrible to work for. "I once said about working for him that he'd called his book *Industry and Humanity*," said Jack Pickersgill, who also worked for King, referring to King's dense 1918 book. "But there was plenty of industry and no humanity [to working for him]." Pickersgill's assessment was not uncommon. Indeed, the portrait of Mackenzie King that emerges from those who knew him is not flattering. The prime minister had no concern for the private or family lives of his staff and worked them constantly. He would think nothing of a calling a man in the middle of the evening to come back to Laurier House to work. Working twelve hour days, seven days a week, was not unusual. A married man found it tough, noted Mike Deacey. There were a lot of "burnt suppers and sometimes an angry wife."

Not only that, the prime minister was not that much fun or able to relax at the end of the day. Work was his life. Gordon Robertson, who worked in King's office from 1945 to 1948, recounted the story of the time he, the prime minister, and Jacques Gréber (a French architect who advised Ottawa's Federal District Commission — now the National Capital Commission — on a new design for the city) were in New York for meetings.

After meeting for about an hour at the Harvard Club, where King liked to stay, it was time for drinks. King asked Gréber and Robertson to repair to the bar. Both of the prime minister's guests grew excited about the prospect of a drink to unwind after a long day. But Scotch or a cold gin and tonic were not on the agenda. King, a teetotaller, said "Well, gentlemen, will we all have lemonade?"

"No one had the courage to suggest a preference for anything else," Robertson recalled in his memoir. "We solemnly drained the sour juice from the elegant glasses with as much show of satisfaction as we could muster. King went off to his bed in the club, and we to ours."

King was also a cheapskate, who tried to avoid any expenses at all times. Robertson learned that if he ever wanted to be reimbursed for money he gave to King — who never had cash with him — he needed get the receipts right away. So Robertson pre-made receipts for King to sign when he turned over money to him.

While King had little regard for those who worked for him, he was a perfectionist and a highly driven man who worked late into the evenings. There was no secretary who could meet his many demands, and there was no such thing as a routine piece of correspondence if his signature appeared at the bottom of the page. Even "the simplest letter of congratulation or message of sympathy was revised with the same painstaking care as the most important speech or state paper." Speech writing was a particularly challenging enterprise for his staff as it was not unusual to have fifteen drafts with corrections during the process, which saw the text going back and forth from the East Block office to

Laurier House. "After every speech he always felt and nearly always said: 'If only there had been one more day.'"

In Cabinet, King was disciplined — and no smoking was allowed. He could be ruthless in the exercise of power and always knew what he wanted to achieve. He let his ministers do their jobs and allowed for a full airing of views. "While he did not intimidate his colleagues," noted Pickersgill, "he certainly dominated the Cabinet."

But there was another side to King — perhaps it was just that this side did not reveal itself enough. He could be funny and engaging in conversation. "To meet Mr. King at close range … to listen to him talk, was to realize the charm he had and to know why he was such a forceful personality at international gatherings," wrote Blair Fraser in *Maclean's*. "In public he was both cold and stiff … his private talk was blunt, forthright, and memorable."[25] Indeed, King — as with other prime ministers — could make you feel as though what he was telling you was for your ears only.

"He was a man who did a great many anonymous acts of deep human kindness," remembered Lester B. Pearson at the unveiling of King's statue on Parliament Hill in 1968. "No one he knew — and indeed many he did not know — ever suffered loss or misfortune without the prime minister sending a message of sympathy and consolation. He could be a very warm human being as well as a cool and calculating politician."[26]

Pearson and Fraser have hit upon the two sides of King. There was little love for him, in contrast to the feelings that Macdonald and Laurier inspired, but there was plenty of respect. It is no surprise that King remains something of an enigma today. He was notoriously difficult to nail down politically — recall his famous phrase about conscription during the Second World War: "Conscription if necessary, but not necessarily conscription" — and nailing down his personality was also a challenge. As a *Globe and Mail* editorial noted upon King's death, he "lacked the capacity to inspire multitudes by personal magnetism," yet he was our longest serving prime minister. The editorial later noted that "his whole life was in his work" and yet "as an individual he was a man of great charm … a skilled host, and excelled at the handling of intimate gatherings." Poet F.R. Scott was prescient when he wrote in his 1957 poem "W.L.M.K.," "Truly he will be remembered / Wherever men honour ingenuity, / Ambiguity, inactivity, and political longevity."

Bennett

R.B. Bennett, who served as prime minister for five years (1930–35) between two of Mackenzie King's periods in office, had a reputation for being a loner and a tight manager. He encroached on the responsibilities of his Cabinet ministers, which upset his colleagues. He also served as his own minister of finance and minister of external affairs. "He erected a personal dictatorship," wrote Bruce Hutchison in *Mr. Prime Minister*, "benign, strictly honest, industrious, competent, but entirely dependent on its boss. What was to be called, in our time, the cult of personality had arrived."[27]

There is a famous 1931 cartoon by Arch Dale that appeared in the *Winnipeg Free Press* in which Bennett is depicted holding a Cabinet meeting where he is surrounded at the table by replications of himself. Bennett viewed his Cabinet as a board of directors, but as his biographer, John Boyko, noted, "He listened and sought opinion, but in the end his was the only voice that mattered." In another anecdote that gets told in many different versions, a passerby near Parliament sees the prime minister walking down the street talking to himself. He asks himself aloud what the man is doing. "That's the prime minister and he's having a Cabinet meeting," comes the reply.

Like King, Bennett was exacting in his expectations of those who worked for him and had a tremendous capacity for work. "A man of amazing vitality, he insisted on attending to details himself and wore out relays of secretaries and stenographers dictating to the last unimportant letter," the *Globe and Mail* recalled in a profile at the time of his death in 1947. He was famous for his prodigious memory but was impatient and acted as though he were the smartest person in the room.

Bennett could be bombastic, particularly in the House of Commons. Liberal MP Chubby Power said of him: "In this house he often exhibits the manners of a Chicago policeman and the temperament of a Hollywood actor."[28] In person, he could be brusque and aloof with others. He promised his mother he would not consume alcohol or smoke, a promise he kept, though he occasionally drank crème de menthe, rationalizing it by saying it was non-alcoholic. His main vice was a near insatiable appetite for chocolates, which he ate often and regularly. He had a girth to prove it.

Behind the scenes, he showed some compassion. As prime minister during the Great Depression, he received hundreds of letters from Canadians asking for assistance. Often he slipped his own money into his replies. Whenever Bennett heard a child was born and given the name Richard Bedford, he sent a silver christening mug to the family. Throughout his life he supported the education of eighteen young people. At Christmas, he would mail out dozens of boxes of chocolates and hundreds of gifts of flowers.[29]

No one was about to run through a wall for Bennett — he "had no capacity for making friends," observed Tommy Douglas. Like King, he was alone at the top and seemed to like it that way. In the end, he died alone in England in the bathtub.

Harper

Stephen Harper has occasionally been compared to both R.B. Bennett and Mackenzie King. Like the former, he preferred to think of himself as the smartest guy in the room; as with the latter, he was no charmer and few voters developed an affection for him. A poll conducted in 2008 found that 55 percent of Canadians agreed with the statement that "there is something about Stephen Harper that I just don't like."

Harper, Bennett, and King would never be accused of being overly sentimental, charismatic, or interested in the team game. Quite the opposite. "Stephen Harper may be the most solitary prime minister we have ever had," wrote Harper biographer and *Globe and Mail* journalist, John Ibbitson. "Although he will ask relevant staff to offer their opinions on an important issue, he hates sitting around with others, blue-skying or talking through an issue. His thought process is linear, and it requires solitude to function."

Like many prime ministers — but perhaps Bennett and King chief among them — Harper had an astonishing ability for work and attention to detail. He methodically pored over his briefing books, notating them in ways that impressed those in the civil service. His preparation and meticulous approach was reminiscent of Louis St.

Laurent and had a similar impact on his Cabinet in that many were intimidated, refraining from speaking lest they should be made to look ill-informed. And, incidentally, like St. Laurent, Harper had a hot temper that could result in a flurry of expletives. Harper was a "Frankenstein monster who terrorized his cabinet and caucus," wrote Conrad Black in the *National Post*.[30] Unlike St. Laurent, however, there was an unfortunate negativity to Harper's disposition that some would argue ultimately led to his political demise in 2015 when it contrasted starkly with "Sunny Ways" 2.0 in Justin Trudeau.

Jeffrey Simpson and Brian Laghi spoke to a number of insiders for their detailed 2008 profile of Harper that appeared in the *Globe and Mail*. "There's a menacing undertone sometimes," noted one civil servant who had sat in on government meetings. "He can go very cold and cut ministers to the quick. He uses an icy, cold voice.... When he gets mad, he speaks softly but he gets very red in the face and goes to that mean, partisan place. He's very capable of making a piercing comment that's part of the intimidation."

To some degree, all prime ministers are misunderstood as people. Canadians will take a disliking to them because of a political policy, or they will fixate on some aspect to their personality that they don't like. Bennett, King, and Harper would be at the top of that list of misunderstood PMs. So would Pierre Trudeau and Brian Mulroney. In reality, the prime minister is never as unlikeable or awful as Canadians like to think. The same was true for Stephen Harper. The cold and robotic persona we usually saw in public masked a funny and soft side seen by his friends and family.

"Within his tight circle of family and friends," Simpson and Laghi continued, "the Prime Minister is seen as warm and caring. To everyone else, he is a buttoned-up, buttoned-down politician who commands respect but little affection."

This is why Canadians were startled to see Harper playing the piano and singing at the National Arts Centre in Ottawa in 2009. It revealed a fun and softer side of the PM they had never witnessed. One Carleton University professor presented a paper about Harper's use of music to the Congress of the Humanities and Social Sciences in 2015 and later told the *National Post*, "There's something about music that gives him the opportunity to present a kind of interior life. Music is just such a powerful emotional shorthand."[31]

Many wondered why this side of the PM was not trotted out more often, but it was simply not in Harper's nature. Private, reserved, and somewhat shy ("A room filled with people he doesn't know is Stephen Harper's idea of hell"), he preferred to stay out of this kind of spotlight.

Former Harper advisor Tom Flanagan once referred to Harper as "Mackenzie King without a Ouija board." One day some historian might write a book comparing the two. But another *Maclean's* writer, Paul Wells, echoed Blair Fraser's earlier description of King when writing about meeting Harper. "A conversation with Stephen Harper is a real conversation. He listens, is curious, asks questions, responds with something that relates to what you said, contests your conclusions if he disagrees, shuts up if you know more."[32]

Like King, he was a perfectionist, inclined to work alone, but capable of compassion. He noticeably choked up when delivering the government's apology for residential schools in 2008. And after the 2014 attack on Parliament Hill, the prime minister crossed the floor to hug NDP Opposition leader Tom Mulcair and Liberal leader Justin Trudeau. But Harper was always something of an enigma to Canadians, much like King. Sometimes you only get out of a relationship as much as you are willing to put into it. Not a backslapper like Macdonald, nor a charmer like Laurier; he needed to be encouraged to pick up the telephone to stroke people, something that was second nature to Mulroney. But Harper was his own man. "People ask me what he's like," said one observer. "And I say 'He's exactly what you think he's like.' Very serious, inscrutable."[33]

ONE OF A KIND: JOHN DIEFENBAKER, PIERRE TRUDEAU, AND JEAN CHRÉTIEN

Diefenbaker

The prime minister has many important functions but one that remains paramount is the ability to manage people. Interpersonal skills are not to be underestimated. No other prime minister failed as spectacularly in this regard as John Diefenbaker, a man who is perhaps the most fascinating character study of all our prime ministers. Moody, petty, insecure, suspicious, and vain, Diefenbaker was also funny, thoughtful, and playful. But his attributes stood in the shadows cast by his liabilities. His inability to trust people and to get the most from them prevented him from being successful at his job. "The right instincts were in him," wrote Peter C. Newman in *Renegade in Power*, "but throughout his stormy stewardship, they languished in the cupboard of his soul."

Diefenbaker was larger than life, and there is no shortage of comments or anecdotes to draw upon to help shed light on his habits and personality. Arrogance and a lack of trust were problems at the top of the list. "He always wanted to run his own show," said his long-time personal secretary, Bunny Pound.

Not surprisingly, he did not get along well with his Cabinet, which was in a state of near-mutiny in 1963 as it lurched from crisis to crisis. Unfortunately, the 1958 landslide election victory, in which Diefenbaker won the largest parliamentary majority in history, changed him. He became intoxicated by power. George Hees, who served as minister of transport and, later, minister of trade, put it well: "He began to think he had all the ideas in his own head, which he hadn't," he said. "It wasn't an attitude he had before, he always listened to advice before, and I think that he lacked [that skill] somewhat in being prime minister, certainly after 1958."[34] As Jean Chrétien later described him: "It looked as if he thought God had chosen him prime minister."

John Diefenbaker had always burnished his reputation for being just an ordinary Canadian. He was known to many as plain "John," and indeed that was part of his appeal across Canada. He was seen as friendly and easy to get along with. But when he became PM this changed. He wanted to be greeted at the airport by a large contingent of staff and Cabinet ministers. When a reporter once referred to him by his first name — certainly a breach of protocol — Diefenbaker called the news agency he worked for and asked for him to be fired.[35] "He interpreted the people's splendid acclaim of him as adequate proof of his greatness and became intoxicated with the authority of his office," wrote Newman. And this was his downfall. A prime minister not comfortable in his own skin, unable to lead or trust his team, will not be successful.

There was a gentler side to Diefenbaker, however. Basil Robinson, a foreign policy adviser to Dief, wrote his own memoir in 1989 titled *Diefenbaker's World*. When *Rogue Tory*, the seminal biography on Diefenbaker, was published in 1995 by Denis Smith, Robinson wrote to the author in a letter that captured the two sides of the Chief:

> One aspect that I wish I had written more of in *Diefenbaker's World* is the personal side of life with Diefenbaker. He was, of course, often impossible, and at first I wondered if I would be able to cope with his moods and suspicions. But as we came to know each other in daily encounters, at home or on the road, he was never inaccessible even when he was otherwise preoccupied — an important point on which I could not say the same for all the ministers I have worked for/with. After a year or so I felt I could talk frankly to him without getting thrown out of the room, and if we had a little crossing of swords he would nearly always find an early way of signaling that he did not want relations to be strained. He could be hilariously funny in moments of relaxation and also remarkably considerate if one were ill or coping with some family crisis. One of my children still speaks gratefully of being taught to fish by the prime minister at Harrington Lake.[36]

Smith replied by writing that he, "too, may not have said enough about his kindnesses and sense of the ridiculous."[37] Indeed, Diefenbaker could be charming and wonderful toward others — particularly if they posed no threat to him. Unfortunately, this aspect of him was not a big enough part of his personality to compensate for his flaws. He was Lear-like in his demands for loyalty and respect, but as far as being prime minister goes, as Newman aptly surmised, "even some of his most loyal disciples began to regard him as a man to be cherished for his symbolic value, rather than for his capabilities as prime minister."

Trudeau

Pierre Trudeau continues to capture the attention of Canadians, more than any other former prime minister. This is just another way of saying, "He haunts us still," a line so common when reading about Trudeau, it starts to grate. Part of this continuing fascination with the man is due to the fact that baby boomers were coming of age at the height of Trudeaumania in 1968, so the sheer number of people who recall him means he continues to play a role in any national discussion of prime ministers. He was a part of their world. He is also the country's third-longest serving PM.

While Trudeau and John Diefenbaker share little in common, it is true that they were both larger-than-life figures whose unique personalities made an indelible impact on Canadians. Who could forget his famous pirouette done behind the back of Queen Elizabeth II in 1977 at the London G7 meeting? At first thought to be a spontaneous gesture, the pirouette was, in fact, something that Trudeau had been planning in the hours beforehand. Despite that, the fact that he would have the audacity to perform such a stunt is indicative of a flair and a sense of the dramatic unique in Canada's prime ministers. Thumbing his nose at the rules of international protocol, Trudeau succeeded in creating an image of someone irreverent and fascinating. That act captures the essence of his public persona that set him apart from all of his predecessors. As Roger Graham once wrote, quoted by Michael Bliss in an essay that appeared in the 1998 book, *Trudeau's Shadow,* "Had there ever been in Canada a national party leader quite like this? ... Sir Wilfrid Laurier, let us say, sliding down a banister? Sir Robert Borden in goggles and flippers? Arthur Meighen in a Mercedes? Mackenzie King at judo? R.B. Bennett on skis?"[38] The answers were always, "No."

Unlike a Macdonald, Laurier, or Mulroney, Trudeau — who has been described as shy — sought and enjoyed his solitude and privacy. "He was not the kind of guy who would hang around to have a beer with you," recalled Jean Chrétien.[39] He was more like Mackenzie King and Stephen Harper in this regard. The image of the prime minister paddling his canoe on his own is a picture that captures the private side of him. There would be no backslapping or calls into his office for chit-chat or small talk of any kind. He feared the intrusions into his private time, and while he enjoyed meeting people, this was true only to a point. He did not require it as fuel, as was the case with some prime ministers. To many people he was remote. Cabinet colleague Donald Macdonald wrote that Trudeau treated all but his closest friends with "patrician reserve."[40]

On the other hand, he was capable of exhibiting personal charm when he wanted to, particularly toward staff at the House of Commons or young people. But as with other prime ministers, some of his best qualities remained hidden from the view of Canadians at large. "He is, at times, a very gentle man, a very shy man," recalled his secretary from his early days, Mary Macdonald. "He's a very strong and powerful man and he changes. The roles are intertwined in him. He's an individual, I'm sure you know he's one of the nicest, easiest people. I really enjoyed my association."

Despite some of the adventurous aspects of Trudeau's personality, there was also a considerable degree of formality to him. "Mr. Trudeau understood well the majesty of the office," said Ivan Head, who served as his special assistant. "In the entire period he was prime minister — whether we were alone, whether we were abroad, whether we were in his office in front of officials or in the presence of press or foreigners — [not once] did I ever refer to him by his first name during that period. He was always prime minister."[41]

Some of this formality was transferred to Trudeau's Cabinet meetings which were much more organized and disciplined than those of his predecessor, Lester B. Pearson. He insisted that everyone be heard and there was an order to conversations, unlike with the Pearson Cabinet where it was not uncommon for two or more conversations to take place at the same time. There was never any doubt about who was leading the council, but Trudeau was not the type to simply say any decision was a *fait accompli*. Writing in his 1985 memoir *Straight from the Heart*, Jean Chrétien, who held various Cabinet portfolios throughout the Trudeau years, noted, "[Trudeau's] nature was to challenge, to provoke, to buck the trend, and he didn't mind making enemies in the process." Continuing, Chrétien added, "But that didn't mean he acted in an authoritarian manner when the debate turned to decision."

There was a combative and competitive element to Trudeau, which would come as no surprise to those who remember him. Whether it was giving the middle finger to protesters in British Columbia or telling a reporter, "Just watch me," when asked how far he would go to end the October Crisis in 1970, Trudeau was always ready for a battle of some kind. Loved by some, loathed by others, Trudeau remains, nearly thirty-five years after he left office, one of the country's few indelible political figures.

Chrétien

While Jean Chrétien had many characteristics common among prime ministers, such as toughness and pride, he was also singular in the folksy, backwoodsman persona that he cultivated — something that he used to great political advantage in becoming prime minister in 1993. "The plain-spoken, rough-hewn Mr. Chrétien, who abjured grand visions in favour of nuts-and-bolts problem-solving, seemed to many voters to be just the antidote the country needed," reflected the *Globe and Mail* as Chrétien's time in office was coming to a close. "Mr. Mulroney was slick; Mr. Chrétien, quite clearly, was not."

He was not slick. Jean Chrétien was combative, stubborn, and ultracompetitive. "Any game he's in, he needs to win," recalled Peter Donolo, his director of communications.[42] The extent of Chrétien's competitive bent was mostly kept from the public, as it conflicted with the relaxed image the prime minister liked to project, an image embodied by the aw-shucks "little guy from Shawinigan" caricature. Former prime minister Joe Clark had a good sense of this and touched upon it in his 2003 tribute to Chrétien given in the House of Commons. "What is remarkable about the prime minister, at least before power changed him, is that he could have been the next-door neighbour, anywhere in Canada. It is not just that he felt at home. Canadians feel at home with him, and this is a real and personal tribute."

Behind the public facade, however, was a man who loved art, architecture, and classical music, something few Canadians knew about Chrétien. One example that captures the dual nature of the man is the fact that he would watch football on television with the sound off so that he could listen to his Mozart and Brahms. ("One-third of the players are named Smith, anyway, so I could still follow it," he quipped in an interview with me.)

Remembering the endless discussion of Pierre Trudeau's sessions, Chrétien's Cabinet meetings were brisk and businesslike, rarely lasting longer than the allotted time of two hours. Ministers were left to do their jobs and Chrétien was always approachable. "He didn't praise and he didn't criticize," recalled Lyle Vanclief who was minister of agriculture from 1997 to 2003. "But you could be candid with him. He was the kind of individual I could always feel comfortable asking for a conversation, to share some of his wisdom on just about anything."[43]

He was stung by criticism that he did not read or request documents with great detail, but it was not his style — he was not a King, Trudeau, or Harper. "He didn't have the time or inclination to be a details person, and was certain that wasn't the job of a prime minister," wrote Eddie Goldenberg, Chrétien's senior political advisor for more than thirty years. "Rather he wanted to manage the big picture, and take time to himself for reflection and strategic thinking."[44] He was resentful of the elites who looked down upon him even as he stoked his everyman reputation. But he was always approachable.

Behind the scenes, Chrétien could be humorous, angry, generous, and dismissive. He would pour a cup of coffee for a colleague at the same time he was denouncing him. He told reporters in 1997, after the RCMP used pepper spray on protesters in Vancouver, "For me, pepper, I put it on my plate." He quietly gave blood after the September 11, 2001, terrorist attacks. But you would not want to have crossed him, for he had streaks of pettiness and revenge that ran through him.

While Chrétien's popularity dipped in his final years in office, when it seemed as though he had lost his common touch and overstayed his welcome, many Canadians who remember him would likely rank him high among prime ministers with whom they would most like to have a beer. He appeared to be more at home in the pool hall than in 24 Sussex Drive, a point made colourfully in Lawrence Martin's biography *Iron Man*. "It was as if he'd been taken straight from the factory floor and plunked down under the chandeliers.... The deluxe sofa he rested on might just as well have been a stool in the corner of the boxing ring, its occupant, age sixty-nine, ready to go a few rounds with anyone dumb enough to take him on."[45]

SHORT-TERM PRIME MINISTERS

Of Canada's twenty-three prime ministers, nine of them — nearly 40 percent — served under two and half years. Their lack of historical significance does not permit a full portrait of them all, but a thumbnail sketch of each is appropriate. Just because they served a short time in office does not mean they were not interesting characters or that they lacked engaging stories. Here's a brief look at the country's short-term prime ministers, in chronological order.

THE CARETAKERS: JOHN ABBOTT, JOHN THOMPSON, MACKENZIE BOWELL, AND CHARLES TUPPER

After the death of Sir John A. Macdonald in 1891, the country was led by a series of four men, whose time ranged from Charles Tupper's sixty-eight days in office — the shortest stint of any PM in history — to Sir John Thompson, who held the job for just over two years.

Macdonald's immediate successor was John Abbott. "Venerable and well-mannered, fond of whist and cribbage," was how historian P.B. Waite described him.[46] Abbott claimed to have never liked politics: "Why should I go where the doing of public work will only make me hated … and where I can gain reputation and credit by practising arts which I detest to acquire popularity?" Abbott was seventy years old when he came into office, and failing health (see chapter 5) meant he resigned after just more than eighteen months as prime minister.

His successor was John Thompson (1892–94). Thompson is the only prime minister other than John A. Macdonald to die in office (see chapter 5). He was highly respected in the House of Commons where his well-argued speeches relied on facts rather than flourishes of rhetoric. "The new Premier is certainly not jaunty, but he is no kill-joy," observed the *Globe* in 1894. The writer of that piece went on to observe that "Sir John Thompson must rely on the impression which he conveys of strength of character, coolness of judgment, and abundant courage." He was a well-organized administrator and seemingly devoid of corruption (he was a former provincial judge). "He won't even consider whether a thing is good for the party until he is quite sure it is good for the country," said one fellow Tory.

John Thompson's death resulted in the appointment of a new prime minister, Sir Mackenzie Bowell. Like Abbott, he was another septuagenarian and, like Thompson, he served briefly — 1894–96. Bowell is usually at the bottom of any ranking of Canada's prime ministers. Vain, arrogant, and utterly lacking in self-awareness, he was probably both the least-liked leader in Canadian history and its least able. "I never recall, without a blush, days of weak and incompetent administration by a Cabinet presided over by a man whose sudden and unlooked for elevation had visibly turned his head," observed Joseph Pope, who at the time was a secretary to the Cabinet. "[It was] a ministry without unity or cohesion of any kind, and prey to internal dissensions until they became a spectacle to the world, to angels and men."

Bowell was inept at managing his team, and half his Cabinet — whom he described as a "nest of traitors" — resigned in protest over his handling of the Manitoba Schools Question in 1896. He was ultimately forced out by the Cabinet and party the same year. Bowell returned to his Senate seat, where he served another twenty-three years. His replacement was Sir Charles Tupper, the last of the caretaker prime ministers in the wake of Macdonald's death.

Hailing from Nova Scotia, Tupper was a former Father of Confederation and the only medical doctor to serve as prime minister. At seventy-four years of age, he remains the oldest person to assume office, a record unlikely to be broken. Once he fixed the Cabinet mess left by Bowell, Tupper faced an election as the Conservative's five year mandate was over. Laurier and the Liberals won, and the shortest term for a Canadian prime minister was over. Tupper, though, lived until 1915 when he was ninety-four years old, therefore holding the distinction of being Canada's longest-living former PM, edging out Mackenzie Bowell by just over three months.

THE OTHERS: ARTHUR MEIGHEN, JOE CLARK, JOHN TURNER, KIM CAMPBELL, AND PAUL MARTIN

Meighen

Arthur Meighen (1920–21; 1926) was — at age forty-six when he gained office — the youngest man to serve as PM at the time. Despite that, he seems to have punched above his weight. This is largely due to his towering intellect, some saying he was the country's brightest mind. He knew all of Shakespeare's plays and quoted from them with ease. His reputation as an orator and debater in the House of Commons was well established. "He is incomparably the most powerful intellect in the House of Commons — not the finest, nor the most spacious, nor the most attractive but the most effective," wrote *Maclean's* magazine in 1921.[47] Not all agreed. Historian Michael Bliss, who devoted half a chapter of his book *Right Honourable Men* to Meighen (and no chapter on Louis St. Laurent), wrote that, "as a debater in the House of Commons, he was no more the equal of Macdonald or Laurier than liquor-store alcohol resembles good scotch."

Many rightly saw Meighen as cold, stern, and lacking the interpersonal skills that a prime minister can use to bend his colleagues to his will. He was industrious and employed logic and facts rather than emotion to rally supporters — those that there were — to his side. Meighen won all the debates, it was once said of him, but Mackenzie King won all the elections. Chubby Power, though an MP belonging to the Liberals, summed it up well when he wrote of Meighen: "I doubt that anyone would have taken off his coat to fight for Meighen had his name been mentioned with disrespect, but such a thing could easily have happened for Laurier or even for King."[48]

There is always another side, though. It was just that only those who were his close friends got to see it. Meighen could be warm and personable. As his biographer, Roger Graham, wrote in a 1955 edition of the *Queen's Quarterly*, they saw him as "friendly, charming, approachable, and quite without pretension, a man of simple tastes who liked informality and loved to tell a good joke, especially at his own expense. This part of himself, Meighen seemed to leave behind when he entered the Commons chamber."[49]

Clark

It would be more than fifty years before another short-term prime minister took the keys to 24 Sussex Drive. In 1979, Progressive Conservative leader Joe Clark (1979–80) defeated the Pierre Trudeau–led Liberals to form a minority government. It lasted just seven months before it was toppled in a non-confidence vote that restored Trudeau to power in the February 1980 election. Clark remains the youngest person ever to be prime minister, taking the job at age thirty-nine.

Clark was initially seen as a bumbler. A series of gaffes while in Opposition contributed to this. His luggage missed a connecting flight while flying from Bangkok to New Delhi in 1979; he bumped into the sharp end of a bayonet when reviewing troops in the Middle East. In truth, Clark was actually pushed by the gaggle of reporters trailing him, but it didn't matter. The media had their narrative and stuck to it.

Notwithstanding the media portrayal, people liked Joe Clark, because, perhaps more than any other prime minister with the exception of Louis St. Laurent, he had a high level of common decency. "Talking to Clark, you are struck by his candor," wrote Sandra Gwyn in *Saturday Night* magazine in 1976, "his grave natural courtesy, and — something I've never remarked before in a politician — his almost total lack of ego."

Clark lost the party leadership to Brian Mulroney in 1983 but served as one of Mulroney's most trusted Cabinet ministers, including a very successful run as external affairs minister. In 1998 he returned to lead the Progressive Conservative party, a job he held until 2003. This was part of his political renaissance, which led the *Globe and Mail* to describe him in a 2001 editorial as "cool."

"Canadians have developed a genuine affection for the battler from High River, Alta., who has proved one of Canada's great political survivors over his thirty-year career."[50]

Turner

John Turner became prime minister when he won the leadership of the Liberal party after Pierre Trudeau resigned in 1984. He served as PM from June to September, before being defeated by Brian Mulroney's Conservatives in the election held the same year. His eleven weeks in office are the second-shortest in history. Being prime minister for such a short time can be a curse. The calling card in the history books will always say that Turner was prime minister, but in his own view it obscures his time as justice minister, during which he made the greatest contribution to the country, particularly during the 1970 October Crisis.

But he was prime minister (though without a seat in the House of Commons), and by virtue of that office, he is in this book. For years pundits telegraphed him as a future PM. His looks, athleticism, and charisma all worked in his favour. "He chats as easily with tycoons as with janitors," wrote Walter Stewart, "smiles a lot, laughs a lot, and is guaranteed not to fade, rust, or drip on the carpet."[51]

His time in office was limited to the length of an election campaign. Years after he was prime minister, however, I got a taste of his charm and jocular nature. At a lunch in Toronto peppered with F-bombs and colourful stories, it was time to order dessert. Turner said he wanted a bowl of berries. "Have you got any berries?" he barked at the waiter. "I'd like to have some berries."

"Yes, we do, Mr. Turner," replied the waiter. "Would you like some whipped cream on them?"

"No, I don't want any of that bullshit on them," he groused. "Just bring me the berries, no bullshit."

When the waiter turned to me for my order, I said, "I'll have the berries, too, but bring them with the full bullshit."

Campbell

Kim Campbell was prime minister a touch longer than John Turner; her term in office is the third-shortest at 132 days. She took power in a manner similar to Turner, by winning the leadership of a party in power — the Progressive Conservatives, following the resignation of Brian Mulroney — in 1993. Like Turner, her time in office would last only a summer — in fact, she never even moved into 24 Sussex Drive, instead living at Harrington Lake when she was not campaigning.

Campbell remains the country's first and only woman to become prime minster, a fact that is still close to her heart. "I put a female face in that prime ministerial corridor to say to people girls can and should think of themselves as doing this," she told me in an interview.

A 1993 profile in *Maclean's* magazine summed up one aspect of Kim Campbell. It said that she was "tough-minded and articulate ... stylish and astute.... She can master issues with ease and flair; she can charm an audience with self-deprecating humor and biting wit. She has demonstrated a lifelong dedication to learning."

There was another side to Campbell, however. In a description that could have been written about Arthur Meighen, Pierre Trudeau, or even Mackenzie King, the authors observed, "She is loath to change her mind once she takes a position. If her opponents are adamant or ill-informed, she often responds with brusque disdain. At times, she seems to resent her critics as much as she does their criticism."

Criticism of Campbell was harsh in the wake of her smashing electoral defeat, in which the PC party won just two seats in the 1993 election. She ranks last on most PM lists. But, like Joe Clark, she experienced a renaissance. A 2017 *Maclean's* article ran under the headline "Canada's coolest PM. (It's not Justin Trudeau.)" noting that Campbell's personality traits, such as frankness and originality, have great appeal with millennials and on Twitter. She is personable, funny, thoughtful, and very mindful of her place in history as the country's first woman prime minister. No woman has come close to becoming PM since her time in office.

Martin

Canadians are lucky that in their history they have been served by a number of prime ministers whom few could argue were not good people. Paul Martin (2003–06) is near the top of that list. He was described in a 2006 *Globe and Mail* editorial as "a decent, honourable man whose long-sought opportunity to be Prime Minister of Canada fell short of expectations." He was the kind of gentleman who would light a woman's cigarette (the few that still smoked) or make sure they walked on the inside part of the sidewalk while he took the side closest to the street. Martin was a gentleman of the old-school variety but his prime ministership did not measure up.

Martin was PM for just over two years, obtaining office following the internecine Liberal party warfare between him and Jean Chrétien. He loved policy more than most prime ministers and dove right into those questions with a relentless curiosity. Like virtually all prime ministers, Martin had tremendous stamina. He worked tirelessly and refuelled by taking naps at a moment's notice, an ability he shared with Diefenbaker.

He was a great listener — some might say he was too good at it — but the price paid for all of the consultation was the nickname "Mr. Dithers," dumped on the prime minster by the *Economist*, the British magazine, in 2005. Anthony Wilson-Smith drove the point home well in a *Maclean's* article just before Martin became PM:

> A genuine interest in others is always an attractive quality in a person, and it's one of the things that draws people to Martin — as well as the fact that he's easy enough in his own skin to welcome contrary views, and to learn from them. But ... Martin has promised to do so much listening to so many disparate groups that if he keeps all his related vows, he'll never have time to accomplish anything.

Martin was always seen as a classy PM bent on doing the right thing. He's remembered as much for his work as finance minister as he is for his brief stint at 24 Sussex.

THE INCUMBENT

Justin Trudeau

Justin Trudeau's full and behind-the-scenes portrait as prime minister is still to be written, but the broad strokes seem already to be in place. His invocation of Laurier's "sunny ways" has been the hallmark of his early years in office. His predilection for hugs and intense stares into the eyes of others show someone who appears to have a high emotional intelligence. He smiles a lot and seems to thrive in the public side of being prime minister. Crowds adore him and treat him like something more than just the country's leader. He is often greeted as a rock star, not too different from the way his father was treated during the brief era of Trudeaumania. Even Conrad Black says Trudeau is impossible not to like, though critics have derided him as a "shiny pony" and opposition members continue to use "selfie" as an epithet toward him, though it does not seem to stick. Some have wondered how genuine all of the "sunny ways" and constant smiling are, but one Cabinet minister told me Trudeau is as genuine as they come. He's a kind person and his smile is real.

Trudeau is naturally curious, and when it comes to issues before his government he always wants to know more. When he is learning something, he is happy — a link, perhaps, to his days as a teacher, a beginning career that Trudeau has never ignored and views as an essential part of who he is. In Cabinet he is pleased when there is a robust discussion and a full airing of views. As the famous 2017 *Rolling Stone* piece observed, "Listening is his seducing."[52] His disposition is firm and he does not tolerate fools.

As the only PM to grow up as the child of a prime minister, Trudeau has a unique insight into the job. In the one conversation he and his father ever had about the possibility of going into politics, Pierre did not have much advice for his son. But the current occupant of the country's most important job realized that "everything I need to know about being prime minister [my dad] had already taught me, about being a good person."[53]

CHAPTER 3

"TERRESTRIAL AND CELESTIAL":
PRIME MINISTERS AND TRAVEL

I return ten times more Canadian. I have imbibed
the air, spirit and enthusiasm of the West.
— Sir Wilfrid Laurier, 1910

It is 1969, and Pierre Trudeau is up before 7:00 a.m. this cool May
morning in Chatham, New Brunswick. Trudeau is not known as
an early bird by any means, so this is something of a hardship for the
prime minister. He pulls on a blue flying suit, black boots, and heads
out from his room at the Canadian Armed Base where he had spent the
night. Trudeaumania, the phenomenon of a year ago, has faded, but
this trip to the Maritimes will see some of its vestiges return.

"Did you sleep well?" Lieutenant Colonel Stuart Millar asks him.
Millar will be the pilot of a CF-101 fighter jet known as a "Voodoo"
that will thrust him and the prime minister into the air.

"Did *you* sleep well? That's more important," Trudeau replied.

The Voodoo has dual controls. The prime minister climbs into the
jet and is strapped in to the navigator's seat. He has added a white

helmet and orange life preserver to his outfit. Trudeau has had a pilot's licence since long before he became prime minister, but as he noted, "That was in the day of the Tiger Moths."

Millar taxis the aircraft down the runway and in ten seconds it soars toward the clouds. It sweeps low over the heads of the assembled media and military personnel and "then Canada's prime minister disappeared almost vertically into a bank of clouds with the afterburners flaming behind."[1]

Moments later, when the plane has reached the height of forty-two thousand feet, the control tower reports that the prime minister is now behind the controls and flying at more than eight hundred miles per hour, breaking the sound barrier. "We have a supersonic prime minister," quips Colonel Arnie Bauer on the ground. After buzzing the base three times, Lieutenant Colonel Millar and the prime minister return — the flight was somewhat abridged, since Trudeau had been ordered back because he was running late for Mass.

Once back down, Bauer asks the PM, "Do you think it's here to stay?"

"Flying?" the prime minister replies. "I think it will last as long as sex."[2]

Pierre Trudeau was not the first prime minister to fly in an airplane, but no other PM can claim to have broken the sound barrier while flying one. The anecdote about his historic flight is a fitting place to start a chapter about the travel experiences of prime ministers. "Travel inside our far-flung country is time consuming but vital," Brian Mulroney wrote in his memoirs. "Both for the country, which sees that the prime minister takes the regions seriously, and for the PM, who avoids being stuck in an Ottawa bubble."

Trudeau escaped the bubble dramatically in his supersonic flight. For prime ministers before him, travel was decidedly slower — only a few had taken planes (none supersonic ones); those before were confined to travel by rails, seas, and roads. Regardless of the form it took, travel for prime ministers reflected both the times and the person and gives us a peek into one aspect of being prime minister that rarely reached the public's attention. Except when it was seen as too expensive.

This chapter will look at how prime ministers have travelled and some of the behind-the-scenes anecdotes from those travels.

As technology improved, the methods prime ministers used to travel changed along with it. A country that was pulled together by a transcontinental railway and whose prime ministers travelled overseas by steamship, eventually developed an intricate system of roads. Later, of course, the PMs travelled by airplane. Prime ministers used all forms of major transportation (though they also travelled by helicopter, yacht, ferry, elephant, motorcycle, snowmobile, subway, and horse-drawn carriage) in order to reach voters, meet with other Canadian leaders, and attend important international gatherings. Like many Canadians, they accumulated their own travel stories.

Sir John A. Macdonald knew that without a transcontinental railway the Dominion of Canada was merely a "geographical expression." The history of the construction of that magnificent "national dream" has been well documented, and most prime ministers made use of the ribbon of steel to meet the citizens across the country, either while campaigning or when simply escaping that Ottawa bubble of which Mulroney spoke.

In 1886, one year after the completion of the Canadian Pacific Railway, Macdonald made a country-wide tour to personally experience his greatest accomplishment as prime minister, a trip mostly remembered today for the fact that Macdonald and his wife, Lady Agnes Macdonald, spent part of the trip riding on the locomotive's cowcatcher, the cone-like protuberance on the front of the train. Travelling through the Prairies at speeds of up to sixty-four kilometres per hour, the prime minister's train moved only during the day so the PM could see the country. The journey took them to the railway's terminus at Port Moody, B.C. Macdonald did not say much about the magnificence of the trip on the CPR, but Joseph Pope in his memoirs wrote, "I could not help feeling as I stood by that old man standing on the shores of the Pacific, with his grey hair blowing over his forehead, what an exultant moment it must have been for him."[3] After ten thousand kilometres and fifty days of travel, Macdonald was back in Ottawa, having made a journey few had ever done before him.

Travel by rail for prime ministers was done in appropriate style, which meant a private railcar provided by the railway companies. In Macdonald's case, this was in the "Jamaica" car. These provided luxurious accommodations, and included a sitting room, bedroom, private baths, and dining rooms. Lady Macdonald described it well as "all somewhat resembling the cabin of a fine ship." Use of private cars was standard for the likes of Wilfrid Laurier, Robert Borden, Mackenzie King, and Louis St. Laurent. The car allowed some measure of privacy for the PM and helped enable him to get work done. At every stop in a major town, telegrams and newspapers were brought to the private car so that the business of being prime minister could continue. The private car also afforded the prime minister a chance to rest, something particularly important during the intense travel of an election campaign. And it allowed for family time. Train travel could be fun, too. During a 1950 trip to St. Louis to pick up an honorary degree, St. Laurent took to the controls of the Detroit–Chicago train, blowing the whistle like an enthusiastic schoolboy along the way.

Travelling with someone can be revealing. A train trip with William Lyon Mackenzie King, for example, was a decidedly sober affair. King was a notorious teetotaller. Gordon Robertson, who served as secretary to King, was in charge of guests when travelling on the prime minister's private Car 101. On one trip back to Ottawa from New York, Robertson inquired about wine for dinner. There was none. Exasperated, Robertson decided to take preemptive measures, making sure that he brought something along on future trips. He recalled that his reputation with the prime minister would have taken a dramatic drop, however, "if he had known that the first item I ever packed for any trip was a bottle of scotch."

A dry private car was certainly one problem not to be ignored, nor was inadequate air conditioning. One of Prime Minister Louis St. Laurent's aide's jobs was to make sure his car "was properly iced by the [Department of Transport] to suit his comfort."

But this was harder than it seemed in the days before air conditioning. The various compartments on the railcar could not be cooled evenly; as a result some parts were too cold and others too hot. Canadian National Railways endeavoured to make the necessary changes for St. Laurent in 1949, including setting the controls so the car could not be cooled below 71 degrees Fahrenheit and adjusting ceiling tiles "so as to maintain a uniform temperature throughout the car."

For all the comfort provided by a private railcar, this form of travel was not without its dangers. On Laurier's grand tour of the West in 1910, a shunting freight train brushed against his railcar leaving the PM shaken but uninjured. Similarly, a large piece of timber from a passing train clipped Macdonald's "Jamaica" car, doing it considerable damage. Fortunately, the prime minister was unharmed.

In more modern times, the dangers faced by the PM came not from the nature of train travel itself, but from angry Canadians. On a 1982 vacation with his sons through British Columbia, Pierre Trudeau's train was pelted with tomatoes and eggs as he emerged from the Connaught Tunnel that runs under the Rogers Pass. Later, in Salmon Arm, he faced more unhappy Canadians, only this time the prime minister responded by giving the protesters the finger, a gesture that soon came to be called the "Salmon Arm Salute." Barbara Hughes, one of the protesters, did not seem too unhappy with Trudeau's gesture. She told the *Globe and Mail* later, "There's not too many people who can claim to be given the finger by the prime minister."[4]

It has been more than fifty years since a prime minister made widespread use of rail travel to carry out some of his duties. In 1963 Prime Minister John Diefenbaker made extensive use of a private railcar for that year's election campaign. Tory organizer Dalton Camp insisted he travel by train that year because he knew Dief and his wife, Olive, were more comfortable travelling by rail. And he was right. The Chief loved the extra opportunity of meeting people that rail travel provided. But on this campaign things got off to a rocky start when Mrs. Diefenbaker asked for their special private car. When told by Camp that it was in for repairs, Olive was upset and appeared to see a conspiracy brewing as quickly as did her husband. "There you go. They're conspiring against us. They just don't want to give us a rail car in which we'll be comfortable." The Diefenbakers were eventually persuaded to get on the new one provided, but Olive complained about the beds. "She would not be happy until she got Car 100 back."[5]

Since then, rail travel by prime ministers has mostly been a shtick or campaign gimmick. During the 1974 election campaign, for example, Pierre Trudeau travelled through the Maritimes by train. The journey ended in Quebec but not before one incident in Sainte-Anne-de-la-Pocatière involving a twenty-eight-year-old reporter named Mike Duffy. After Duffy filed his story using a woman's home telephone, her husband thought he had other ideas and chased after Duffy as he tried to catch the train. Trudeau reached his arm over the back of the gate on the train to try to lift the reporter to safety, but the train was moving too quickly and Duffy stumbled and fell. "It was pure Mack Sennett[*] as Trudeau urged the puffing Duffy on, only relenting at the last minute and ordering the train to stop," remembered *Toronto Star* journalist Val Sears.[6] Duffy survived the incident but would go on to have other travel stories in his own political career some fifty years later.

While rail travel was the number one method for prime ministers to see the country, for nearly a century the historic, colonial, and political ties to Great Britain necessitated regular travel to London. For the first eighty years of Confederation these trips were made exclusively by ship. The voyages, which took anywhere from seven to ten days to complete — depending on the weather and sea conditions — were sometimes uneventful, while at other times they proved more challenging. A transatlantic crossing, though, can test the fortitude of anyone, including prime ministers.

Wilfrid Laurier loved Britain. He was a popular visitor when there, and he enjoyed the country and its institutions. It was getting there that was the problem; Sir Wilfrid hated travel by sea — "billow and brine he cannot breast."[7] During his fifteen years as prime minister, Laurier made just three trips across the Atlantic, and endured some form of seasickness on each of them. In 1897, he and his wife, Zoé, sailed

---

* Mack Sennett was a Canadian-born film actor best known for slapstick comedy.

to England onboard the Cunard Line's *Lucania* for Queen Victoria's Diamond Jubilee, as well as to attend that year's Imperial Conference. He got seasick. Five years later, he sailed overseas for the coronation of Edward VII (and to attend the Imperial Conference) and the trip was not much better. When he returned to Canada, the prime minister disembarked early at Rimouski in order to get him back on dry land, so rough had been the crossing.

When Robert Borden finally saw him in Ottawa a few days later he "was so greatly shocked that [he] averted [his] gaze." Newspapers reported that Laurier looked thin.

No doubt. He probably spent most of the voyage unable to leave his bedside. The trip had started off well enough but then strong winds set the ship tossing and sprayed water over its bow. Few passengers ventured up to the deck for three days, and Laurier, like all passengers, suffered. The *Globe* reported that the voyage had been "immensely rough, but, strange to say, Sir Wilfrid, though a poor sailor, bore it better than that across, for the *Lake Erie* is very steady."[8] Laurier would make one more transatlantic voyage during his years as prime minister. In 1911 he travelled to England for the coronation of George V.

The turbulent waters — and the resulting seasickness — was just one of the drawbacks of ocean-going travel at the turn of the century. But for Prime Minister Robert Borden there was something far more dangerous to consider when crossing the Atlantic: German U-boats. A trip across the ocean during the First World War (1914–18) was to literally risk your life. As R.C. Brown wrote in his two-volume biography of Borden: "An Atlantic crossing on a British liner by a dominion prime minister was considered dangerous in the best circumstances, and the sinking of the *Lusitania* in May 1915 made the voyage appear even more perilous." Borden noted in his memoirs that many people felt he should have taken passage on a U.S. ship to better avoid the submarine threat (the U.S. did not join the war until 1917), but "I felt very strongly that I should sail under my own flag and did so."

Departing from New York aboard the *Adriatic*, Borden's first trip overseas took place in July 1915. It is not that often, if at all, that one considers the impact of dangerous travel on a prime minister and his family. For the Bordens, the risk of this crossing was very much on their minds. "Laura could hardly keep tears back but was very brave," Borden wrote in his diary. "I found the parting very hard." He wrote to his "dearest wife" regularly while away.

What was it like to travel the Atlantic during a time of war? To avoid detection by U-boats, precautions were taken, which included sailing with no lights at night. The captain's travel orders were sealed. He was instructed to burn them afterward and report having done so to the British Admiralty. Passengers wore lifebelts for much of the journey.

Borden noted the preparations: "This morning, eight boats equipped with water, provisions, oil, lamps, compass, sail, rockets are hanging along each side of ship ready to be lowered at a moment's notice. Several passengers wearing waistcoats which can be inflated in sixty seconds and will support two persons."

It must have frayed the nerves of all passengers who were, according to Borden, "much divided in opinion as to whether my presence on board increases or diminishes danger." As the *Adriatic* got closer to England, three destroyers escorted it. "Passengers greatly relieved by their presence which is attributed to me."

Despite the very real dangers, Borden did not shy away from overseas travel. In February of 1917, two months before the great battle of Vimy Ridge, Borden made another transatlantic voyage. Much like later trips by Stephen Harper to Afghanistan, this one occurred under the cloak of secrecy as Borden made his way to Halifax, boarded the *Calgarian*, and made the dangerous and uncomfortable winter crossing to England in seven days. While the ship continued to wait for its escort of destroyers to guide it in — and their absence was a growing concern — Borden took precautions by packing a small bag of necessities in case he needed "to take to the boats" in the event of an attack by German submarines. The *Calgarian* arrived safely, but the crossing challenged the prime minister for a good night's sleep. His room was near the ship's expansion joints, and their constant creeping in the middle of the night forced Borden to take refuge in the smoking room.

Because of the length of these trips, the sojourns lasted much longer than would any trip to Europe by a prime minster today. Borden was away from Ottawa for close to three months, visiting Canada's soldiers at hospitals, attending meetings of the Imperial War Cabinet, as well as fitting in some leisure time. On each of these trips he admitted to being lonely or homesick and missing Laura. But it was not all hardship. Ocean travel meant leisurely games of bridge and shuffleboard or walks along the deck where one could see an inky night sky with brilliant stars. Prime ministers occupied themselves with reading, cards, correspondence, and conversation. Borden once even played a bit of cricket onboard ship but this resulted in a pulled leg muscle requiring "electric massage."

Borden made two more overseas trips: one in 1918 for more meetings of the Imperial War Cabinet, for which he stayed for two months; another in 1919 when, with the war over, he travelled to Paris to take part in six months of negotiations for the Treaty of Versailles. The visit to France was much more pleasurable than those he had made to London. For one thing, Borden stayed in a much better hotel, the Majestic. In London he had been staying at Claridge's, where the rooms were so cold his staff had to scrounge up firewood from the Canadian military nearby. But Paris had its pleasures. He attended *Cyrano de Bergerac* and other theatre performances regularly and even took some French lessons, all the while leading the Canadian delegation at the treaty negotiations. In all, Borden was there for four months before he returned to Canada.

Robert Borden's successor, Arthur Meighen, was not prime minister for long — just over two years — but that was enough to make one voyage across the Atlantic, which he did in 1921 for an Imperial Conference. But this trip revealed another side of Meighen, one not usually seen by the public. As Roger Graham writes in his biography of the Conservative PM:

> An ocean voyage, it is said, can strangely affect one's behavior. Thus it was that Meighen, not normally an early riser, was one of the first to reach the deck in the morning; that, usually indifferent to organized games, "he spent a great deal of time playing shuttlecock ... at which he exhibited considerable skill"; that, ordinarily not fond of dancing, "he was among the most enthusiastic of dancers...." But one of his activities was more in keeping with his usual fancy: "Later in the night," [Grattan] O'Leary wrote, with a sly jibe

that Meighen would greatly enjoy, "[he] would dis-
close his puritanical upbringing by playing the second
worst game of bridge on boat."

Historians have portrayed Meighen as a cutting and humourless
figure. He does not appear to have been the sort of person with whom
you would want to make an ocean voyage — a remote Stephen Harper
figure of his day — yet this 1921 trip tells a different story. Here was
the cool and collected Meighen playing shuttlecock and lousy hands of
bridge with various passengers, who grew fond of him as he relaxed and
let his guard down. "Those even briefly exposed to this aspect of the
man looked upon him with affection," Graham wrote.

There is a lesson there for all prime ministers. Showing your
human side is a winning strategy. Meighen had another opportunity to
demonstrate this. During this crossing on the *Empress of Britain*, one
passenger gave birth to a son. The name? William Meighen Smith. The
prime minister was touched by the gesture and shortly thereafter made
a visit to the mother and newborn, presenting them with a gift.

Travel by ship was a regular occurrence for Canada's earliest prime ministers who
needed to get to London for Imperial Conferences or celebrations for monarchs. R.B.
Bennett is seen here aboard the *Empress of Australia* in 1930.

On a 1921 transatlantic voyage to England, a woman gave birth to a child and named the boy William Meighen Smith, the middle name inspired by Prime Minister Arthur Meighen, who was also onboard. The delighted prime minister visited the mother and child to present them with a gift.

While travelling with Arthur Meighen may have been more fun than expected, a trip on the seas with W.L.M. King was no better than those by rail. Late in King's prime ministership in 1948 — his final year in office — he was sailing back from England to Canada aboard the *Queen Elizabeth*. At the time, King was still recovering from an illness and he asked senior advisor Gordon Robertson and private secretary Edouard Handy to report to his stateroom each morning at 9:00 a.m. with any news.* Handy and Robertson reported to King's room at the appropriate time only to find it locked, though they knew he was inside. Was King playing games? There was no answer after knocking, either. While the two men left to discuss the next course of action King unlocked the latch. When they returned he had the gall to ask why they were late. Later, near the very end of the trip, the ship was fogbound for twenty-four hours in open seas and Robertson wondered "if anyone's patience could endure that extra day a short distance from New York."

---

* One piece of news they delivered to the prime minister was the surprising election of Harry Truman.

While travel by rail and sea dominated the first eighty to ninety years of Canadian history, air travel is the usual mode of transportation today, with prime ministers flying thousands of kilometres on a regular basis. Pierre Trudeau flew more than 150,000 kilometres in less than three years in office between 1968 and 1971, while Justin Trudeau's first ten months in office saw him flying off to no less than eleven different countries. Prime ministers are truly road warriors, and this intensifies during an election campaign. Paul Martin gave some perspective to the grind of travel during these intense periods:

> You are jammed into an airplane for week after week, with forty of your best friends — the press corps — riding just five or six rows behind you. You may wake up at an ungodly hour in Halifax, have "media availability" on the wharf, give a luncheon speech to a service club in Thunder Bay, and end the day with a rally in Winnipeg. Although I have long ago seen the toned body of my youth metamorphose into something, shall we say, less toned, I have always been blessed with a strong constitution and lots of energy. I can go long hours without exhausting myself, which is what you have to do on an election campaign. I can also sleep on planes.

The whirlwind of travel and campaigning can make remembering names a challenge, so Martin picked up a trick to help him. When he got up to the lectern to give his stump speech and say wonderful things about the local candidate, he just looked out to the audience and read their waving campaign signs to remind him of the candidate's name.

Despite the media portrayal of prime ministerial travel as some sort of glamorous perquisite of the job, quite the opposite is true. As one advance team specialist put it, travel for this job is "brutal."[9] Each visit by a PM involves detailed preparation by an advance team, who travel to the destination to deal with the logistics of a visit from the PM.

Usually, the prime minister will go directly from his flight to a meeting or to attend to some other matter of state business. There is no rest day in advance or downtime to get ready. It is a grind, but that is not what the Canadian public would think because that is not what they see.

Travel is a challenge for prime ministers — particularly those with children — because they are away from them for so long, but it is easier for them than, say, an ordinary MP or Canadian citizen. In fact, it was one of the first things noticed by Justin Trudeau when he became prime minister on November 4, 2015. In an interview with his long-time friend and Montreal radio host Terry DiMonte in December 2015 (DiMonte noted that security dogs had sniffed out the studio beforehand), Trudeau was asked about the trappings of power, and he drew a comparison between his new and old experiences in air travel. A trip from Ottawa to Montreal was typical.

The prime minister, speaking of how travel operated as an MP or party leader, said, "Whereas in the past if I had an event that finished at 8 o'clock in the evening in Toronto or Montreal, [there] was half an hour to the airport, [and] you have to be there a good half hour to forty-five minutes in advance [of the flight], then hopefully there's a flight around 10:00 or 10:30, then you get back, you're home by midnight, just past midnight.

"Now, if I finish an event at 8 o'clock in Toronto," he continued, speaking of his time as prime minister, "I'm at airport at 8:30, I'm in the plane and lifting off at 8:32 and I'm home in time to go to bed with Sophie at 10:00."

Trudeau spoke how all of this helped him to be a better parent, a point not be taken lightly when examining the conditions of being prime minister. And while all of this air travel may seem routine in today's world, that was decidedly not the case for the country's first prime minister to — in the words of John Magee's 1941 poem — "have slipped the surly bonds of Earth / And danced the skies on laughter-silvered wings."

In his diary the day before he left on a flight for England in August of 1941, Mackenzie King made sure his will was up to date, and he noted that University of Toronto vice-chancellor William Mulock "spoke about God's protecting care and he asked me to cable him when

I arrived." King took one "last look at the pictures of the family and my mother's painting and said a quiet prayer for guidance." For the prime minister this was no ordinary excursion. He had read about a number of plane crashes, including a transatlantic flight that killed twenty-two passengers. King was fatalistic:

> I have, however, no real fear. While I should like to continue to live and complete the work that I believe is a part and purpose of my life, if it is God's will that my time on earth should close in the fulfillment of an obvious duty to my country, to the Commonwealth, and to humanity at this time ... I shall feel no concern about having my earthly journey brought to its close at this stage.

The first flight for a Canadian prime minister was taken on a B-24 bomber, also known as a Liberator (King loved the name), which was a four-engined, long-range bomber with twin tail design built for the war. The prime minister was scheduled to travel from Montreal to Scotland, with a refuelling stop in Gander, Newfoundland. Onboard, the plane had been slightly modified with a comfortable reclining chair and a divan that King decided was "most attractive." Despite those earlier plane crashes mentioned in the prime minister's diary, was there anything to be concerned about?[*]

"Nothing in the least felt unpleasant and [I] did not feel the slightest bit of timidity," wrote King. "Indeed, thoroughly enjoyed the ascent itself and from the moment we began to fly on the level, enjoyed the whole sensation of floating through and above the clouds, getting glimpses of the country below. I was impressed with how plainly everything was visible."

Without a doubt, King enjoyed his flying experience and wrote about it at length in his diary. "In the course of travel through the morning, I felt no unpleasant sensation, on the contrary, real enjoyment and inspiration.

---

[*] King had previously banned air travel overseas by his Cabinet, but after trade minister C.D. Howe's ship was torpedoed in a 1940 Atlantic crossing, he changed his mind and allowed it. Howe survived the U-boat attack and continued on to England.

The words that kept coming to my mind were: terrestrial and celestial; seeing a new heaven and a new earth." He also recognized the uniqueness of the experience, remarking, "Had anyone told me I should have been writing on an aeroplane, a bomber, I could never have believed them. The whole was a surprise beyond words." King then sat back and enjoyed the flight, remarking on the glory of God and the spiritual nature of flight. He decided he would not fall asleep until he had seen the stars. "The only words that could describe one's feeling were: majestic and celestial."

When King landed in Scotland, the first flight by a sitting Canadian prime minister — a transatlantic one no less — was complete. The trip was graceful, but King's exit from the aircraft was not like what we are used to seeing today. Rather than an executive wave and walk down stairs, King emerged posterior-first from the belly of the B24 and for a moment looked as though he might get stuck. But the stocky PM succeeded with his exit and reviewed Canadian troops.

King's successful flight was the beginning of airplane travel for prime ministers and it came as commercial flying was beginning in Canada. Trans-Canada Airlines — renamed Air Canada in 1965 — was formed in 1937 (Canadian Pacific Airlines followed in 1942). The first commercial transcontinental flights offered by the airline began in 1939 with service from Montreal to Vancouver, a fifteen-hour flight that included stops in Ottawa, North Bay, Kapuskasing, Winnipeg, Regina, Lethbridge, and Edmonton. The airline began making flights across the Atlantic in 1943 as it assisted in getting war material to Great Britain, and by 1946 there were daily flights to across the pond. The age of passenger flight was taking off.

A few years after King's initial flight, a B-24 bomber was permanently remodelled for exclusive use by the PM. Comfortable seating and a special office for King and his secretary was installed, in addition to windows on each side of the fuselage. The plane featured a kitchen and washroom, as well. The Canadian Red Ensign was painted on the nose of the aircraft, with a lightning bolt farther back along the polished aluminum exterior.[10] Mackenzie King flew in the "Silver Saloon," as it was nicknamed, for the rest of his time in office. When his term concluded in 1948, the plane was flown to CFB Trenton where it was put in storage. In 1951 it was sold to Chile.

While King was the first sitting prime minister to travel by airplane, he very nearly was not. During the First World War, Bonar Law, a member of the British War Cabinet and friend of Robert Borden's, frequently travelled between London and Paris by "flying machine."

"I sometimes had a half-formed intention to journey from Paris to London by air," wrote Robert Borden in 1933, "but I was always deterred by the extreme uncertainty of the English weather."

In any case, Borden was the first person to have served as prime minister to fly in a plane: in 1933 he flew from his favourite fishing spot at Echo Beach, not far from Huntsville, Ontario, back to Ottawa. "I first closed my eyes as we rose from the water," he remembered, "but very soon I opened them and found that I was neither giddy nor nervous. This was quite a surprise, as ordinarily I dread any considerable height and am much relieved to reach terra firma once more."[11]

Plane travel was still something of an adventure in the late 1940s and early 1950s. Memoirs of the time usually have a story about an air trip filled with some measure of drama. On Prime Minister Louis St. Laurent's trip home from Paris in January 1950, the plane stopped at Keflavík Airport in Iceland to refuel. The pilot suggested that since weather and winds were favourable, a non-stop flight to Ottawa, without the usual stop in Newfoundland, would be possible. Not long after the flight took off, passengers were told to fasten their seat belts without explanation. Moments later, the plane was back in Iceland because one of the engines had failed. To fix it, parts would have to come from North America, so the prime minister was stuck in Iceland for another day before a Trans-Canada Airlines plane with three available seats came to fetch St. Laurent and two of his entourage. In his memoirs, Jack Pickersgill noted that the Canadair North Star planes they flew home in were quite a bit noisier than the RCAF CF-5s in which they had come over in (the CF-5s had Pratt and Whitney engines while the North Stars had Merlin engines, known to be very noisy). On the flight home, though, St. Laurent had turned to him and said he found "the noise of the North Star was very reassuring."

Air transportation was destined to grow, and with it prime ministerial travel by plane. In fact, domestic intercity air travel increased by more than 100 percent during Pierre Trudeau's first six years in office, according to the 1991 Royal Commission on National Passenger Transportation. It also meant a new area to be politicized by the media and opposition parties.

From Pierre Trudeau to Justin Trudeau, no prime minister was excused from being criticized for travel by air. It was either too much, too expensive, or too luxurious. Trudeau *pater* faced some of the toughest grilling, in part because he was the first prime minister to truly embrace foreign travel to such a degree, but also because his prime ministership was more public than any of his predecessors. He was watched more closely. A 1970 front-page article in the *Globe and Mail* became the template for the sort of attacks all subsequent PMs would face for their air travels. Titled "How the PM gets around and who pays," the article by reporter John Burns noted that the PM had been using the Department of Transport's JetStars for what appeared to be holiday excursions in addition to legitimate political travel. "Mr. Trudeau is by no means the first prime minister to use government transportation for personal or political trips," Burns wrote, "but he has done it more frequently than his predecessors, and in a forthright way which raises some old questions about privileges and perquisites of the office."

Ah, yes. The "perks" of office. This is a question that has dogged all Canadian PMs, particularly when it comes to travel. In what style — if one can really call it that — should the prime minister of the country travel? "There are people in Canada," Brian Mulroney once said, "who will not be satisfied until the prime minister of Canada travels around in a provincial autobus and stays at the YMCA."[12] The Trudeau trip that was the basis of the *Globe* article was a jaunt by the PM to Belize in which he took with him Tim Porteous, his executive assistant; Gérard Pelletier, who was secretary of state; and both their wives. An RCMP security officer was also onboard.

The response from those close to the prime minister provides not only some insight into the nature of the job of prime minister but also into how some things have changed. The basic talking point on Trudeau's frequent flying habit and use of government aircraft was that all of this was for security and the efficient use of the prime minister's time. Many of the newspaper articles from this period included the equivalent option for travel had the prime minister flown commercial, with the implication that perhaps the PM should be travelling that way with everyone else. Trudeau's handlers constantly talked about the "special nature of the job." As his secretary, Mary Macdonald, put it so succinctly. "The prime minister is the prime minister. His case is different from anyone else."[13]

The Trudeau travel chronicles got plenty of debate going in the editorial pages. Letters to the editor ran the gamut, but more letters were published in support of the prime minister and his travel needs. "Why any good, competent man should run for the office of Prime Minister of Canada is a complete mystery to me," wrote one disgruntled Canadian who was fed up with the scrutiny and criticism.[14] Those in support of the PM agreed that there is a need for the leader of the country to have special allowances made for his transportation, including security and the need to get places quickly. But the media reports on this aspect of the life of a prime minister were just beginning, and the use of government-owned jets for travel would become a convenient and regular instrument with which the opposition parties would attempt to damage the reputation of the PM.

Brian Mulroney, Kim Campbell, Jean Chrétien, Stephen Harper, and Justin Trudeau all faced admonishment due to their perceived jet-setting. Mulroney, who once joked that the government's Challenger jets were "sacred instruments of travel," paid the price for the comment when a journalist reported it without mentioning his joking tone. Mulroney noted that the aircraft he flew on for international trips, a thirty-year-old Boeing 707, was so old and broken down that condensation used to leak all over his papers when they took off. He couldn't even take or make a telephone call because it wasn't equipped to do so.* Mulroney said the press gallery was always asking him to get rid of the plane because they were concerned about its reliability. "The chances were, if it went down, we'd all get killed and they didn't mind me but they didn't want it happening to them."

---

* So bad was the situation that, when Indian prime minister Indira Gandhi was assassinated, Mulroney had to take the call in the cockpit of the airplane with the pilots listening in.

The fact was, the 707 Mulroney used for long-haul trips was so awful that it was banned from landing at airports, such as London's Heathrow, unless the prime minister was onboard. There were huge environmental concerns about it, too. "You could tell when [the 707] was coming because the black smoke poured out of the engine. The exhaust fumes were black," recalled Scott Munnoch, who was part of the Mulroney advance team from 1989 to 1993. Munnoch recounted one instance when the prime minister and his entourage were travelling from a NATO summit in London to a G7 meeting in Houston. Partway over the Atlantic a high, whistling noise was coming from the emergency exit door near the wing. "That got everyone's attention," Munnoch remembered. "The crew member came back — and I'll never forget this — he took a napkin and stuffed it in the seal. It stopped the whistle and we kept on going," he chuckled.[15] In another incident, after the 1985 Commonwealth Heads of Government meeting in Nassau, it was decided that Mulroney and his wife, Mila, would leave as soon as possible on a Challenger jet and that the media and rest of the PM's entourage would follow on the 707. But then someone realized that if the PM was not on the 707, it wouldn't be able to fly so the plan was scrapped.[16]

The plane was an embarrassment, so not long after Wardair was purchased by Canadian Airlines in 1990 the Mulroney government bought three of its Airbus 310s (and later bought two more to make a fleet of five), which became the standard aircraft prime ministers travelled on for long-haul flights. And it was here that one of the great myths about Brian Mulroney was born: The Myth of the Taj Mahal. One of the Airbuses was retrofitted for VIP travel. A small cabin with a shower and office was installed on the plane, but it was hardly opulent. Those who have been in it scoff at the description of it as some sort of Air Force One, the American president's plane. But then–Opposition leader Jean Chrétien dubbed it the "flying Taj Mahal," in an attempt to brand Mulroney as an extravagant traveller and wasteful spender on perks. The mud stuck and Mulroney was forever linked to the "Taj Mahal." But there was only one thing: Mulroney never flew in it.*

---

* Mulroney did fly in it once. When he attended Nelson Mandela's funeral in 2013, Prime Minister Stephen Harper brought him, along with Kim Campbell and Jean Chrétien.

It was not the 310s that got all the attention, however, it was the Challenger jets. These were the Bombardier jets (older versions were made by Canadair, which Bombardier bought in 1986) that prime ministers used for domestic and short-haul travel. When most Canadians think of PMs and travel, it is the Challenger that will come to mind. Why? Because the media and politicians have been taking PMs to task for their trips on the Challenger forever. Unfortunately, for Brian Mulroney at least, the Challenger jets were not in much better condition than that old Boeing 707. In fact, Mulroney's Challenger jet was so unreliable that it began to impinge upon his ability to do his job. He was delayed several times, and at one point had to hitch a ride on an executive jet after a visit to northern Quebec. A solution was needed. For a while "shadow jets" accompanied him on his travels. In other words, a second airplane followed the PM to any location. If the first one broke down, the other was called into service. When word leaked out about this, the practice was halted and a better solution found, but not before it became another *cause célèbre* in the media. The cost of the PM's plane continued to be an issue after Mulroney's term ended. Ironically, Jean Chrétien, who had attacked Mulroney for his approval of the purchase of new jets, also became the object of criticism when, during his years as prime minister, he approved the purchase of two new Challengers at a cost of $100 million.* One newspaper headline, not surprisingly, referred to them as "luxury jets."[17]

If you thought politicians might have eventually outgrown the use of prime ministerial travel as a hammer with which to bludgeon a PM, you would be mistaken. On April 1, 2014, NDP MP Charlie Angus brought forward an opposition motion to debate Stephen Harper's use of the Challenger. Perhaps there were no other burning issues to debate in Parliament but the House spent the better part of seven hours debating the motion.

"This is about a contempt for the Canadian people," Angus intoned in the House. "The prime minister told Canadians in 2006 that he would clean up this culture of entitlement. Instead, his attitude

---

* It's understandable that Chrétien may have wanted new aircraft. On a flight home from Sweden in 2001 his plane plunged thousands of feet in mere seconds after the decompression system malfunctioned at twenty-seven thousand feet.

was that he would clean up the Liberals, and once they were done, then he and his friends would pork out at the trough."

Of course, as Angus deftly noted in the debate, Harper, while in opposition, had chastised the government of Jean Chrétien for its use of Challenger jets to "fly the prime minister and his Cabinet around in luxury."

The issue for Angus and the opposition was a familiar, if unimaginative, line of attack. Ostensibly, the opposition was taking issue with the fact that a friend of Stephen Harper who had raised money for the Conservative party had joined him on the Challenger. That the PM had reimbursed the Treasury for the flight costs at commercial rates (a rule implemented by the Harper Tories) was lost in the politicization of the use of jets by a prime minister. But all of this is politics. A Conservative MP summed up the debate in one word: "silly."

Like a zombie that cannot be killed, the topic of PMs and travel remains an issue no opposition can refuse. It took just six weeks for Prime Minister Justin Trudeau to hear criticism of his use of a Challenger jet. In March of 2016, Trudeau took a family vacation in St. Kitts and Nevis, flying down on the Challenger, as he is required to do for security reasons. Trudeau paid economy-class equivalent for his family members, following the Harper precedent. But news reports noted that the taxpayer was still on the hook to cover the costs of the flight crew that had to stay there while the PM and his family were on vacation. Conservative MP and former Speaker of the House Andrew Scheer (now Tory leader), weighed in on the issue. "To keep two pilots around the clock on the payroll when you're off for ten days like that might not have been the best signal for Canadians," he said. Some things never change.[18]

In 2017, Trudeau was again under fire, this time for expenses incurred when he stayed on the private island of the Aga Khan in the Bahamas during a 2016 Christmas holiday. The opposition went after him for the costs incurred while the prime minister replied that the expenditures were unavoidable because of the need for security. In December 2017, parliamentary ethics commissioner Mary Dawson issued her long-awaited investigation of the matter and found that Trudeau's acceptance of the vacation on the Aga Khan's island "could reasonably be seen to have been given to influence Mr. Trudeau in his capacity as prime minister." The media and opposition parties continued to highlight the story and the prime minister said he would try to do better. The fact remains, though, that a prime minister needs safe and expedient travel at all times. Criticizing the travel of prime ministers is the laziest kind of politics.

Like many Canadians who have travelled overseas, prime ministers have returned with a few great tales, and part of the intriguing behind-the-scenes history of being prime minister is the colourful stories from when they have been in foreign countries. There is no shortage of anecdotes, two of which involved hunting animals.

In 1958, John Diefenbaker was on his famous world tour that lasted seven weeks and took him to about a dozen countries. It also presented him with the opportunity to hunt a Bengal tiger. "Governments of several Commonwealth countries in South and Southeast Asia are reported to be pressing with alacrity and enthusiasm the idea that a tiger hunt might be in order on the occasion of the prime minister's visit," wrote the *Ottawa Citizen*. The paper indicated that Canadian authorities were essentially trying to avoid the whole spectacle, using Diefenbaker's busy schedule as an excuse. But it was to no avail. The tiger hunt proceeded, and, perhaps luckily for Diefenbaker's reputation, he came away empty handed. Under the headline "PM Doesn't Bag Tiger But Enjoys Big Hunt," the *Globe and Mail* reported that "Bengal tigers, more interested in their love life than in being shot, stayed out of sight of Prime Minister Diefenbaker today as the Canadian leader went on his first tiger hunt."

The hunt lasted three hours and took place in India along the Chambal River near Kota. "I was quite happy to bag nothing," the prime minister recalled in his memoirs. "It was a most relaxing day, without official duties or the need to dress in anything more stylish than old fishing clothes and a rumpled straw hat."

In 1993, another Conservative prime minister on a tour of European capitals would participate in a hunting expedition pursuing wild animals. This time the intended prey was a wild boar and the prime minister in search of game was Brian Mulroney, who joined Russian president Boris Yeltsin and their wives at Yeltsin's dacha. The incident became something of a media issue when a photograph appeared of Mulroney and Yeltsin standing proudly over the two dead animals with rifles positioned just so. Did Mulroney actually shoot the boar? I was keen to find out and asked him in one of our interviews.

"I shot the boar," he told me, recalling the incident. "I'm no novice with a rifle," he continued, alluding to the fact he hunted with his father up in Baie-Comeau, Quebec, when he was younger. "But I'm not a crack shot, either."

On the day of the hunt, Yeltsin took Mulroney out to a tower, where they stood while the wild boars get flushed out into their view. Luck was on Mulroney's side that day; a boar came within range, he pulled the trigger, and indeed bagged his boar. Someone in the press asked him if he had actually done the deed — had he killed a boar? "No," he quipped. "I've counted and see all the press corps is accounted for."

According to his memoirs there remains a boar hide stored "in a secure facility controlled by Library and Archives Canada. Despite the extensive use I have made of their records for [my memoirs], I must confess that I have not visited the boar's hide recently."

In another travel story involving an animal, Prime Minister Paul Martin was in Tripoli, Libya, for a 2004 meeting with Muammar Gaddafi. A lengthy meeting with the Libyan leader led to no results of any substance, and the PM worried about what he would tell the media. But in the end it turned out that there was nothing to worry about. Their attention had long since turned from Martin's meeting to the priapic spectacle of two camels engaged in an act of procreation. "This proved to be far more interesting to the Canadian press corps than anything I could ever say," Martin deadpanned in his memoirs.

Despite the portrayal of prime ministerial travel in the media as fancy and luxurious — what with the so-called "Flying Taj Mahal" and thoughts of expensive hotels — the reality is that a prime minister must be a road warrior and many simply did not enjoy this aspect of the job, though it is an essential component of being prime minister. Take Mackenzie King for example. "He hated the fatigue and discomfort of travelling," wrote one of his biographers. (Flying was another matter, but King mostly travelled by rail.) "The constant worrying [over] preparing and delivering speeches, the imposition on his time by individuals and delegations, and the problem of remembering names and chatting with strangers." Stephen Harper, who resembled King in many ways, also disliked this part of the job and how it complicated his routines and schedules. The jet lag and food was no source of happiness either. Harper simply was not as keen as other PMs before him to take advantage of some of the sights. "He would rather look down at a book than up at the Eiffel Tower," noted John Ibbitson in his biography of the former PM.

Louis St. Laurent was no fan, either. For one thing, his wife, Jeanne, refused to fly, so she never accompanied him on his travels when they involved aircraft. But St. Laurent was a man of impeccable character. In 1953, so that Mrs. St. Laurent could attend the coronation of Queen Elizabeth II, the PM travelled to England with her by ship. That was the last time a prime minister made a transatlantic crossing by sea for official business.[*]

Despite the fact he was less than enthusiastic about travel, he was a globetrotter as PM, making numerous trips abroad, including a highly publicized world tour in 1954 during which he visited twelve countries. He left just two days after his seventy-second birthday and would not return to Canada for six weeks, during which time he travelled to places such as India, Pakistan, Ceylon (now Sri Lanka), and Korea. The trip began, however, in London, where the prime minister lunched with British prime minister Winston Churchill, who gave St. Laurent some advice that would be useful for any PM. Churchill had made many of these lengthy worldwide trips, he told St. Laurent, and he found that the schedules were always too overloaded to allow for any type of relaxation. "As a result, he made it a practice when travelling never to walk when it was possible to ride, never to stand when it was possible to sit down, never to sit when he could lie down, and never

---

[*] Mrs. St. Laurent was not the only person close to a PM to fear flying. Diefenbaker's long-time personal secretary, Marjorie "Bunny" Pound, hated to fly, so she made Dief do all of his dictation during flights to distract her.

to miss an opportunity to visit a washroom, as there was no knowing when the next opportunity would occur."[19]

All of that excellent advice could do nothing to help St. Laurent when faced with a dilemma a number of Canadians have also met at one time or another: a missing piece of clothing. The prime minister was dressing for a formal dinner hosted by Indian prime minister Jawaharlal Nehru when he discovered his pants were nowhere to be found. "Like Sir Walter Raleigh throwing down his cloak for Queen Elizabeth to walk upon, I said, 'Take mine, prime minister,'" Charles Ritchie recorded in his diary, "but a second look at his girth and mine showed that this was a physical impossibility." A call went out to a servant for help acquiring a pair from the palace where they were but with no success. The only other solution was to go to a New Delhi bazaar to purchase a pair.

> The moments ticked by. The prime minister was already eleven minutes late for dinner. Finally the servant returned bearing with him an extremely greasy pair of second- or third-hand trousers of such circumference that they had to be fastened round the prime minister's waist with safety-pins. During the whole of this agonizing ordeal Mr. St. Laurent remained perfectly unperturbed and patient, with never a word of complaint. My mind boggled at the thought of what Mackenzie King would have said in these circumstances.[20]

The trousers fiasco would be the least of St. Laurent's problems encountered while on a voyage that would challenge a man half his age. Used to a simple diet back in Canada, he did not eat much on the tour. The weather was also a problem: the heat and humidity in places such as New Delhi and Jakarta were wearing him down, and by the time he had finished visiting Canadian troops in Korea, where the weather was wintry and cold, St. Laurent was physically spent. He wrote to Mrs. St. Laurent about how much he yearned to get home. When he reached Tokyo, St. Laurent suffered a bout of dysentery, which left him a weakened man. But he soldiered on with his itinerary in Japan.

The trip had been remarkable not only for its length and distance travelled but also for the reception St. Laurent received when he arrived at Uplands airport in Ottawa. On hand to greet him were not only Cabinet colleagues such as C.D. Howe and Lester Pearson, but also George Drew, the leader of the Opposition, who enthusiastically shook his hand. Jeanne St. Laurent received a more-than-usual affectionate public kiss from the prime minister, along with a lei he picked up on the stopover in Hawaii on the way home. Much like any Canadian who has been away from home for an extended period of time, St. Laurent was thrilled to be back on Canadian soil and excitedly recounted impressions of the trip in the House of Commons. But the travel had taken its toll on him and the aging prime minister was entering a period of irrevocable decline.

Although foreign travel occupies an important place in the itineraries of Canada's prime ministers, Canada is where they spend the majority of their time, and travel around Ottawa, the capital, is done primarily by car. Virtually every day, the PM is chauffeured from home to Parliament Hill in an armoured limousine with doors so heavy it is best to let an RCMP officer open and close them. The commute from 24 Sussex takes about five minutes, but the routes vary for security reasons.*

The earliest prime ministers to get chauffeured around in cars were Wilfrid Laurier and Robert Borden. Laurier, though, was known for taking public transit to work, and "it was no unusual thing to step on a streetcar and have the prime minister of Canada offer a seat with old-world courtesy."[21] For Borden's part, he occasionally rode a bicycle to the Hill before he became PM.

Car rides did not always go smoothly. In one long-forgotten but at the time — in 1957 — front-page news story, the Cadillac ferrying Prime Minister Louis St. Laurent was forced off the road by another vehicle and into the ditch off Highway 90, near Barrie, Ontario. The grass on the side of the road was wet and soft, so St. Laurent escaped injury, though one

---

* On Mulroney's last day in office, his motorcade had a minor fender-bender when a vehicle unexpectedly cut in front of it, causing one of the security cars to crash into the one carrying the PM. "That hasn't happened before," said an unruffled Mulroney.

reporter, Victor Mackie of the *Winnipeg Free Press*, suffered two broken vertebrae when his typewriter went flying into his back.

The PM, ever the diplomat, had the presence of mind and political acumen to exchange pleasantries with the other driver, noted the *Toronto Star* story with the headline "St. Laurent Rumpled In Crash, Woman Driver Is Praised." That "woman driver" was Pearl Payette, who avoided the heavy wires from telephone poles and "kept [the car] from rolling into a deep culvert head on."[22]

Looking back, a couple of things stand out from this incident. First is the fact the PM was being driven in a private car by a private citizen on a road not cleared by security. That just doesn't happen anymore. The second astonishing thing is that St. Laurent was sitting in the front of the Cadillac, something newspaper writers of the day called "the suicide seat." Indeed, St. Laurent would only ride shotgun: when the journey continued in another car, he took his usual place — in the front seat.

As Brian Mulroney noted at the outset of this chapter, travel for the prime minister is an essential part of the job. While it provides a necessary escape from the capital, it also has the benefit of showing him the country in ways few others ever see it. There are few Canadians who get to see all of the geography of this magnificent country in its full splendour. For those who do, it has an impact.

When Wilfrid Laurier travelled by rail to western Canada for the first time in 1910 it changed him. He saw Port Arthur and Fort William on the north shore of Lake Superior; ten thousand people greeted him in Winnipeg. In Saskatoon, he met a young newspaper boy. "You have remarkable newsboys here," Laurier remarked. "This one talked to me for half an hour at the railway station and then said, 'Well, Mr. Prime Minister, I can't waste any more time. I have to deliver my papers.'" It was John Diefenbaker. Laurier rested at Banff in the mountain air of the Rockies; he saw Vancouver and Victoria. It was the trip of a lifetime and one many Canadians today still dream of doing. "I return ten times more Canadian," Laurier said at the time. "I have imbibed the air, spirit, and enthusiasm of the West."

The same was true for Mackenzie King on that inaugural transatlantic flight by a prime minister. "It really does give one an entirely new vision of one's country, its extent, and its grandeur," he confided in his diary. Indeed, the ability and privilege of meeting Canadians from all corners of the country is one of the unique benefits of being prime minister. The challenge is to be able to articulate the wonder of a far-flung, sparsely populated, but magnificent country to all of its citizens. Surely, if every Canadian could see Canada the way the prime minister does, much of our regional prejudice and ignorance would melt away.

CHAPTER 4

"YOU'LL NEVER WALK ALONE":
PRIME MINISTERS AND SECURITY

A Canadian prime minister once remarked in a private
conversation that the techniques to protect him were
intelligently conceived and conscientiously carried
out but that they would be nevertheless entirely futile
if an assassin were determined to take his life.

— *Globe and Mail* editorial, 1966

Prime Minister John Diefenbaker is sitting on a beach in
Nassau, Bahamas. It is December 1957 and the Conservative
leader is still enjoying the aftermath of his electoral victory in June
that ended twenty-two years of Liberal rule. After six months of governing, it is time for a vacation, though the prime minister is not
very good at relaxing. At this moment, posed in a small chair, he is
dictating notes to his assistant, the unflappable Bunny Pound, in an
effort to keep busy, as is his wont. Inside, his wife, Olive, is knitting.
A few minutes later, Diefenbaker leaves the beach to check on her. An

American couple approaches the PM's assistant and one asks, "Who is that gentleman? He seems rather important."

"Oh, he's the new prime minister of Canada," comes the reply.

The American tourist drops his coffee cup to the ground in shock. "Well, where are all the security staff?"

"It's me," says Ms. Pound to the stunned Americans.[1]

Few have given much thought about Canadian prime ministers and their personal security. As was the case on John Diefenbaker's Nassau vacation, it has generally been assumed that our leaders could carry on as virtually any other private citizen, unbothered by others and feeling safe. The truth, though, is that threats to the lives of prime ministers have been a constant since the days of Sir John A. Macdonald. While no Canadian prime minister has ever been killed by an assassin — whereas in the United States four presidents have been murdered — our PMs have been targets and, on a couple of occasions, the would-be assailants nearly achieved their objectives.

It is not surprising that Canadians might take the security of their prime minister for granted. This is a country, after all, that has witnessed only two political assassinations in more than 150 years of existence. Thomas D'Arcy McGee, the Irish immigrant and Father of Confederation, was gunned down outside his boarding house at the corner of Sparks and Metcalfe Streets in Ottawa in 1868. Prime Minister John A. Macdonald rushed to the scene in his carriage, holding McGee's wounded head until a doctor arrived and pronounced him dead.

McGee had met a fate that Agnes Macdonald always worried would befall her husband. There were certainly threats to Macdonald's life. The fate of Métis leader Louis Riel — who was hanged in 1885 when the prime minister would not commute his sentence — precipitated a number of menacing letters being sent to the prime minister. "Beware Old Man," began one. "The death of Riel by hanging would be your own death. I give you fair warning so beware. And if Riel is hanged prepare to appear before your Creator without further notice. You will be liable to fall at any moment. Remember that this is no snake story."[2]

The other political assassination in Canadian history occurred during the 1970 October Crisis (the apex of an ongoing terrorist campaign in support of an independent Quebec led by the Front de Libération du Québec, or FLQ), when Quebec Cabinet minister Pierre Laporte was kidnapped and subsequently strangled to death by the Chénier cell of the FLQ. He was taken in broad daylight while he played ball with his nephew on his front lawn in Westmount, the tiny municipality where the city's Anglo elite live. As the crisis escalated, Prime Minister Pierre Trudeau ordered the military to start guarding politicians in Ottawa, as well as at embassies and other prominent homes in the capital. Cabinet ministers got special protection, as did the homes of former prime minister Lester Pearson and Opposition leader Robert Stanfield.*

While threats to prime ministers have been common, actual attempts on their lives have been rare. Canadian prime ministers, consequently, have gone mostly unguarded — something Canadians may find strange, given the security bubble surrounding the current PM. For the first one hundred years of the country's history, it was the standard practice for a prime minister to have no security detail at all unless moments of severe political unrest warranted it. For example, during the 1917–18 conscription crisis of the First World War, a guard was placed outside the Ottawa home of Prime Minister Robert Borden on Wurtemburg Street, and he was forced to travel to Parliament in a motor vehicle filled with police officers for his protection. This was the result of receiving a number of anonymous death threats in the mail. After the 1917 bombing of the residence of Lord Atholstan, owner of the *Montreal Star*, police learned that the same group also had plans to bomb Parliament and assassinate Borden.[3] But this was an extreme and unique situation during a time of war and domestic unrest.

Nonetheless, the residue of conscription stuck to Borden's successor, Arthur Meighen, who became prime minister in 1920. Meighen had been instrumental in the drafting of the conscription bill in 1917 —

---

* In fact, as early as 1963 when Pearson was PM, 24 Sussex Drive got extra patrols from the RCMP due to activities of the FLQ.

reviled in Quebec — but now, as prime minister, he was campaigning in the 1921 election. Meighen showed courage by appearing in Montreal, where circulating throughout the great French-speaking metropolis were posters that said, "Meighen is coming. Bring eggs." The hall where he was to speak was surrounded by police who were anticipating trouble but none transpired. Later, at Sherbrooke, Quebec, a rock came crashing through a window, flying over the prime minister's head and striking the canopy covering the platform party. No one was injured but the security risks for Meighen were plain to see.

In a typically Canadian way, the *lack* of security afforded prime ministers, at least in the early history of the country, is the most striking (and amusing) aspect of any discussion about PMs and protection in Canada. William Lyon Mackenzie King loathed any suggestion of security and resisted any such offers, even when travelling abroad to Washington or London. King liked to be seen as open to Canadians (even if that did not mean he actually wanted to speak with them). He was one of the few unprotected heads of government in the world during his time in office, which included the years of the Second World War.

When Louis St. Laurent became prime minister in 1948, he insisted on continuing with the practice of going without personal security. It became customary around Ottawa to see the prime minister walking to work while being greeted by various passersby as he tipped his hat. On one of his first days as prime minister, however, St. Laurent noticed that there seemed to be a man trailing him. He picked up the telephone and called the RCMP commissioner to ask what was going on since he had specifically asked for no security detail.

"But I haven't anybody following you, sir," replied the commissioner.

"Well, somebody is following me," St. Laurent insisted.

The head of the RCMP was immediately concerned that there may be a "lunatic" — a popular term in those days for someone we might call a "lone wolf" today — or a potential assassin following the PM. The next day they apprehended a man near St. Laurent. It was an American magazine reporter researching his story.[4]

The lack of security for the PM was captured in a quaint 1957 National Film Board tourist film about Ottawa titled *Capital City*. In it, bystanders are outside 24 Sussex Drive when one says of the PM's official residence, "Why, it looks so unofficial. You would never know. You could walk right up to the front door. I thought there'd be a guard or something."

"Why, yes now," says another, referring to security guards. "Where are they concealed?"

"Well, there aren't any as far as I know."

Just then, St. Laurent pulls out of Sussex in his chauffeur-driven car. "This business about the guards is remarkable. And none in the car, either!" says the dumbfounded citizen.[5]

There were similar moments for St. Laurent's successor, John Diefenbaker. Dief received violent threats through the mail (as all prime ministers have) and was occasionally stopped by strangers on his walks. The prime minister's assistants did not like the tone of the letters and decided the RCMP should assign some plainclothes officers to shadow Diefenbaker from a distance. The Chief was told of the arrangement so that he would not wonder who the strangers were while out on his walk. But a few days later, the prime minister told his office that he had seen no one out there protecting him. Thomas Van Dusen, Dief's advisor, told the RCMP to be more obvious about their tracking of the PM. "In a day or so," Van Dusen recounted, "[Diefenbaker] reported that he had 'caught' the RCMP dogging his tracks. He was quite pleased with his own astuteness."[6]

Another incident involving Diefenbaker and the RCMP occurred in Trail, B.C., during the 1962 election campaign. Elections often present security personnel with additional headaches because of the crowds and the candidates' desire to interact with the people. In this instance, fortunately, the prime minister's life was not threatened.

Diefenbaker was giving a speech in front of a crowd of about 1,900 when five Doukhobor women — the Doukhobors were a sect of Russian dissenters who emigrated to Canada at the turn of the twentieth century — marched naked in front of him. "The middle-aged women remained unclothed," noted the *Globe and Mail* news report, "wailing at the prime minister, for almost five minutes before Royal Canadian Mounted Police escorted them outside Trail Memorial Arena."

The women involved in the protest were members of the Sons of Freedom, a radical sect of Doukhobors. Such nude protests were part of the sect's philosophical stance against the materialism of society. In this case, they were protesting the fact that their husbands were in jail facing terrorist charges. Diefenbaker was surprised at first by the chorus of women, but then found his footing. "That is no novelty to me," he said after seeing the women.

RCMP officers tried to get the women to cover themselves but had no luck as some in the crowd laughed while others were beginning to get a little impatient. The prime minister, meanwhile, along with those on the platform with him, including Mrs. Diefenbaker, smiled gamely.

"I was raised on a homestead in Saskatchewan. That's why I know what those things are," Diefenbaker told the crowd, the assumption being that he was referring to the style of the protest as the Sons of Freedom were notorious for naked demonstrations. By this time, six more RCMP officers, in both plainclothes and uniform, surrounded the women and ushered them out. Diefenbaker's life was never in danger, but the incident spiced up an otherwise sleepy campaign event. "The prime minister had difficulty arousing the crowd early in his speech. Then came the stripping and the rally woke up."[7]

What forces a prime minister to have security? In the early days, it was usually in response to specific threats, as was the case with Robert Borden, noted earlier. During the 1960s, the world was rocked by the assassinations of John F. Kennedy in 1963, and both Martin Luther King Jr. and Robert F. Kennedy in 1968. Not surprisingly, President Kennedy's assassination brought increased security for Lester Pearson, who was assigned an RCMP guard to escort him everywhere he went. Prior to the president's murder in Dallas, Pearson, as was the case for all previous prime ministers, had no formal personal security. In fact, just two weeks after Kennedy's death, Pearson asked for the guard — whom he had only accepted with reluctance — to be removed, a request that was granted.

It seems, though, that the Kennedy assassination motivated some unbalanced citizens in their correspondence to the prime minister.

One person wrote to Pearson in January 1964 saying, "You know what happened to Mr. John F. Kennedy a short while ago; well if you do not take any actions in order to give us a national flag, you will also receive a bullet in your head like the president of the United States."[8]

The threat was only one of many Pearson received during his time as PM. On July 12, 1964, a man called 24 Sussex Drive asking to speak to the prime minister. When told he was away in England, the caller responded by saying, "Mr. Pearson was lucky because the house would blow up at 11:25 p.m." The threat turned out to be a prank call, and in a sign of the innocence of the times the RCMP police report of the incident noted that "Marjory Culshaw and other members of the household staff did not appear to be unduly alarmed by the bomb threat, [and] she suggested that one of the evening TV programs which she had seen had probably sparked the call."[9]

Pearson was involved in a few other security matters during his five years as prime minister. In 1966, a forty-five-year-old man named Paul Chartier made it into Parliament with a homemade bomb consisting of ten sticks of dynamite. "Suddenly, there was a noise that I can hardly describe. It wasn't sharp, it seemed more like a dull thud," recalled Alastair Fraser who was Clerk Assistant of the House of Commons at the time. "I thought there had possibly been an explosion outside the building or something of that kind."[10] With Prime Minister Pearson and Opposition Leader John Diefenbaker both in the House of Commons at the time, it was fortunate that Chartier's bomb exploded in the third-floor washroom, killing only the would-be assassin. With some typical Canadian decorum and respect for process, Diefenbaker suggested that the House adjourn and Pearson agreed, and there appeared to be no great alarm. The washroom in which the bomb exploded was only about twenty metres from the prime minister's office, though Pearson did not appear to have been the specific target — Chartier wanted to take out as many MPs as possible, but extra security was assigned to Pearson in the days that followed.

Chartier had written letters and speeches critical of the federal government. A note had been found in his pocket that began, "When I am the president of Canada ..." A doctor later testified at an inquiry that Chartier had a "mild mental disorder," but he was not diagnosed with

JANUARY 1964

W A R N I N G   W A R N I N G   W A R N I N G

SUBJECT: NATIONAL FLAG

DEAR MR. PEARSON:

         YOU KNOW WHAT HAPPENED TO MR. JOHN F. KENNEDY A SHORT WHILE AGO; WELL IF YOU DO NOT TAKE ANY ACTIONS IN ORDER TO GIVE US A NATIONAL FLAG, YOU WILL ALSO RECEIVE A BULLET IN YOUR HEAD LIKE THE PRESIDENT OF THE UNITED STATES.

         INDEED, WE HAVE WAITED LONG ENOUGH FOR THAT AND YOU WILL HAVE TO TAKE THE NECESSARY PROCEDURES, IN ORDER TO ACCOMPLISH THAT WORK.

         BEFORE ENDING, I AM WAITING SOME NEWS FROM YOU THROUGH THE NEWSPAPERS MEDIA.

         IT IS A FINAL WARNING AND I AM WAITING YOUR COOPERATION FOR THE BENEFIT OF ALL THE CANADIANS OF THIS COUNTRY.

            SIGNATURE,

            MR. DECIDED.

MR. Lester Pearson,
Parliament Building,
Ottawa, Ontario.

(PERSONAL)

Prime ministers throughout Canadian history have received many threats against their lives, often through the mail. This particularly menacing 1964 letter to Lester B. Pearson came just a couple of months after the assassination of President John F. Kennedy.

insanity. In a lengthy letter he wrote to the *Edmonton Journal*, he talked about killing as many members of Parliament as possible.

As far as the prime minister's personal security was concerned at this time, much of the public discussion of the issue focused on three things: one, threats cannot be reduced to zero in the face of a determined criminal; two, it is not the Canadian way to have the PM insulated from the public in a protective bubble; and three, this is not the United States. The sentiments were captured well in a George Bain column from the *Globe and Mail*:

> Our prime ministers have usually moved about the capital (and everywhere else) as free as the breeze. No motorcycle escort accompanies the prime minister's black Buick when he travels between home and office, and if he chooses to walk between the East Block and the Centre Block, he walks.
>
> Probably any prime minister under a parliamentary system is in a safer position for psychological reasons … than is a President of the United States. Very simply, he affords a less inviting target to the unbalanced person seeking to hit back at an oppressive world.[11]

Pearson certainly found out about security and the president of the United States when Lyndon B. Johnson made a short-notice visit to the prime minister during Expo 67, the world's fair that doubled as the country's centennial party. Johnson's bilateral meeting with Pearson took place at Harrington Lake, the prime minister's country retreat. It turned out to be an unforgettable visit. "This old cottage will never be the same again," Pearson quipped to reporters before the president had even arrived.

Harrington was a beehive of activity, "overrun with police, reporters, officials, cars, buses, and helicopters." Pearson tried to relax and read on the porch in the view of reporters.

Then over the hills from the southeast came two U.S. Marine helicopters. They circled the lake once and came in for the landing, the president's helicopter clipping the top branches of a maple tree. The prime minister stood in the shelter of another tree, protecting himself from the leaves and debris thrown up by the whirlybirds' blades, then trotted across the field to greet his guest.[12]

The security, a combination of RCMP and U.S. Secret Service, along with Johnson's intrusive entrance, was more than the mild-mannered Pearson could stomach. A "couple of Mounties could have done the job," he said. But it got worse: "I went in to the house and up the stairs. At the top a hard-faced chap said: 'Who are you? Where are you going?' I replied 'I live here and I'm going to the bathroom.' I was pretty indignant that [the Secret Service] penetrated our dwelling to that extent."

If Pearson was perhaps a little too naive toward security, he was only reflecting a general ambivalence about the issue shared by Canadians, including the RCMP. A May 1963 RCMP document outlining how to carry out security for 24 Sussex Drive benignly says, "Unexpected or doubtful visitors arriving after the prime minister has retired for the night are to be politely and firmly discouraged and informed that the prime minister has retired for the night and [told] that they are to obtain an appointment by telephoning the next day to his secretary."[13]

Pearson was a glass half-full type of man who avoided controversy, a skill developed in his career as a distinguished diplomat in the Department of External Affairs in the 1930s and 1940s. He represented an idealistic and gentle side of Canada, a side that was about to be swept away by heated politics in Quebec and a flamboyant prime minister who was not afraid to stick his neck out. In such circumstances, the target becomes much more visible. Security for the prime minister was about to change. No longer would they travel around "as free as the breeze."

It did not take long for the new reality to become apparent. Pierre Trudeau became prime minister in April of 1968 and quickly called an election for June 25. On June 6, U.S. Senator Robert F. Kennedy was gunned down in a Los Angeles hotel, shocking the world and once more raising the question of the safety of leaders. At a Trudeau campaign visit to Mississauga, Ontario, in mid-June, security reached a "fever pitch." Police sharpshooters patrolled rooftops and officers were on every highway overpass as the PM's motorcade drove down the Queen Elizabeth Way. Of Kennedy, one officer said, "It was in our minds. I don't want to be melodramatic. I would prefer to say that we were watching in case a heckler decided to throw something."[14]

Part of the issue was Trudeau's popularity. This was at the height of Trudeaumania, and it is hard to imagine the frenzy that followed the prime minister wherever he went in 1968. He was mobbed everywhere as he electrified an electorate that had been fed the likes of the often uninspiring Lester Pearson, John Diefenbaker, and Louis St. Laurent for the past twenty years — all respectable gentlemen but hardly the types of personalities to get the heart pumping. Trudeau was more like a member of the Beatles. Protecting him was a serious security problem for the RCMP. "The masses of people that crush around him wherever he goes make it almost impossible for police at any particular time to keep a complete security screen," observed the *Toronto Star*. Indeed, the prime minister often seemed in danger "of being dragged off the back of his moving convertible as hundreds [tried] to grab his hand along procession routes."[15]

As a point of comparison, during a 1962 campaign stop at a Mississauga high school by prime minister John Diefenbaker — a PM who could at least excite a crowd with his oratory, if not his looks — there were twenty guards from the local constabulary. For Trudeau's visit to a Mississauga shopping plaza six years later there were forty-five local police officers, ten detectives, fifteen Ontario Provincial Police officers, "and an unknown number of RCMP."[16]

June was a tough month for ensuring the safety of the prime minister. The day before the June 25 vote, the PM attended the Saint-Jean-Baptiste parade in Montreal, despite a request from Mayor Jean Drapeau not to come, as it might encourage demonstrations by

Quebec separatists. "I'm certainly not going to admit, by backing down, that the prime minister of Canada can't watch the festival of Saint-Jean in his own home town!" Trudeau wrote in his memoirs. "I've been watching this parade since I was six years old."

Violence erupted during the parade directly in front of the viewing stand where Trudeau sat, along with the archbishop of Montreal, Paul Grégoire; Drapeau; and Quebec premier Daniel Johnson. Trudeau and the other VIPs were pelted with bottles and other projectiles while angry crowds shouted, "*Trudeau au Poteau*" (Trudeau to the gallows). The RCMP moved in to protect the PM and get him to a safer location, but in just one of many scenes that captured the feistiness of the new prime minister, he gesticulated adamantly with his left arm that there was no way he was leaving. "I would not have it," Trudeau later said. "I had absolutely no desire to give in to such a ridiculous display of violence."

Extensive security precautions were already in place for Trudeau's visit as a result of death threats telephoned into news organizations. These were not uncommon throughout his time in office. Visits to his home province were particularly fraught with danger, as the FLQ continued its terrorist activities, which included such actions as blowing up mailboxes and bombing the Montreal Stock Exchange. Large public events always presented greater security challenges, and Trudeau faced another in 1969 when he attended the first Grey Cup game held in Montreal in thirty-four years.

Relations between French and English Canada were on the minds of many. This was the same year that the Trudeau government introduced the Official Languages Act, which made Canada officially bilingual, enshrining the equal status of French and English. Bringing the country's marquee sports event to the heart of French Canada was just another example of attempts to build national unity during a fragile time in the nation's history. The game, played between the Russ Jackson–led Ottawa Rough Riders and Ron Lancaster's Saskatchewan Roughriders, raised concerns not only for the protection of the prime minister, but also the players. The Autostade, where the game would be played, featured the largest security force ever for a sporting event in Canada up to that time. As an indication of how skittish police in

Montreal were, three weeks prior to the Grey Cup game, the Santa Claus parade, of all things, was cancelled.

With Trudeau in attendance, sitting next to CFL commissioner Jake Gaudaur, the game went off without incident. The prime minister even nailed the ceremonial kickoff.* Plainclothes officers on the sidelines went unnoticed by the players. Trudeau, dressed in a jaunty white knit tam cap and matching scarf was photographed presenting the trophy to Russ Jackson, who led Ottawa to victory. Jackson asked Trudeau if he could trade his helmet for the PM's tam but the prime minister turned him down, saying he couldn't do it since Margaret had knit it for him.

There were similar concerns at the 1970 Grey Cup held in Toronto the following year. This time the game came only a few weeks after the October Crisis, so tensions were running very high. Trudeau's attendance at the contest was intended to burnish his image. This was the Grey Cup at which Trudeau famously arrived wearing a fedora and "Dracula-like cape," landing the PM on the front pages the next day. Security remained very tight for the contest. "In addition to the usual uniformed men in the stands and along the field sidelines, there were police on roofs and other vantage points surrounding CNE Stadium, on the roof of the [nearby] Coliseum, and on hills at Ontario Place," one news report noted.[17] Away from the public, the prime minister's security detail was not taking any chances. At a dinner held at historian Ramsay Cook's residence, RCMP officers even searched through a parcel of Dinky Toys brought by one guest as a gift for Cook's kids.

Pierre Trudeau's love of the outdoors contributed to some security issues, including one incident from the late 1970s when Trudeau and his sons Justin and Sacha were on a canoe trip. The RCMP dropped the Trudeaus off and chose a fixed rendezvous point down the Picanoc River in Quebec, about an hour's drive north of Ottawa. When the prime minister and his sons arrived, there was no security detail in sight. Trudeau was angry because he was with his sons. He made his way to a nearby

---

* Trudeau blundered quite badly in the 1968 game. Rumour was he practised intensely for the 1969 Grey Cup kickoff. It paid off. He kicked it twenty-eight yards.

cottage, where a surprised couple greeted the PM and allowed him to use their phone. As it turned out, the RCMP cruiser had gotten stuck in the mud. Once they were freed, they went to the wrong spot and had to be fetched by Bill Mason, one of Trudeau's travelling companions.

In stark contrast to his immediate predecessors, Pierre Trudeau was concerned about his privacy as much as his security. At Harrington Lake, he increased his protective detail to include patrols of the water and asked for the construction of a small security compound. But the occasional lost hiker or cross-country skier sometimes ended up at the cottage.* There were other encroachments to worry about, as well. In the summer of 1974 a Laval University researcher was granted permission to continue his study of beaver lodges in the area. Once his observations were completed, he and his field partner noticed what they thought was a bald eagle flying by. Upon closer examination, it turned out to be an osprey, so the two researchers continued to follow the flight path of the bird with their binoculars.

Not far in the distance, however, the prime minister and his wife, Margaret, were taking a dip in the lake, "apparently skinny," when they espied two pairs of binoculars seemingly trained on them. The RCMP were called and, as Canadian Press reporter Dave McIntosh remembered, the incident was written up in a report by the assistant manager of the National Capital Commission, which said, in part:

> At a small island [the researchers] were met by the RCMP security patrol boat. They were questioned about their presence on the lake and the work they were performing. They requested the patrol to tow them to the north end of the lake in that they might leave the lake as soon as possible. They were questioned on their use of binoculars and stated that they had not

---

* A 1965 memo to Lester Pearson from the Privy Council Office acknowledged the "difficulty with tourists and sightseers intruding at Harrington Lake." Their solution was to erect a "Private Entrance" sign at the main gate.

seen anyone on the lake or along the shoreline during their visit. It was established that the … canoe did not have any fishing or camera equipment in it.

The report further indicated that to avoid these "untoward occurrences" in the future, approvals of visitors to the lake for research would be cleared with the PM or staff first and that trees for better privacy would be planted at the cottage. All of this "to ensure that [the PM's] privacy and enjoyment are not impaired."[18]

Pierre Trudeau's prime ministership was a turning point in the security of Canada's head of government. The political climate at home and abroad changed drastically during his era, one that featured terrorist attacks and a political assassination on Canadian soil. Although the country has believed that peace, order, and good government have been three of its defining characteristics since the Constitution Act (originally named the British North America Act) was signed in 1867, it turns out that Canada was not immune to the political violence spawned during that era.

In 1971, for example, it again became clear how vulnerable leaders were. The Soviet premier Alexei Kosygin, who was visiting Ottawa at the time, was attacked by a protester, who jumped on him while he and Trudeau walked in front of a crowd on Parliament Hill. Security was tight, yet somehow the assailant, Geza Matrai, slipped through. Trudeau attempted to help Kosygin defend himself before the RCMP wrestled the attacker to the ground in a security breach that dominated news reports the next day.

In the United States, the situation was much worse: within a few years the country had seen the assassination of the two Kennedys, as well as Martin Luther King Jr. In 1978, George Moscone, the mayor of San Francisco, was shot and killed along with city supervisor Harvey Milk. These were disconcerting years in North America, necessitating for the first time the serious and sustained protection of the prime minister. Trudeau was a highly visible star and stars need protection. He was also not afraid to take on hecklers or other dissenters, making him a target. But all subsequent prime ministers would continue to struggle with their desire to meet the people and the RCMP's mandate to keep the PM safe.

While death threats against prime ministers are not uncommon and most, if not all PMs, have faced them, only one leader has actually come frighteningly close to assassination. When it did happen, in 1995, the gravity of the breach to the prime minister's security was downplayed. Instead, it was treated as though it were some kind of prank. This attitude toward safety was colourfully captured by *Globe and Mail* columnist George Bain — with reference to a 1960s-era lapse in security — as the "bovine characteristics of Canadians."[19] In other words, Canadians were quite complacent about security. An assassination attempt couldn't really happen in Canada, could it? And with a folksy PM like Jean Chrétien, was there really something to worry about?

Chrétien — a long-time Cabinet minister before he became PM in 1993 — was well aware of the risks faced by people such as him. "The threat of assassination haunts every political leader, and every nation has to devote a lot of money and effort to protection," he wrote in his memoirs. Unfortunately for Chrétien and his wife, Aline, the spectre of it came a little too close to home on November 5, 1995, when an intruder armed with a long knife somehow broke into 24 Sussex Drive and made it to the hallway outside the prime minister's bedroom.

That night the PM was tired and had gone to bed, taking a sleeping pill to help him have a sound sleep. This had been a particularly stressful time for the country and its prime minister. The week before, the Quebec referendum result put the nation on tenterhooks. While separation had been defeated, the result had been very close, with only 50.6 percent of Quebeckers narrowly choosing to stay part of Canada. The next day Chrétien was to head to Israel for the funeral of Yitzhak Rabin, who had been assassinated on November 4. There was understandable anxiety in the Chrétien household.

At around 3:00 a.m, Aline Chrétien was awoken when she heard some noise in the hallway outside of their bedroom. When she investigated, she discovered a man wearing glasses and a toque. He was also carrying a knife. She hurriedly turned around, locked the door behind her, and called the RCMP security. She roused her husband, telling him there was an intruder. He looked like Forrest Gump, she told him.

In an instinctive move of self-defence, the prime minister picked up a heavy Inuit sculpture, ready to do what was necessary to save his and his wife's lives. He recalled:

> [The intruder] may have suspected I was armed; and he
> certainly knew he was trapped. Without even trying to
> open the door — which was probably a lucky thing for
> him, given that the carving might well have killed him
> — he silently walked over to a bench at the top of the
> staircase, sat down, and waited for the guards to arrive.

Everyone else waited, too. Aline called security a second time — "Come right now! We're afraid!" — as they still had not arrived after several minutes. And when the RCMP finally did show up at the doors of 24 Sussex Drive, about ten minutes after the initial call, the Keystone Cops discovered that they did not have a proper set of keys for the door. The security for the prime minister had lapsed completely. The outcome could have been the death of Jean Chrétien.

The assailant was André Dallaire, a thirty-four-year-old convenience store clerk. He told police after his arrest that he "would have jumped him and slit his throat" had he crossed paths with the prime minister that night. He was charged with attempted murder, breaking and entering, being unlawfully in a dwelling, and possession of weapon.[20]

The hopelessly ill-prepared RCMP played down the incident. "Right away the RCMP was saying the prime minister's life was never under threat, that there never was any issue of his safety, and I thought 'bullshit,'" recalled Chrétien's communications director, Peter Donolo. "They were minimizing it like mad. I thought it was important that the truth came out."[21]

It is no wonder that the RCMP wanted to play down the incident. During Dallaire's trial it was revealed that he had thrown rocks over the fence at Sussex to see if anyone would notice. He waved at the security cameras and got no reaction. And he broke into the house and spent an hour walking around the basement and other floors before he was finally discovered by Aline Chrétien.

Perhaps a break-in such as this should not have come as a big shock. Ben Mulroney, son of Prime Minister Brian Mulroney, shed some light on security at 24 Sussex. "Security was not what it is today. There was no capital 'S' in security," Mulroney said in a 2015 interview on CPAC.

> When we first got there, security at 24 Sussex amounted to having a Crown Vic at one end of the semicircle — you would come in one gate and exit the other — there was a Crown Vic at one end with two RCMP and a Crown Vic at the other, and if you wanted to get into the prime minister's residence you would flash your high beams or you'd wave at the cop and he'd look at you and I don't know by what criteria they established that they would let you in … they'd come up, open the gate, and let you in and then the other guy at the other end would let you out. That was security [when we were there].[22]

Despite the seriousness of the Dallaire break-in, it wasn't long before the media were having fun with what had happened. "In a very typical Canadian manner we quickly turned it into a joke," observed Donolo.[23] Less than a week after the assassination attempt, humorous accounts made their way into the newspaper. In the *Globe and Mail's* "National Notebook," a roundup of the week's political news, the paper wrote, "Mr. Chrétien might pause to acknowledge the quintessentially Canadian wit that has been generated in the wake of the story." Some of the humour was related to a recently signed licensing agreement with the Walt Disney Company, and that led to references to the RCMP as "Mickey Mouse security" and the bodyguards as "Goofy" and "Dumbo." The paper also quoted some as saying, "An Inuit bird in the hand is worth two RCMP officers in the bush." And "for the political historians," the *Globe* mused, "Pierre Trudeau had his night of long knives, Mr. Chrétien had his night of the jackknives."[24]

None of this was found to be too humorous by the Chrétiens. Aline subsequently had trouble sleeping and had to spend some time out at Harrington Lake to deal with the stress. But part of the reaction was also likely due to the folksy attitude projected by Jean Chrétien, who included a picture of him and television comedienne Mary Walsh joking about the break-in in his memoirs. Moreover, coming long before such tragic events as the 2001 terrorist attacks or the 2014 attack on Parliament Hill, it is easy looking back to see a touch of the "bovine characteristics" among Canadians concerning what remains the most serious threat to the life of a prime minister in the history of the country. The view of such things would be much different now.

Security issues seemed to dog Jean Chrétien during his first few years in office. As if a direct threat on his life was not enough, three months later the prime minister got into another security snafu when he manhandled a protester at a February 1996 Flag Day event in Gatineau, Quebec. There had been some concern before Chrétien arrived at the event. He had a sense something wasn't right and asked his security detail if everything was good. They replied that it was.

Sometimes, small details matter. Advance planning for the event — which happens for all PM visits — did not pick up on the fact that the sun would be shining in the platform party's face. This would necessitate Chrétien wearing his sunglasses, something they tried to avoid because it made him look sinister. While heading back to his car after giving a short speech — sunglasses on — Chrétien recalled he and his bodyguards were "besieged by children, all wanting me to sign their flags." The PM stopped to sign a few, but then all hell broke loose as protesters rushed into the kids, yelling through a bullhorn, including Bill Clennett, who got right up in the prime minister's face. "In my surprise and anger," Chrétien recounted, "I grabbed the nearer one with my two hands and flipped him to the side, though I don't remember the exact sequence. It had been only three months since someone had tried to assassinate me, so my reaction was instinctive and probably angrier than it would have been otherwise."

It would come to be known as the "Shawinigan handshake," as Chrétien grabbed Clennett by the throat, angry grimace on his face, and threw him aside like he was in a street fight. This time it led not only to the expected humorous reactions but also concerns about national unity, coming just four months after the razor-thin Quebec referendum. "Chrétien manhandles protester: National-unity fallout expected as PM takes matters into his own hands in Flag Day ceremony in Quebec" read one *Globe and Mail* headline. At CJMF radio in Quebec City, a call-in show received more than 1,500 calls and 64 percent of them were calling on Chrétien to resign. The show's host, Robert Gillet, called him "Mad Dog Chrétien."[25]

On the lighter side, one Liberal staffer joked that he could get a fortune if he were allowed to auction off the sunglasses the prime minister wore during the incident in which Chrétien biographer Lawrence Martin described the PM as looking like a "Mafia hit man."[26] Peter Donolo told the PM not to worry about reported damage to the protester's dental bridge: "Don't worry, Prime Minister, we'll cover it through the infrastructure program." President Bill Clinton said the protesters had learned a lesson. And on it went.

As for the RCMP, they considered the case closed and claimed that Clennett, the man assaulted by Jean Chrétien, did not pose a security threat. But had the RCMP done their job, the incident would never have happened. One historian said at the time that the whole thing was "trivial, blown all out of proportion," and that Chrétien's actions were far less egregious than the time Pierre Trudeau gave the finger to protesters in Salmon Arm, B.C.[27] The event would surely be analyzed differently today.

The moment was not lost on the prime minister, however, who reflected in his memoirs about the importance of synergy between the prime minister and his security detail. This was especially important for Chrétien — and most PMs — because of his preference for wading into crowds. "Working a crowd became a kind of instinctive collaboration between the bodyguards and me," he wrote. "Since they all had their own techniques, their own reactions, and their own understanding of how I moved and behaved, I found the system worked best when there wasn't a constant turnover [of officers]."

Chrétien felt this was part of what led to yet another security breach when, in 2000, he was pelted in the face with a pie on Prince Edward Island. He bristled at yet another letdown in his protection but showed he could still muster a sense of humour when he said, "Gee, you guys are strange. Here you serve the pie before the soup!" But the incident revealed the challenges of protecting a PM who wants to meet people and even sometimes deviate from the pre-arranged route he is supposed to take as planned by the RCMP. "We can't put him in a glass bubble and say nobody will ever have access to him," said Staff-Sergeant Andre Guertin after the incident. While that may be true, one former security officer was stunned that someone got that close to the PM with something as large as a pie.

The media, however, were starting to change their tone after so many lapses in security. "We in the media have to stop treating them as innocent mischief makers. The police have to stop treating them as petty nuisances and the courts have to stop treating them as inconsequential offenders," weighed in the *Toronto Star*. "Pie-throwing may be funny on television or onstage, but accosting a politician in a public place — whether it is with a pie, a clenched fist, or a knife — is neither harmless nor humorous."[28]

All of these security breakdowns took place before September 11, 2001, the day of terrorist attacks that struck New York and Washington. The government's and the public's attitude toward security took a significant turn at that time, and no longer would Canadians view the protection of public spaces or public figures in the same way.

Even so, there were still mind-boggling security breaches afterward. In 2002, a man left a grenade on the front desk of the Langevin Block building (now the called the Office of the Prime Minister and Privy Council). The grenade did not contain explosives but the incident raised alarm bells on Parliament Hill. In a criticism that would return later, one MP questioned why there were four different security forces in charge of protecting the Hill (RCMP, House of Commons security, Senate security, and local Ottawa police). How was that efficient?

Harrington Lake and 24 Sussex Drive were also deemed to need more security in the years following 9/11, according to a threat assessment done by the RCMP in 2009. As a country deeply involved in the war on terror, it was no surprise that the report noted that Sussex should have an "antiram, antiscaling" fence installed to reduce the chance of a terrorist attack. "For the Prime Minister and the associated residences, one adversary that has been identified is al-Qaeda,"[29] the report noted.

As worries about terrorism grew, if anyone still thought of security as something perpetrated by "innocent mischief makers," October 22, 2014, would change all of that.

The nation was shocked that day when Michael Zehaf-Bibeau stormed into the Parliament Buildings armed with a rifle and long knife. He had already shot and killed Corporal Nathan Cirillo, who was standing guard at the Tomb of the Unknown Soldier, not far away. Zehaf-Bibeau then headed to Parliament Hill. Prime Minister Stephen Harper was in the Parliamentary Reading Room in the main corridor of the building addressing his caucus of MPs when gunfire was heard. Remarkably, Harper was not with his security detail, which was outside of Parliament. He was, essentially, unprotected. Glen McGregor of the *Ottawa Citizen* gave one of the best accounts of the moment after speaking to an unidentified House of Commons security guard:

> "Where is he?" the constable asked, meaning Prime Minister Stephen Harper.
>
> Fingers pointed towards the northeast corner of the room, where a door inset in the wood-panelled wall stood slightly ajar.
>
> The closet is barely four feet in each direction, further cramped by conduit and wiring panels on the walls. With the door closed, it is completely dark and the only sound is a low hum of a cooling fan.
>
> Harper stood inside, facing the door. He seemed calm, not frightened, the constable recalls.

"He was waiting for whoever was supposed to protect him," the constable said. "His eyes were looking at me like he wanted to know what was going on.

"I looked at him and said, 'Are you OK?' He looked at me and said, 'Yes.'"

Again, the constable says, he feared a group of terrorists barging in and taking Harper hostage.

"I said, 'Stay there.' He nodded."[30]

Harper's protection detail, along with House of Commons security, arrived minutes later. The PM was then rushed to 24 Sussex Drive. Moments before, Zehaf-Bibeau had been shot and killed by Sergeant-at-Arms Kevin Vickers, just down the hallway from where Harper was. It was the closest an assassin had come to threatening the life of a prime minister since the Chrétien incident twenty years previous. Increased security measures went into place, and once more Canadians wrestled with the question of how open their Parliament should be.

Like prime ministers before him, Stephen Harper faced his share of threats, as well as disappointments with his security detail. The officers were slow during their shift changes, which delayed the Harpers; they couldn't keep up with Laureen Harper on her hikes around Harrington Lake; and, on one occasion, an officer showed up late for her because the officer was too hungover. As a result, Harper instituted changes by appointing Bruno Saccomani to fix up the prime minister's protection detail (PMPD). No leader in Canada before had been as elaborately protected as he was.

During Harper's first six years in office, the cost of PMPD doubled to $20 million. The unit got new weapons, bigger vehicles, and their training became more tactical, "involving mock attacks, target practice and paintball drills. There is a growing use of SWAT teams in the Prime Minister's motorcade, and the Mounties on the detail are fitter and better trained than ever," reported the *Globe and Mail*.[31]

Despite that, as Jean Chrétien also knows, people can penetrate the security blanket. Two protesters got behind Stephen Harper while he was delivering a speech in Vancouver in 2014. They had dressed in black to blend in with the hotel catering staff. To some extent, these breaches are inevitable. As one former RCMP security officer said, "There's always going to be breaches like that, but it's all about democracy…. We don't limit people's movements in a democracy, we don't ask people for their papers at every corner and leaders of democratic nations understand that they're putting themselves in harm's way just by taking office, because you can't predict what's going to happen."[32]

"I always think of that song, 'You'll Never Walk Alone,'" said Prime Minister Kim Campbell in 1993, referring to her security detail. "And believe me, I never do."[33] She wasn't joking and went on to mention the RCMP officers who were standing behind potted plants — just like in the cartoons — when she once took her sister to dinner. So it is no surprise that from time to time prime ministers have tried to escape those whose job it is to keep them safe.

"I sometimes had the same impulse for freedom that had caused me to run away from the school where I boarded as a young man when I was courting Aline," Jean Chrétien once admitted. At the 1998 G8 summit in Birmingham, England, Chrétien and U.S. President Bill Clinton did try to run away. The two were having a chat when they noticed there did not seem to be any security around. "Bill, let's make a run for it," Chrétien suggested. "We rushed into the woods, as excited as two boys running away from their teachers, and went for a long walk by ourselves."

This bilateral escape led to a much-talked-about photograph of Chrétien and Clinton trying to hop a wall. According to Chrétien, he challenged the president: "Come on, Bill, let's see who can get to the top fastest." Chrétien is shown in the photo gamely overcoming the wall while the president is doing his best but can't seem to pull it off.

On another occasion, Chrétien and his grandson decided to bolt from the hotel at a 2008 G8 Summit in Genoa, Italy. "For a half-hour or so we enjoyed a lovely stroll through the narrow streets of the nearby village and, gee, we had fun," he recalled. When the escape was noticed, panic ensued. "The PM has left the room!" But Chrétien returned and all was well.

Prime Minister Jean Chrétien and U.S. president Bill Clinton decided to dodge their security and go for a walk during the 1998 Birmingham, England, G8 conference. When they returned, the sixty-one-year-old Chrétien showed his athleticism, making the leap over this wall look rather easy compared to his forty-eight-year-old American counterpart.

When you are prime minister, the ordinary can become extra-ordinary. Chrétien liked to drop into taverns in Ottawa or Gatineau to have a beer and hear what the locals had to say, for example. Stephen Harper shopped at the local drug store in the New Edinburgh neighbourhood, picking items out like anyone else. Security was always close by but these moments are hard to get when you are the prime minister.

Pierre Trudeau occasionally tried to elude his security, as well. In 1970, during the October Crisis, he and Margaret found the protection quite oppressive when they were at Harrington Lake, so they took off into the woods for an escape. But the two got lost coming back and security panicked. When Pierre and Margaret finally emerged from the forest they heard gunshots. They were coming from the middle of the lake where an officer was firing his weapon in an effort to guide them home.

The athleticism of both of these former prime ministers proved to be a problem when they chose to hit the slopes. Jean Chrétien needed RCMP officers who were accomplished skiers. During a Colorado

Christmas holiday in 1997, one RCMP officer broke a leg and another her wrist. When Justin Trudeau became prime minister, a call went out to RCMP members looking for skiers who could handle triple black diamond hills to keep up with a PM who was a former snowboard instructor at Whistler during his youth. When asked if he were causing a problem for his protection detail, Trudeau responded, "I have many times and will continue to praise the RCMP for the extraordinary work they do. They're just as good on the slopes as anywhere in the world."[34]

Sometimes the RCMP have stood in the way of a prime minister wanting to have some fun. Once during Paul Martin's time as PM, he was relaxing at his farm in Knowlton, Quebec, his preferred place to escape from the demands of being prime minister. On one occasion a hot-air balloon got blown off course. "All of a sudden there was a massive mobilization of the Mounties," Martin recalled. "And all of the sudden this balloon appeared over the farm. They didn't know what the heck was the story. So I went out and they said, 'Oh, no, you can't come by here, Mr. Martin.' And I said I want to come see this on the farm." The balloon ended up landing on Martin's property with the help of the Mounties. "From my point of view, it was great fun," he said.[35]

Despite their not uncommon desire to escape the protective bubble of their security teams, prime ministers develop friendships with their protectors. Jean Chrétien, despite his protective detail problems, became quite friendly with a number of the officers around him. Paul Martin thought highly of his RCMP officers, who held him in high regard in return. The fact that officers assigned are usually there for several years helps to develop the relationship. The changes in PMPD for Stephen Harper led to a better relationship between Harper and his family and the officers, who were well liked by the family. But this contributed to internal RCMP rivalries, as well as rumours of an affair between Laureen Harper and an officer.

The election of Prime Minister Justin Trudeau brought back a number of security challenges for PMPD because of his fondness for wandering into crowds, not exactly Stephen Harper's modus operandi. As the first prime minister to march in Toronto's Gay Pride parade, Trudeau exposed himself to security risks — by marching openly in a parade attended by thousands — like few PMs before him. But getting any specific information from the RCMP about how they handle his protection is a difficult task. Whereas there once was a time when some details about the security of the PM were printed in the newspapers, the RCMP are understandably very tight-lipped about this now. Interview questions for this book were turned down by the RCMP, but after speaking to some police officers who worked in VIP security, a portrait of what happens emerges.[36]

Before events such as the Pride parade, the RCMP search for any potential threats developing in places such as the "dark web" or other Internet chat areas. A march in a public parade is a high-risk activity, and if, through intelligence, security deemed that there was a likely potential threat to the PM, his appearance would be cancelled. At large events such as this, the prime minister is surrounded by about a dozen officers from PMPD for his immediate protection. There are numerous other plainclothes officers dispersed throughout the crowd. An escape route through the streets is always planned in advance. If there ever were an incident, the PMPD's sole responsibility is to get the prime minister to safety. Other local police handle the situation on the ground in terms of apprehending anyone.

Much of what happens in the protection of the prime minister goes on behind the scenes. The public never see it. Those escape routes mentioned previously, for example, are tested and driven in advance during the time of day the PM is scheduled to visit. A few days before, officers walk around the location the PM is scheduled to visit to do reconnaissance and get a sense of who is hanging around the area. "There's a lot that goes into a prime minister's visit," said one officer, noting the sweeps of buildings with bomb-sniffing dogs. Sometimes garbage cans on the street will be removed and mailboxes could be sealed up.

Officers are trained to watch people's eyes and hands, which are often indicators of a potential threat. "Usually if somebody is going to do something bad, they will sort of unintentionally or unknowingly glance down at what they're doing before they do what they're going to do," a former officer said. "You have to watch the eyes and the hands.

Even people with sunglasses on, you can tell, because there's an almost imperceptible nod of the head or movement of the head — and that's when you would glance at the hands to see what was coming before someone is going to do something."

Has security changed much in the past thirty years? "Back in the day, you had to have boots on the ground to gather your intelligence," noted the former officer. "People talked to each other on landline phones and now it's on cell phones." The officer said this technology cuts both ways: it is easier to track potential threats to a prime minister but there is a lot more chatter to weed through "in order to get rid of the ones who are just people spouting off" as opposed to legitimate threats. Or, as the RCMP wrote to me in the one question they would answer about security changes, "Over the past decades, there has been an escalation in the complexity and unpredictability of criminal threats and the expertise required to mitigate them. With the multifaceted and evolving nature of crime today," the written answer continued, "police services must adapt to ensure that they can continue to detect, disrupt, and prevent criminal activity early and effectively."[37]

Presumably this applies to pie throwers, as well.

Security continues to be at top of mind, as it always is with prime ministers in today's world. In 2017, two years after the Trudeaus moved into Rideau Cottage, $2 million was spent on security upgrades. Most of the enhancements appeared to be of a physical nature, such as removable barriers. "RCMP security measures put in place for the prime minister and his family are intelligence-led and commensurate with threat assessments," their memo to me said. "These measures are not only dictated by threat assessments, but can also vary from one year to another, depending on the type and number of political obligations of a prime minister."

Prime ministers of Canada will continue to work with their protective detail in order to strike the balance between access to Canadians — who genuinely enjoy seeing, greeting, and being with their prime minister — and ensuring that the PMs and their families are safe. Most often — and this is the intended outcome — Canadians barely know that the prime minister is being protected, which is how the RCMP wants it.

As sophisticated as security has become, though, prime ministers are always under threat. The history of prime ministers and their security reveals that being prime minister involves a certain amount of personal risk. It always has. And over time, the risk has only increased. "It is accepted by most men in public life that part of the price they pay is their vulnerability to those who, for thousands of reasons, might wish to focus their hatred upon them," wrote the *Globe and Mail* in a 1966 editorial.[38] While the country and its prime ministers have faced a few close calls (those we know of, as well as those we do not), Canada has been fortunate to avoid the staggering shock of losing one of its leaders to an assassin's bullet as has been the case with the United States on four occasions. May it always be so.

Chapter 5

"A Hard and Trying Job": Prime Ministers and Health

At 8:15 went to Dr. Kidd's office where I met Dr. Caven who made careful and complete examination of my condition. Then he conferred with Dr. Kidd and informed me that it was necessary that I should retire from public life or I would become a nervous wreck and have a serious illness.

— Robert Borden, diary entry, December 11, 1919

Sir John A. Macdonald is standing in his East Block office on Parliament Hill. It is May 6, 1870. He has been prime minister for almost three years. As legislation about bringing Manitoba into Confederation is introduced in the House of Commons, one observer notes that Macdonald "seemed feeble, and looked ill, but spoke with great skill." As for the prime minister, he, too, has realized a recent absence of good health. Sharp pains have been coming and going, piercing his upper back. Now, the pains have returned. John A. stands up to relieve the discomfort. Someone walking by the prime minister's office hears a sudden noise, walks into his office, and finds Macdonald collapsed on the floor. The situation seems grave and the prime minister's doctor, upon examining him, tells the governor general there is "little hope" Sir John A. Macdonald will survive.

The health of the prime minister of Canada is not a topic that garners much attention in today's world — one in which the average life expectancy of a Canadian is more than eighty years — much longer than in the age of Macdonald and Laurier, when it was closer to fifty, due to misfortunes such as higher infant mortality rates and widespread illness. What is more, with advances in health and science we know a lot more about how life can be prolonged. Like his father before him, Prime Minister Justin Trudeau is a good example of someone who appears to take his physical health seriously. And it's a good thing, too, because as John Diefenbaker said after a couple of years in office: "Two years is a long time, and while I have enjoyed every minute of it — being prime minister is a hard and trying job."

The days are long — more than twelve hours — the travel is punishing, including being in and out of many time zones, and the burdens of office are relentless as the prime minister is responsible for the entire country. "It's an awful lot of work, and it can be draining. Everyone who does the job takes it very seriously," said Joe Clark in an interview with me. In the later stages of the Mulroney government in the early 1990s, Clark, who was in the Cabinet, noted the toll the stress of the job was taking on Mulroney. "I was concerned about the consequences of Brian working too hard at his job," he recalled. "He'd come in more tired in the morning consistently than he should have been. He'd been up reading his briefs." Like many PMs, Mulroney did not shy away from work. "He read the long briefs," Clark said. "He was not a golf course prime minister."

While "being prime minister" has never been listed as a cause of death for any of our leaders, two men died in office, both within a few years of each other and both in the 1890s. By comparison, two American presidents, Warren G. Harding and Franklin Roosevelt, died of natural causes while still in office, the former in 1923, the latter in 1945.

Diefenbaker's comment alludes to the stress of the job. Many PMs dealt with this through exercise. Some walked, some swam, and others golfed. A holiday was always useful. In the case of Robert Borden, however, the stress of being prime minister, particularly during the intense period of the First World War and its aftermath, nearly led to his death.

Borden was often ill, whether it was a cold, the grippe (an old-fashioned word for influenza), sciatica, rheumatism, or, as was many times the case, carbuncles (boils). Borden complained of them regularly in his diary. "In bed nearly all day," he wrote on October 21, 1913. "[Dr.] Laidlaw came and lanced a carbuncle and injected serum into my arm. Neck very sore." Three days later he noted that he was still in the care of physicians and that the carbuncles were still bothering him.[1] Once the war started in 1914, things got worse.

Being prime minister during the Great War exacted a toll on Robert Borden and his health sometimes kept him from his work. In January 1916 he noted in his diary how much pain he was in: "confined to a bed under charge of doctor and trained nurse." He was "giving no attention at all to [his] work."[2] During the conscription crisis in 1917, when Borden introduced mandatory military service, the strain of the decision and resulting death threats against him led to his collapse in September of that year. He was ordered to rest in bed. After, he spent a few relaxing days fishing with Cabinet minister and friend Arthur Meighen to get away from the travails of the job.

Ultimately, the burden and stress of being prime minister, combined with Borden's relentless and dutiful approach to the job, led to doctors advising him that he "could not remain or continue in public life." Advice, it seems, that would be unlikely to be given to a PM today. Borden recorded the meeting in his diary:

> At 8:15 went to Dr. Kidd's office where I met Dr. Caven who made careful and complete examination of my condition. Then he conferred with Dr. Kidd and informed me that it was necessary that I should retire from public life or I would become a nervous wreck and have a serious illness.... He made careful enquiry

as to my work and my duties during the past years. Then he said very emphatically — "except for your splendid inheritance you would have been dead before this. As it is, you have no organic disease at present, but organic disease will ensue very soon unless you give up public life and have absolute rest and freedom from worry for a very long period. Otherwise you will become a nervous wreck and have a complete collapse."

With the decision to step down made, Borden informed his Cabinet and wisely left Ottawa in early January 1920 for West Palm Beach, Florida. His journey continued to Cuba, Jamaica, and Trinidad before he sailed rough seas for England. This trip was followed by several weeks in Asheville, North Carolina, and all the while he was still prime minister. He officially resigned on July 10, 1920, at which time Arthur Meighen replaced him. The doctor's orders and the six-month vacation seem to have helped. Borden was sixty when he retired and would live another seventeen years.

Robert Borden was not the only prime minister to suffer serious ailment as a result of the stress of being prime minister. Another Conservative, R.B. Bennett, paid the price as well when, in 1935, he had a heart attack. Never known as someone to eschew hard work, Bennett may have overdone it. Of course, serving as PM during the greatest economic crisis of the twentieth century probably did not help either. Nor did the fact that Bennett was overweight. He did not smoke or drink alcohol, but he was not much of a man for exercise and did enjoy eating copious amounts of chocolate.

In February 1935, Bennett was diagnosed with a respiratory infection and ordered to bed by doctors. But he was a hard man to keep down. As John Boyko noted, "He had for some time been a heart attack waiting to happen." During his last physical, in 1934, an irregular heart rhythm had been detected but nothing was prescribed. "It is unlikely Bennett would have listened anyway." In March he had a heart attack.

The illness kept Bennett out of the public eye for weeks and he dealt only with urgent matters. He tired easily and made no appearances in public or the House of Commons. Essentially, he was invisible. He surfaced six weeks later to meet reporters before he left for England to consult with specialists there and to observe the Silver Jubilee of King George V. In the Tudor Room of the Château Laurier hotel, where Bennett kept a multi-room suite, he barbed with the press. Harry W. Anderson, editor of the *Globe*, noted that the PM "was still a little shaky about the legs."

As for Bennett, he revealed a touch of his sense of humour when he told the assembled reporters, "Let's talk — let's talk about anything and everything except politics, international affairs, the weather, and my health."[3]

Another journalist teased when he told Bennett it was great to be able to speak to the PM when he was "unable to roar back at us."

Bennett responded by saying, "Don't be too confident. I'm feeling better and stronger every day." He replied to another question about legislation proposing an eight-hour workday by saying "it did not apply to prime ministers and newspapermen."[4]

Bennett travelled to England, but when he returned the prime minister was not noticeably better. "I saw two specialists in London and they reported that my heart was organically sound," Bennett told reporters later. "It was, however, a tired heart. Just what it will be capable of accomplishing remains to be seen." He later wrote to a friend: "I really should not be at work.... I doubt very much whether I will be able to go on. If I get a chance to rest for six months, I will be all right, but as there is an election before that time, it looks to me as though I might have to retire."

Remarkably, Bennett recovered enough from his heart attack to run in the 1935 election. With the country in the depths of the Great Depression, though, he was unable to overcome the formidable economic forces that left so many Canadian unemployed and destitute. Images of "Bennett buggies" (a motor car with the engine and windows taken out so it could be pulled by horses) and unrest in the form of major protests, such as the Regina Riot, sealed Bennett's fate. He was defeated by Mackenzie King's Liberals.

After serving three years as leader of the Opposition, Bennett left Canada for England. In 1941 he became Viscount Bennett, serving faithfully in the British House of Lords. His health was still in decline and in 1944 he was diagnosed with diabetes. He died in his bathtub in 1947 in Mickleham, England. He is the only Canadian prime minister who rests outside Canada.

Mackenzie King, who returned to office in 1935 after defeating R.B. Bennett (he was previously prime minister from 1921–30, with a brief interlude by Arthur Meighen in 1926), found it harder as the years went on to meet the demands of being prime minister. He struggled with his weight, which often ballooned above two hundred pounds, about forty pounds more than would be ideal for a man who was five-foot-eight. Doctors encouraged him to eat better and exercise more. King suffered bouts of sciatica that kept him confined to bed for days at a time. In 1934, at age sixty, he strained his knee and complained of back pain. He was subsequently diagnosed with arthritis. He went on a strict diet to take some of the weight off his joints and lost more than thirty pounds but he would eventually put it all back on.

Despite his trouble keeping his weight down, King paid close attention to his health — if the number of times he commented on it in his diary is any indication. In that regard he was much like Borden. He and Borden might have enjoyed discussing each other's problems. King had another connection with Borden: he was also a wartime leader and being prime minister during the period from 1939–45 placed immense responsibility on him. By October 1944, King wondered if he would be able to continue. "When I was in bed this morning," he wrote, "I felt then that perhaps I had reached the point that I could not go any further. That Council [Cabinet] might have to carry on tomorrow without my being present."

His health was bothering him, particularly his leg. Dealing with the conscription issue, as he was, meant added strain. He was not sure if he could muster the strength to fight, and, at seventy years old, he wrote in his diary: "I felt bound to say in the light of the medical advice I had received that while I was prepared to go up to the point where my physical strength enabled me to continue to carry on, I could not go beyond that."

King's health problems climaxed during his final months in office. Louis St. Laurent was selected as the new leader of the Liberal party in August 1948, but King insisted that he remain prime minister until at least after he attended a U.N. conference in Paris and a Commonwealth Conference in London that fall. It was an unwise decision, born from King's love of power and inability to give it up. He noted in his diary that he was short of breath when giving his address to the General Assembly of the U.N. and wondered "if he'd be able to get through." He continued to complain of poor health and arrived in London on October 5. Two days later he saw Winston Churchill's physician, Lord Moran:

> The only questions he asked me was whether I felt any pain at any time in the frontal part of my chest beneath the chest bone. I told him I had not been conscious of that at any time. I had had, however, a nasty experience of acute indigestion while at luncheon in Paris, where I had to stand up to get my breath, and felt I might choke, and had had similar experiences here in London at luncheon Churchill had given, and had had similar experiences eating in my home in Ottawa. The doctors had told me they had gathered this was a heart symptom.

Moran diagnosed King with serious heart troubles. He told him he could not attend the conference, and that he would need nursing care in his hotel room, a suggestion the prime minister initially rebuffed. King was given an injection of morphine so that he would sleep better. The doctor felt "the continuous loss of sleep was something that had to be overcome as quickly as possible." Louis St. Laurent was summoned from Canada to take his place.

Despite the health setback, King continued to receive guests in his room at the Dorchester Hotel. His visitors included King George VI — "an extremely pleasant one" and Winston Churchill who was, by this time, no longer prime minister, having lost the 1945 election.* According to King — who certainly had the tendency to exaggerate — Churchill was quite choked up by the meeting. "He came to my bedside and his eyes filled up with tears. He shook my hands very warmly and affectionately. As he went out the door, I could see that he was restraining feelings of emotion."

King kept up with the news of the Commonwealth conference as much as possible and continued to meet with important political figures such as Clement Attlee, the British prime minister, and Jawaharlal Nehru, his Indian counterpart. He even entertained some of his favourite British mediums, who conducted a seance at his bedside.[5] King returned to Ottawa in early November, his health still lagging. He held his last Cabinet meeting on November 12. On November 15, Louis St. Laurent succeeded him. Less than two years later, on July 22, 1950, Canada's longest-serving prime minister passed away. He is interred at Mount Pleasant Cemetery in Toronto.

Not to be underestimated in the health of a prime minister — or anyone — is the need for companionship. King was a bachelor — as was Bennett — and while he had friends, he was mostly a loner. But that has consequences. "I mentioned to [Cabinet minister] St. Laurent later in the evening how very difficult it was for me all alone at Laurier House with no one to talk to and by myself to face over too long a period the kind of situation I am faced with today," he wrote in his diary in November 1944.

No married prime minister has ever gone without mentioning the support received from his spouse. While Maryon Pearson once quipped that "behind every successful man stands a surprised woman," the reality is that every prime minister who was supported by a spouse talks about the key role they played. As can be seen with Brian Mulroney and Mila, and with Jean Chrétien and Aline, these relationships are

---

* Churchill was not amused when he was told he could not take his cigar into the room to see King. He glared at the person giving the request, put the cigar in an ashtray, and said to his bodyguard: "Watch it."

vital to the success of a prime minister. The importance of supportive spouses came up repeatedly in my research, including in my interviews with former prime ministers and those who worked alongside them.

Louis St. Laurent was sixty-six years old when he became prime minister in 1948, the oldest of any PM upon assuming office, save for the three caretaker PMs who took over after John A. Macdonald died in 1891. In the 1949 election campaign, St. Laurent's time was carefully parcelled out so as to not overtax his stamina. No campaign event started before 10:00 a.m. and time was set aside each day for the prime minster to rest in his private railcar. When seeing one jam-packed itinerary for St. Laurent, Jack Pickersgill, his special assistant, said they would not do it. "I replied it would be better to lose one seat than to kill the prime minister."

St. Laurent lived, but he got laryngitis, which, according to one account, led to his acquisition of the "Uncle Louis" moniker.* St. Laurent was told to stop giving speeches for a while to let his voice rest. He should just shake hands and "give the impression of being benevolent, old Uncle Louis."[6] St. Laurent biographer Dale C. Thomson said a reporter gave St. Laurent the nickname during a trip through western Canada earlier the same year. Whether true or not, the nickname stuck and had great appeal to Canadians.

While St. Laurent was fit — he golfed regularly and swam lengths in the pool at the Château Laurier hotel in Ottawa — age and the rigours of office wore him down visibly. The 1954 world tour that he undertook at age seventy-two — unprecedented for a Canadian prime minster — would prove to be too much. A long road trip for a prime minister today might be ten days. St. Laurent's trip was forty-two days and included stops in twelve different countries. The itinerary included little to no downtime, except for the time spent on the airplane. It was a tour that would challenge a man half his age. The foreign diet, extreme heat in Asia, and constant packing and unpacking wore

---

* A number of Canadians wrote letters to St. Laurent with home remedies for his laryngitis, as well as some for reported high blood pressure.

St. Laurent out. He even suffered a bout of dysentery during his final days in Tokyo. It was all too much. "The poor man was never the same since," recalled one journalist. "After the tour he came back totally exhausted. His health was ruined and he was just a scarecrow."[7]

In the House of Commons, St. Laurent also evinced a tired and worn-out disposition. He seemed passive and uninterested in the proceedings and debates, speaking only when he had to. Newspaper reporters started noticing, and the prime minister was convinced to see a doctor, who revealed that St. Laurent had an ulcer. He changed his diet and tried to quit smoking (he never gave up the habit but was able to cut down, trimming his consumption to a few per day from his usual fifteen).

Two years later, in 1957, when St. Laurent visited U.S. president Dwight Eisenhower, Canadian ambassador Arnold Heeney described him as "an almost pathetic spectacle."[8] While there was no formal diagnosis, it appears likely that St. Laurent suffered from depression. It might have been seasonal affective disorder, as often these bouts of lethargy came during the winter months. He battled the dips through exercise, diet, and winter vacations to the south. Whatever it was, it affected his ability to govern in the way that he had in the past, when some referred to him as the most efficient man ever to lead the country.

After losing the 1957 election, the defeated prime minister arrived back in Ottawa where there were only a handful of people to meet him at the train station and St. Laurent had to walk some distance along the railway tracks to get to his car. He fell into a deep funk and was eventually convinced to retire as Liberal leader. Giving up the reins of power seemed to liberate him. The man who was only the second prime minister to serve in office at age seventy-five lived another sixteen years until he passed away in 1973 at age ninety-one.*

Compared to Louis St. Laurent's seventy-five years of age, John Diefenbaker was relatively youthful at sixty-one when he became prime minister. But he would not be without his health issues.

---

* Mackenzie Bowell lived to ninety-three and Charles Tupper to ninety-four; they are the only nonagenarian former prime ministers in addition to St. Laurent.

For one thing, he was hard of hearing. When he first held Cabinet meetings he sat at the end of the long table but soon moved to the middle so he could hear better. He preferred to meet in small groups, with people to the right of him so he could understand the conversation more easily. Some took advantage of his condition. At the 1962 Commonwealth prime ministers' conference, British PM Harold Macmillan had no qualms about racing through the conference communiqué since he knew Dief's deafness allowed him to "pass from one clause to another fairly rapidly."

There were also rumours that Diefenbaker had Parkinson's disease. In 1963, as his Cabinet was imploding around him under the weight of six years in government and weak leadership from the PM, newspaper reports said Cabinet ministers were calling for his resignation, in part due to him having Parkinson's disease. Diefenbaker blamed the Liberals for starting the rumour, which was front-page news. Liberal leader Lester B. Pearson, not surprisingly, denied having anything to do with it. But the Chief was concerned. He secretly went to see two doctors at St. Michael's Hospital in Toronto to be examined. They produced a letter that said the prime minister "was found to be in excellent health. At no time during this or past examinations has there been any evidence of chronic illness."[9]

Diefenbaker's hands and head did shake, but he did not have the disease.* Medical research has now confirmed that he suffered from something known as "essential tremors" — a condition resulting from having elevated levels of noradrenaline in the brain, which caused the shaking.[10] But the rumours during the final months of his time as prime minister were certainly a distraction. That, combined with an irascible personality prone to making rash decisions, contributed to Diefenbaker's problems.

One other health setback dogged Diefenbaker, occurring before the Parkinson's rumours. In the summer of 1962, while at Harrington Lake, he stepped into a gopher hole (there are no gophers in eastern Canada, so it was some kind of hole dug by an animal) and broke his leg. The injury hurt him mentally as much as it did physically.

---

* Canadian comic Rich Little sometimes took heat for his impersonation of Diefenbaker, which exaggerated his shaking hands and head.

Rather than putting him in a walking cast, his doctors prescribed bed-rest. "Their advice was medically sound but politically disastrous," Diefenbaker wrote in his memoirs. "An invalid's bedroom is neither an ideal place for Cabinet meetings nor a location suited to keeping track of political manoeuvrings about one. But flat on my back I remained." Making matters worse was the fact that two weeks before then, Senator William Brunt, his closest confidant and friend, was killed in a car accident. Diefenbaker held Cabinet meetings at 24 Sussex Drive and even held a press conference from his bedside propped up against pillows and wearing his dressing gown.

Diefenbaker tried to put his best foot forward and made a public appearance a few weeks later for the swearing-in of a new Cabinet. He drew attention to the fact that he was using the cane of Sir John A. Macdonald, one of his political heroes. But the injury wore on him and put him in a melancholy mood. He stayed away from his East Block office for about five weeks. "He just stayed at home and it was a bit of sulk, really," recalled Bunny Pound.[11] Later, Pound told the story of the time Lester B. Pearson invited her back to Harrington Lake while he was prime minister. "Now, Bunny," he said, "I want you to show me the gopher hole!"[12] The Chief would not have been amused by the joke at his expense.

Lester B. Pearson, who was a life-long athlete, had a mostly healthy five years as prime minister. He was a senior when he was sworn in, a day before his sixty-sixth birthday. Perhaps the key for Pearson was his self-deprecating sense of humour, a useful remedy for anyone to have, including prime ministers needing to defuse stressful moments. He suffered the usual colds and illnesses but his health merits barely a mention in his memoirs and biographies. But Pearson underwent surgery in 1963, spending two days in hospital. He was there for an operation to remove an obstructed salivary gland and a cyst from his neck. The scar from the surgery was clearly visible in the 1963 documentary film *Mr. Pearson: Profile of a Man and an Office.*

The surgery was front-page news, not in the least because of the rarity of a sitting prime minister facing the operating table. One can only imagine the coverage such an event would receive today in the twenty-four-hour news cycle. Additionally, since Pearson was the leader of a new minority government, his absence was of greater concern than it would have been otherwise. Pearson went to Harrington Lake to recover and kept tabs on the goings-on in the House of Commons. Five days later he hosted a Cabinet meeting at the country retreat and by ten days after his operation, he was back in Parliament.

On Pearson's return, Opposition leader John Diefenbaker touched upon the added dimension of being prime minister and looking after both your own health and that of the country. "I know something of the tremendous load of responsibility that rests on a prime minister," intoned Diefenbaker in the House of Commons. "I realize that for the past few days the prime minister has been in a position where, had the course of Parliament been otherwise, he would probably have entered hospital earlier. These are some of the things that those in private life do not understand, and foremost is the sense of responsibility that rests on those who have the office of prime minister."[13]

That Pearsonian sense of humour would be on display in 1970, a couple of years after he had left office when he had an eye removed because of a malignant tumor. Pearson went to a Montreal Expos game and met umpire Al Barlick before the contest. "How are you?" asked the ump.*

"I'm fine," Pearson replied. "But I've recently had an operation that qualifies me for your business. I ... had my eye out."[14]

Sir John A. Macdonald's brush with death in 1870 opened this chapter, and it is time to revisit the scene to see if he survived. Lying on the floor in his office, the situation was quite grave, as his doctor noted. The story is told well in E.B. Biggar's *Anecdotal Life of Sir John A. Macdonald.* There he quotes from a lecture given by the editor of the *Saint John Telegraph* in New Brunswick:

---

* Barlick is in the Baseball Hall of Fame and was the umpire at first base when Jackie Robinson, the former Montreal Royal, broke the major league colour barrier in 1947 with the Brooklyn Dodgers.

Everyone by a common impulse moved to the East Block to make inquiries, but there the doors were closed and guarded. A great throng about the entrance, anxious and awestruck, bore on their faces the confirmation of the first alarming report. In and about the Parliament Building, in saddened groups, men gathered and spoke to one another with bated breath, while women wept, and the very atmosphere seem choked with gloom.... At nearly five o'clock the House was opened, amid such gloom as had not invaded the chamber since the tragic death of Thomas D'Arcy McGee.

The news of Macdonald's perilous health caught the country's attention. According to the doctor, he had passed a gallstone — a very large one that caused immense pain. The prime minister was treated with morphine. Daily reports were given on his condition and published in the newspapers. The health watch was compared to that of Abraham Lincoln, who had been assassinated in 1865. A few days into his recovery, while he still lay in his office, Lady Macdonald rubbed whisky on his chest. "Oh, do that again," he whispered to her, "it seems to do me good." Later when his doctor indicated his lunch would consist of half an oyster, the PM quipped that "it seems strange that the hopes of Canada should depend on half an oyster."

As Macdonald recovered, he was eventually moved from his East Block office to the more comfortable Speaker's quarters, where he stayed for a few weeks. He was taken out behind the Parliament Buildings to enjoy the view and breeze. When he had improved enough to travel, Lady Macdonald arranged a holiday for them on Prince Edward Island, where they stayed for several weeks.

But the damage had been done. "The attack I had last year has left its mark on me for life," he told a friend. Macdonald had already lived a hard life of drinking and had dealt with difficult personal circumstances, including the death of his first-born son in 1847 and then, ten years later, his first wife. He did not look after himself very well. Now he slowed down a step or two. As Richard Gwyn, his most recent biographer wrote, "The lion wasn't yet in winter, but he was well into the fall."

While this was the most serious of John A.'s health scares, it was not the only one. Alcohol consumption was at the heart of his health problems and it affected his capacity to govern. During the 1872 election campaign he broke his own pledge not to make important decisions while on a drinking binge. He acted "desperate" and "unbalanced."

The Pacific Scandal of 1873–74, in which Macdonald exchanged railway contract favours for political campaign donations, cost him his government. As the scandal unfolded, the prime minister took hard to the bottle. "The days passed drunkenly with the black depression of awakening consciousness alternating with the muddled forgetfulness of stupor," wrote Donald Creighton in his magisterial biography of Canada's first PM.[15]

The pressure led to what came to be known as "Sir John A.'s lost weekend," a two-day period during an August escape to his cottage in Rivière-du-Loup, Quebec, when no one — not even his wife — knew the whereabouts of the prime minister. Rumours abounded, including one that appeared in the *Montreal Witness* stating that Macdonald had committed suicide by jumping into the St. Lawrence River. Lord Dufferin, the governor general, wrote to the colonial secretary, saying that Macdonald was "*perdu* with a friend in the neighbourhood of Quebec."

Little is known about those lost days, including whether the PM actually tried to take his life. Macdonald later issued a statement saying the rumours of a suicide were "an infamous falsehood. I was never better in my life." However, the combination of the high tensions of office with a serious drinking problem proved to be a dangerous mix for the prime minister. Macdonald resigned from office in 1873 due to the scandal and lost the ensuing election in 1874 to Alexander Mackenzie.

Macdonald's drinking problem serves as a propitious moment for a brief aside to look at prime ministers and booze.

Many were teetotallers — Diefenbaker and Bennett are two of the best known. In fact, Dief's abstinence led to one humorous moment during a 1958 trip which began in Ulster, Northern Ireland. The prime minister and his entourage arrived late in the morning, but the Women's Air Force had a bar set up ready to serve Irish coffees with billowing clouds of cream on top.

"I, of course, knew what it was," recalled Dief aide Mike Deacey. "The prime minister was not aware and neither was [accompanying physician, fellow MP, and teetotaller] Dr. Rhinehart, who [was] a very strict teetotaller. He'd never had a drink in his life."

Deacey's quick gulp was well received after an overnight flight combined with the cold, misty morning. But Rhinehart told him it tasted awful.

"Don't say that to any of the Irishmen around. They'll kill you," said Deacey.

"Why?" Rhinehart asked.

"Well, it has a good stroking of Irish whiskey in it."

This presented a problem for Diefenbaker. But what was he to do? He couldn't very well ignore the Irish hospitality he had in his hand. Thankfully for the Chief, he was in conversation with a loquacious RAF officer. Diefenbaker feigned that he was just about to sip from the cup of Irish coffee. When his interlocutor stopped talking, the PM lowered his cup back on his saucer and began to give his side of the conversation. The RAF officer would start talking once more and "Mr. Diefenbaker would start to lift his cup and again he'd stop and the cup went down to the saucer. Mr. Diefenbaker never touched it," Deacey recalled.

By this time Olive Diefenbaker was looking at Deacey, as she knew there was something amiss, while Rhinehart "was poking me in the ribs and saying, 'Mike, you have to do something about this.'"

A prime minister should not be interrupted when he is being received by his host, but Deacey felt action had to be taken. He walked over and with "deepest apologies" to the RAF officer, he said that Diefenbaker's coffee was getting cold. "Do you mind if I have it changed?"

No objection was raised, "so I motioned to one of the girls and she came over and took the two cups an she went back to the bar and I went back with her and I said, this time leave the Irish whiskey out."

As well as the teetotallers, there were former drinkers who had since sworn off the stuff, as was the case with Brian Mulroney. John Turner was known to enjoy a few drinks, perhaps more than others, but the history of Canada's prime ministers and drinking is mostly about having a beer or some wine — or nothing at all. Mackenzie King occasionally had sherry; Lester B. Pearson enjoyed a rye and ginger ale, "the Air Canada drink" as his son Geoffrey called it; Stephen Harper relaxed with a beer while jamming with his band, the Van Cats, but he was mostly a teetotaller; Paul Martin took a glass of red wine or a beer but also enjoyed the occasional Scotch. But there is too much work to do with too much on the line to allow for anything more.

As Opposition leader from 1873 to 1878, Sir John A. Macdonald continued to drink heavily and to generally embarrass himself, but eventually he began to turn things around. "He certainly can drink wine at dinner without being tempted to exceed, which hitherto he has never been able to do, and during the present [1877] session he has never given way as in former times," wrote Lord Dufferin. Ironically, when the 1878 Temperance Act was passed, Macdonald had to be carried out of the House of Commons to spend the night in the Deputy Speaker's office after a bout of insobriety. But Macdonald was not alone as a member of Parliament who imbibed. It was the habit of the times and Macdonald only the best-known among the bibulous.

Macdonald was once more prime minister after winning the 1878 election. Into the 1880s he began to look the way he is portrayed now on Canadian banknotes: grey hair, worn look, an aging man. His strength was waning. In 1881, at age sixty-six, he collapsed. His physician suspected he might have cancer. Macdonald went to London to see doctors there. They prescribed a better diet and some rest. Various ailments continued to plague him but Macdonald continued on. He gamely fought the 1891 election at age seventy-six under the slogan "The Old Flag, The Old Policy, The Old Leader." But the contest was too much for him and in February he took ill and would not fully recover.

His physician, Dr. Robert Wynard Powell, was not surprised that Macdonald got sick. The constant train travel for the election campaign was too strenuous for someone of the prime minister's age. Adding to the strain was the fact that the campaign took place during the winter months (election day was March 6), which necessitated Macdonald enduring outdoor speeches, cold rooms, and nasty weather. "It is not at all surprising that his strength broke down," wrote the doctor in his report of the PM's final days, "or that he contracted a severe cold from the strain and exposure." In fact, Macdonald was diagnosed with bronchitis and a loss of voice. "There was no doubt of a congested lung and a threatened pneumonia," the doctor's report continued, "but absolute rest in bed, perfect quiet and active medicinal treatment averted such a catastrophe, and in a very few days he was sufficiently convalescent to venture downstairs, though still far from well. That Sir John was seriously ill on this occasion there can be no doubt."[16]

Macdonald's Conservatives won the election and the prime minister returned to Ottawa from Kingston in a considerably weakened state. He was well enough to attend the opening of Parliament on April 29 and sign the registry with his son, Hugh John Macdonald, a special moment for them and one of only two occasions when a sitting prime minister enjoyed the company of a son or daughter in the House (Louis St. Laurent was the other — his son Jean-Paul was an MP from 1955 to 1958).

Macdonald continued to decline. On May 12, he had a minor stroke and his physician ordered complete rest. "[The PM's] reply was that complete rest, or absence from Ottawa while Parliament was in session, 'was out of the question, an impossibility.'"

On May 28, the prime minister's doctor was summoned at 3:00 a.m. when Macdonald awoke with no feeling in his left arm and leg. A second, more severe stroke had occurred. The doctor informed the Cabinet of the seriousness of the situation and a bulletin was issued to the public.

"Sir John Macdonald has had a return of his attack of physical and nervous prostration and we have enjoined positively complete rest for the present and entire freedom from public business." On May 29, he suffered another severe stroke from which he would not recover. He could no longer speak. His nourishment consisted of milk containing a small amount of whisky along with tea. The bells on streetcars that passed by Earnscliffe, his residence, were removed and the whistles on steamers sailing down the Ottawa River went silent so as to not disturb Canada's ailing premier. Dr. Wynard recorded on June 6, 1891: "The respirations now evidently changed in character, becoming much slower and deeper. I summoned his family and told them the end was approaching. He remained breathing quite slowly till 10 p.m. when the respirations became very shallow, and death closed the scene at 10:15 p.m. No autopsy was permitted."

The prime minister's death sent the nation into mourning. Its first and much-loved leader had just died in office. The House of Commons was draped in black and Macdonald's body lay in state. There were innumerable encomiums to Macdonald, but the man who would become prime minister five years hence uttered the words that have stood the test of time. "The place of Sir John Macdonald in this country was so large and so absorbing," Wilfrid Laurier said, "that it is almost impossible to conceive that the political life of this country, the fate of this country, can continue without him ... as if indeed one of the institutions of the land had given way."[17]

Macdonald lived a remarkably long time and battled serious health issues throughout his life. The old slogan someone yelled out during the 1891 campaign — "You'll never die, John A.!" seemed to ring true. His death left a big hole in both the country and in his own Conservative party. In some respects, neither was ever filled.

That chasm left by Sir John A. Macdonald's passing led to a game of musical chairs in the prime minister's East Block office, and the health of the next two prime ministers played a significant role in shaping who sat in the chair. Governor General Lord Stanley's first choice for PM was John Thompson, who turned the offer down because he was a Roman Catholic and might therefore cause divisions in Cabinet. As a result, Macdonald's immediate successor was John Joseph Caldwell Abbott, a prime minister who did not even want the job. "I hate politics," he once wrote, "and what are considered their appropriate methods. I hate notoriety, public meetings, public speeches, caucuses, and everything that I know of that is apparently the necessary incident of politics — except doing public work to the best of my ability."[18]

On June 16, 1891, Abbott was sworn in as prime minister at age seventy, leading the government from the Senate. He has the distinction of being the country's first Canadian-born PM.* But barely a year into office, his health began to deteriorate and doctors advised a long rest to recover from "cerebral congestion and consequent exhaustion of the brain and nervous system." In the fall of 1892 he departed for London to see doctors and left behind an undated resignation letter. Abbott never returned to his office as PM. His health had essentially removed him from the position of prime minister.

Left with no other choice in Abbott's absence, Governor General Lord Stanley once again asked John Thompson, a man many thought should have had the job in the first place, to form a government. Thompson was highly regarded by most and had dexterously executed his responsibilities as justice minister in Macdonald's government from 1885–91. The governor general swore him in as prime minister on December 4, 1892.

The encumbrances of being prime minister — that "hard and trying job" — got to Thompson. In 1885, when he had first arrived in Ottawa, he was 190 pounds. By 1894, his weight had ballooned to 225 pounds, on a five-foot-seven frame. "Over the years he had punished his excellent constitution with massive doses of work, and food," observed historian P.B. Waite.[19] His limbs began to swell and concern about the prime minister's health grew.

In December 1894, Thompson went to Windsor Castle to be made a member of the Imperial Privy Council by Queen Victoria. When sitting down to lunch after the ceremony, he fainted. He recovered enough to return to the table, but before he could eat again he collapsed and died of a massive heart attack. For the second time in three and half years, Canada's prime minister had died in office. Thompson, due to the brevity of his time in office — just over two years — is little remembered in history, but historians Jack Granatstein and Norman Hillmer called him the "great might have been of Canadian prime ministers," because of the leadership talents he was said to have had.[20] A 2016 ranking of Canada's prime ministers, conducted by *Maclean's* magazine, placed Thompson third among ten leaders who were short-term PMs.

---

* Abbott's great-grandson is Academy Award–winning actor Christopher Plummer.

Once referred to as "the great might have been" of Canadian prime ministers, John Thompson was the second and last prime minister to die in office. He had a heart attack at Windsor Castle in 1894 while having lunch with Queen Victoria.

John Thompson was the last prime minster to die in office. But throughout Canadian history it is easy to see the negative consequences on the health of those who have served as PM — and these are just the cases we know about. Other minor ailments, or cracks under pressure, suffered alone or with a supportive spouse, have possibly occurred but remained private. One good example of this was Brian Mulroney's balance — he was "a little wobbly" in the words of his former press secretary Bill Fox due to an inner ear condition. No one was told about it, but that was why it was often arranged to have Mulroney's wife, Mila, standing beside him. Before one trip to the White House in 1984, the prime minister's advance team told President Ronald Reagan's team that the two little lecterns set up would not be sufficient for the prime minister — "otherwise, my guy's going to end up in the tuba," Fox recalled. They asked if a chair could be put out for Mulroney. "Sure," came the reply from the White House team. "But we'll have to leak to the media that it's for your guy because the Soviets analyze everything we do."[21]

Prime ministers will always try to project an image of vitality to the public while the difficult side gets hidden from view. We need only look into our own experiences to see the stresses life can bring. It is surely the same — or worse — for the prime minister, given the exigencies of the job. The workload is staggering, and managing to stay healthy by exercising and eating well can be a challenge, even with all the help prime ministers have in their lives. There is often a spouse and children to worry about, as well.

"Being in charge can be a burden," said Pearson at the end his five years in office. But no prime minister has ever said they wished they hadn't had the job.

CHAPTER 6

"CELEBRITY IN CHIEF":
PRIME MINISTERS AND CELEBRITIES

I like his grim jaw, kind eyes, sugar-daddy hair and
suave features. If he'd put his bow tie away forever,
and have his wardrobe overhauled, he'd go places.
Neither Marlon Brando nor John F. Kennedy could
compete with him.
— Jayne Mansfield on Lester B. Pearson, 1963

It is just a few days before Christmas in 1969 and Prime Minister
Pierre Trudeau is waiting in his Centre Block office for a famous
couple on a mission to spread peace. Trudeau's schedule is a little lighter
due to the coming holidays, so he has told his principal secretary, Marc
Lalonde, to take a break from this midmorning meeting while he receives
his guests. The appointment is scheduled to take ten minutes but will
end up taking closer to fifty. The prime minister is wearing a dapper
three-piece suit and polka-dot tie. A newspaper report of the meeting will
say afterward that if it had been the PM's intention to lower the voting
age before the next election, "the meeting yesterday did him no harm."

Through the oak doors of Room 311-S walk John Lennon and Yoko Ono, who are warmly greeted by the prime minister. The member of the Beatles is wearing a black suit and a broad black tie. His long hair and full beard are signatures of the hippie era. His wife is similarly clad in a black dress. Trudeau smiles broadly with his right thumb tucked into his waistcoat pocket, clearly enjoying the meeting. A collection of photographers snap pictures. Lennon and Ono grin as the PM gestures and continues to welcome them. Later, Yoko Ono will say, "If all politicians were like Mr. Trudeau, there would be world peace ... you people in Canada don't realize how lucky you are to have a man like Mr. Trudeau."[1]

The story of prime ministers and celebrities appears to be a modern one, born in the age of television as politicians have attempted to ride the coattails of famous rock stars or athletes, hoping for an uptick in the polls. The reality, however, is that Canadian prime ministers have met with the famous from home and abroad at least since the early days of Mackenzie King in the 1920s. Indeed, meeting with celebrities is part of the job of being prime minister, and these encounters give us not only insights into the political preoccupations of the times in which the meetings took place, but also into the character and sensibilities of the office holders themselves.

Of course, the prime minister is also a celebrity. "There is, at any given time, only one person who is the prime minister of Canada," wrote Kim Campbell in her memoirs. "That, and the fact that constant TV appearances have a way of conferring an aura of celebrity, make the opportunity to get close to the prime minister exciting for most people, regardless of their partisan loyalties."

Whereas fame was once confined to movie stars and athletes, the growth in consumer demand for more and more news about the lives of the famous has meant that the net has had to be cast wider to produce more celebrities — hence the creation of celebrity politicians.[2] In fact, this very chapter — perhaps even the entire book — is a reflection of the interest there is in the personal and private lives of people who are famous. While prime ministers back to Sir John A. Macdonald have been famous across the country, the projection of fame goes much further today. There is no better example of this in Canadian history than the celebrity story emerging in the prime ministership of Justin Trudeau, once dubbed by an opposition MP as the "celebrity-in-chief" of Canada.[3] It has also made him a target for criticism, which seemed to peak with his appearance on the cover of *Rolling Stone* magazine in the summer of 2017. One pundit advised readers to grab a "barf bucket," while the *Toronto Sun*, no fan of Mr. Trudeau, wrote in an editorial, "As Justin Trudeau has been prime minister for almost twenty-one months, we suggest it's past time for him to get down to work. Yes, it's all fun and games when some media are forever gushing over you — see the latest *Rolling Stone* cover story on Trudeau, whom it dubs Canada's 'North Star' — but seriously, enough."[4] Whether it is selfies in Davos or Dundas or appearances on the covers of magazines such as *GQ* or *Hello!*, Trudeau is the avatar for the celebrity PM.

Celebrity culture is a huge part of the political landscape. But one must go back to the late 1910s to first see the notion of celebrity as we might recognize it today. This coincided with the emergence of the Hollywood star system and the rise of technology, such as radio. Immersed in this era of change was Prime Minister Mackenzie King, who, because of the times during which he served as PM, as well as his longevity in office, met some of Canada's and the world's most famous people. And, not surprisingly, there was usually a political calculation to his meetings.

On Saturday, July 2, 1927, less than two months after he became the first person to fly solo across the Atlantic, Charles Lindbergh, the celebrated American aviator and international hero, arrived in Ottawa for a celebration of an achievement that King had called "the greatest single exploit in the world's history." Lindbergh was also in Ottawa to help celebrate the country's Diamond Jubilee. The city was ready. The famous flier literally flew into town that sunny afternoon, touching down in his *Spirit of St. Louis* airplane at Ottawa's Hunt Club Landing Field where he was greeted by a throng of thousands of noisy and enthusiastic citizens.

Moments after "Lindy" arrived, however, tragedy struck. One of Lindbergh's air escorts, Lieutenant Thad Johnson, was killed when his plane crashed. "It was the most tragic kind of incident," King wrote. Johnson's body was eventually taken to the PM's East Block office where it lay in a casket in a nearby corridor as people came by to pay their respects. The next day Johnson received full national and military honours in a ceremony at Parliament Hill that was attended by thousands of people who lined the streets to pay their respects.

How famous was Charles Lindbergh in 1927? Once he completed his incredible aeronautical feat, his life was never the same. Everywhere he went, people wanted to see him. "From the moment he left his room in the morning, he was touched and jostled and bothered," wrote Bill Bryson in *One Summer: America, 1927*.

> He had no private life anymore. Shirts he sent to the laundry never came back. Chicken bones and napkins from his dinner plate were fought over in kitchens. He could not go for a walk or pop into a drugstore. If he went into a men's room, people followed. Checks he wrote were rarely cashed; recipients preferred to frame them instead. No part of his life was normal; and there was no prospect that it ever would be again.

Lindbergh made an immediate impression on the prime minister, which was not hard to do since King was susceptible to the aura of fame and brushes with history. "A more beautiful character I have never seen," he gushed in his diary. "He was like a young god who had appeared from the skies in human form — all that could be desired in youthful appearance, in manner, in charm, in character, as noble a type of the highest manhood as I have ever seen."

Lindbergh was greeted enthusiastically at Parliament Hill as he kept up appearances despite his grief over the tragic death of Thad Johnson.* He was presented with a lifetime pass on Canadian National Railways, a pass that was engraved in gold. But what followed reminds us of how much protocol has changed for prime

---

* A street is named for Johnson near Ottawa's international airport.

ministers and political events. They were simpler times in 1927. Once the speeches were done, no arrangements had been made for the transport of the aviator and prime minister to the governor general's residence. No one knew "who [was] to go with who, or places to sit, etc. It was terrible confusion," wrote King. And this for a visit of the most famous man in the world.

In addition to the lack of organization, it is the intimacy of the Lindbergh visit that stands out today. The celebrated American pilot returned to Laurier House after the day's festivities for a private chat, during which the two men engaged in pleasant conversation, including the possibility of a family connection.* At King's residence, the two men dressed for the evening, with the prime minister loaning Lindbergh his tuxedo studs. Then it was off to Parliament Hill for a dinner where, upon arrival, Lindbergh noted to King just how sore his hands were from all the greetings he had done.

Dinner that night was a celebratory occasion. Glasses clinked and cases of champagne were consumed in toasts to Lindbergh, Canada-U.S. relations, and the Diamond Jubilee of Confederation. It was then time for the escape — no easy matter when dealing with the most famous man in the world. King whisked his guest off to the Library of Parliament to escape the throngs of people.

King battled fatigue the whole evening but was somewhat fortified by the grape that night, a rare but not entirely unknown departure from his usual temperance. "I doubt if I could have gotten thro' without the aid of champagne, tho' I have never allowed myself to believe that it was necessary," he chided himself in his diary. "I believe, however, it helped me tonight."

The "after-party" was held back at Laurier House, where a number of guests attended. Once everyone left, Lindbergh and King, clearly getting along well, talked into the night before retiring at 2:00 a.m. They had breakfast together before the next morning's events, which included the ceremony for Lieutenant Johnson. When the train carrying his body left the station in Ottawa, the great aviator, in his silver *Spirit of St. Louis*, flew low overhead, dropping flowers on the train. "Nothing could have been more moving, more impressive," wrote King.

---

* Lindbergh's grandfather, Charles Land, was Canadian.

Lindbergh made an indelible impression on Mackenzie King. "He is more truly the god-man, than anything I have ever seen. Indeed, it seems to me as if Lindbergh was a young god from the skies, bringing anew the message of Peace & Goodwill."

Mackenzie King delighted in these encounters with the famous, and thanks to his fifty-thousand-page diary* (all of which is available online) we have incredibly detailed accounts of his feelings about such encounters during his time as prime minister. He met Lindbergh just six years after becoming prime minister and was tickled by the whole affair. "It was the triumph of nationhood, the sixtieth anniversary of Confederation, the beginning of a new epoch in our history — our international relations of peace & good will — How strange all should centre about Laurier House & myself, even to Col Lindbergh being my guest there!" Coming as it did during one of the country's biggest celebrations, Lindbergh's visit and the opportunity it afforded for King to rub shoulders with him was a feather in the cap for the prime minister. As for Lindbergh, his biographies mention the trip to Ottawa but there is no account of the aviator's behind-the-scenes time with the prime minister.

In 1944, with the Second World War still raging, Mackenzie King met the American actress Shirley Temple, who was in Ottawa to promote the launch of the Seventh Victory Loan campaign. The war was King's great preoccupation. Temple was the Depression-era child actress star and still just sixteen years old when she shared a platform with the PM to add some stardust to the loan campaign. King, old enough to be her grandfather, was smitten:

> I was greatly attracted by Shirley Temple — a young girl of great charm, very pretty, very natural.... I have seldom found anyone more natural than Shirley Temple was, or quick to adapt herself to every situation. We walked out together to the platform facing Parliament Hill and I sat to her right and St. Laurent to her left. It was quite interesting to watch her methods to rouse the boys to cheer. Very self-possessed, full of joyous freedom and expression in every way.

---

* When the diaries are laid out in a row, they span seven metres in length.

William Lyon Mackenzie King met with many celebrities during his twenty-one years in office, including Charles Lindbergh and Mary Pickford. Here he is pictured with Jack Benny's comedy troupe and two civil servants. From left to right are Sam Hearn, Walter Turnbull, Jack Benny, Don Wilson, Eddie Anderson (aka Rochester), and Prime Minister King. Mary Livingstone is seated.

As with King's visit with Charles Lindbergh, advance planning was absent after the Parliament Hill ceremony when King, Temple, and her parents got into a car to head over to the Château Laurier hotel for a scheduled lunch. Crowds were able to rush around the vehicle, since there had been no police plan for this trip. "I was afraid children would get crushed under the car," King wrote. "But the worst situation came in front of the Château and inside. There the crowd was such that to move the car at all would have meant someone would have been killed or crushed to pieces. We got out on the platform with the help of huge powerful policemen. I expected to find it easy once in the hotel, but there the situation was worse than ever."

King once campaigned on the slogan "King or chaos." Inside the hotel, there were both. The prime minister lost sight of Temple and was carried by the crowd to the elevator where he took Temple's parents up to their hotel suite. King, by this time, was out of breath and feeling the strain of the moment (he was nearly seventy years old at the time). In retrospect, it is difficult to get a clear picture of just how fearful it actually was — King was, after all, something of an exaggerator. Regardless, the lack of security and planning tells us just how different circumstances were in the 1940s as compared to today.

The lunch in the Tudor Room of the hotel went smoothly, the prime minister describing his lunch companion as "delightfully informed and quick in her perceptions." In King's speech he lauded Shirley Temple and praised her career. He confided in his diary that he felt he had spoken very well. "It was really very fine of Mr. and Mrs. Temple and the little girl to come all the way from California by train, and back again, to make this contribution to the seventh victory loan."

King called Temple later in the day to invite her and her parents over to Laurier House to tea, an invitation they accepted. They all drank tea in the dining room. In the library King confided in Temple his visions and coincidences and noted that she had "very definite views

In 1944, former child actress Shirley Temple came to Ottawa to help promote the Seventh Victory Loan campaign in support of Canada's Second World War effort. Temple was sixteen years old at the time. Her most successful films were behind her, but she made an impression on Mackenzie King. "I have seldom found someone as natural as Shirley Temple," he wrote in his diary.

and feelings herself about these things. I could see she had done a lot of thinking; was quite earnest, and very great in perceptions."

Looking back, it is very hard to imagine the sixty-nine-year-old King and the sixteen-year-old Temple having a meeting of the minds, but the prime minister had the tendency to interpret events in ways that reflected well upon him. In the end, before departing, Temple promised to send him a photograph of herself.

The office of the prime minister evidently likes stardust and Temple was not the only Hollywood star to receive King's hospitality and attention. In January of 1948, his final year in office, King entertained "America's Sweetheart" Mary Pickford, the famous film actress. She visited Ottawa to promote a UNESCO effort to help the children of Europe after the war and to gather attention for her most recent film, *Sleep, My Love* (Pickford was one of the producers of the film but did not star in it). Pickford had also visited Canada in 1943, when she dropped in on a munitions plant in Scarborough. For the prime minster, there was something about Mary "which made [meeting her] a real incident in my life."

A major star in the 1910s and 1920s, Pickford was one of Canada's most famous exports to the world of Hollywood film. Born Gladys Louise Smith in Toronto in 1892, the "girl with the curls," as she was once known, earned the title of best-known Canadian in a 1917 issue of *Maclean's* magazine. She starred in a number of silent films and was one of the first wave of actors in Hollywood's new star system. In 1919 she, along with Douglas Fairbanks (whom she would famously marry in 1920), Charlie Chaplin, and D.W. Griffith formed United Artists, which became a very successful film studio. Once talkies (films with audible dialogue) grew in popularity, Pickford's career began a decline but not before she would claim an Oscar in 1929 for her role in *Coquette*, although, ostensibly, the statue was for her career achievements. By 1948, when King met her, she and Fairbanks had long-since divorced and her career was essentially over. Pickford was also in the midst of a long, slow, alcohol-fuelled decline. If King knew how much she drank, he would certainly have disapproved, but there is no mention of this in his diary. However, tellingly, he noted she seemed to suffer from a "touch of the flu."

The public greeting between Pickford and the prime minister portended a happy affair. They shared a mutual interest in the well-being of sick children and a passion for Christian faith. At the UNESCO luncheon Pickford was in town to promote, King gave what he thought was one of his best speeches ever (weren't they all?). "Miss Pickford was evidently greatly pleased," he gushed in his diary. "I could see it in her face when I was speaking."

It was a face he did not necessarily find to his liking, though. "I found she did not strike me as being particularly beautiful nor indeed a vivacious person as pictured." It is unknown what Pickford thought about her luncheon companion, but if she had said the same thing about King it would not have come as a surprise.

Pickford was invited back to Laurier House for tea, along with three others. King and she shared stories of people they had met, including Mussolini. The actress also mentioned that she had recently toured the bunker at Hitler's Chancellery in Berlin and that the tour guide had indicated that while Eva Braun, Hitler's wife, had committed suicide, perhaps Hitler had escaped through tunnels that vented the bunker. The prime minister told her that this was not true and later gave her a copy of H.R. Trevor-Roper's *The Last Days of Hitler* to set her straight.

King and Pickford shared enthusiasm for a life devoted to God, as well as an interest in mysticism and numerology. It's no wonder they got along so well. In conversation she "deplored the irreligion of today" and gave King a copy of a book to which she lent her name called *Why Not Try God?* She invited him to come to spend time with her and her husband, Buddy Rogers, in California. For his part, King gave her a copy of his *Industry and Humanity*, an unreadable book that she very likely put aside unread. He also showed her books that Mussolini had given him, as well as the autographed photograph Hitler bestowed on him during his 1937 visit to Berlin. Then it was time for "America's Sweetheart" to head back to the Château Laurier, but not before the prime minister had to rescue her from the gaggle of autograph seekers who had gathered outside Laurier House. Even then, there was no escaping celebrity hounds.

There is an amusing side note to Mary Pickford's visit for tea at Laurier House. Early in the visit she continually referred to the prime minister as "His Excellency," a term used only for the governor general. "I told her to drop that," King wrote. So they got on to discussing what to call people — no wonder, since MP Thomas Vien had been calling him "the Chief," a term the PM said would not do either. Pickford had told King her name was Mary so for him that made it easy. "Well, my friends call me Rex," he told her. "So on going into dinner tonight she addressed me as Rex. I called her Mary for the rest of the evening...."

For Mackenzie King and Mary Pickford, there was still a film to watch — *Sleep, My Love*. Film footage of the premiere reveals the star power "America's Sweetheart" still had. Emerging from a limousine, Pickford looks glamorous in her white mink coat as she is assisted by a Mountie who takes her black-gloved hand.[*] King smiles broadly for the cameras and seems very pleased to be amidst all the stardust.[5] The *Toronto Star* wrote that Pickford had the "aura of an old time film star."

But the PM was not impressed by her production. "This picture I must confess I could make neither head nor tail of. All series of exciting scenes.... It was the last thing in the world from anything Mary Pickford would have associated with," he judged in his diary. Much more to his liking was the Mickey Mouse cartoon he saw before Pickford's film. "Enjoyed immensely," King wrote.

That was the end of his time with Mary Pickford, but the visit made an impression on him. "I came away feeling that the day had been quite worthwhile and apart from the pleasure it imparted in different ways, was one of real significance."

It is nearly impossible for a prime minister to pass up an opportunity to meet with a famous athlete and Mackenzie King entertained one who had electrified Canada like no one before her and, arguably, no one since. There were some surprisingly political elements to the celebration as well.

---

* One friend of Pickford's said he knew wine had been served at dinner when he saw her arrive at the premiere wearing the governor general's hat.

King actually had a couple of meetings with Barbara Ann Scott, the 1948 gold medal champion in figure skating at the St. Moritz Olympics. It is hard to overstate the impact she had on the country. The diminutive and beautiful nineteen-year-old skater from Ottawa returned to a hero's welcome when she came back to Canada. There were civic receptions everywhere she went and she was celebrated in the House of Commons. King told the House on February 6, 1948, that he had sent a cable to her and "that from one end of the country to the other it was felt that she had done honour not only to herself but to her country, and that the government joined with the people in extending her the warmest congratulations." He noted in his diary that he "did not think there is a single individual whose life and art and talent has been watched as closely by the Canadian people as Barbara Ann Scott, or who has brought as much of a thrill to the entire nation as she has in what she has achieved, and the way in which she has carried her Honours."

After Scott won the world figure skating championships just over a week later, another MP asked King if it would be "possible for her to appear before the House of Commons or the Senate?" King replied that he would introduce the MP to her privately if he wished.

Behind the scenes, King gave a lot of thought to how he or Parliament should honour Barbara Ann Scott. There were thoughts of awarding her the Canada Medal (a precursor to the Order of Canada; it was never awarded and abolished in 1966), creating a postage stamp in her honour, or having some sort of address or official recognition in the House. Some reservations were raised by both caucus and Cabinet that perhaps too much fawning and recognition might be given to Scott. King also received a letter from a Manitoba woman questioning the wisdom of a postage stamp for Scott. "Spoke of the Canadians who had given their lives. Of Banting having given insulin — no stamps for them, etc. Asking whether Canadians were losing their sense of values," he recorded in his diary. The issue clearly troubled the prime minister.

Some in the Liberal caucus and Cabinet also raised some political concerns. It was all predictably cautious and Canadian. Other objectors were petty: King should be careful about honours for Scott because of the close relationship her parents had with former prime minister and King antagonist, Arthur Meighen, as well as the family's closeness to a Conservative MP. The prime minister was persuaded by these reservations, so there was no official award, recognition, or welcome in Parliament for Scott.*

But that did not mean King would not be making close contact with her. Ever the shrewd politician, he recognized her value to him as prime minister. Presaging the feelings of many of his successors, King reflected to himself, "perhaps, as PM, I should identify myself with Barbara Ann's success this year. She has really performed a national service."

On March 9, 1948, Barbara Ann Scott arrived home to Ottawa to be celebrated by her hometown and the entire Dominion. The prime minister, the mayor of Ottawa, and a host of photographers and fans were on hand to welcome the most popular woman in the country. King had cabled Scott to say, "Canadians await your return to accord you a truly national welcome."[6] At the train station downtown, across from the Château Laurier hotel, the photographers shouted to the mayor and PM that they wanted to see hugs. Public displays of affection were not something at which King excelled — he was no Pierre or Justin Trudeau — and his diary entry takes on a judgmental tone when recounting that the mayor "took matters into his hands or rather Barbara into [his] own arms. I presented my cheek for the purposes required. It was something I would have preferred to escape but there was no escaping in the circumstances." Pictures of the moment tell a decidedly different story in which the prime minister is clearly enjoying the occasion.

These visits between prime ministers and the celebrity of the moment are often reflective of their times and a message that the political partner in the meeting might want to achieve. King not only highlighted Barbara Ann Scott's considerable athletic accomplishments but also used his post-lunch speech to make use of her Olympic victory to spread a much-needed positive word. He spoke of the importance of her victory coming as it did in 1948, as the Cold War had renewed tensions worldwide, noting that "she shone forth in her triumphs as a bright star in a troubled world. She helped to bring cheer

---

* In fact, Barbara Ann Scott would "appear" before the House of Commons in 2009 when she brought the Olympic torch into the chamber two months before the Vancouver Games.

and brightness." King concluded by speaking "of her own personality and what it expressed of the youth of Canada. Spirit of Canada. What it expressed of beautiful personality. What it had set in the way of example through practice, self-control and the like. Thoughtfulness of others, always giving credit to the country, etc."

Some might wonder why King spent so much time with Barbara Ann Scott, a woman he would later refer to as "Our Lady of the Snows," a reference to the Rudyard Kipling poem. It is clear she captured his attention to a considerable degree. But this should not come as a surprise. Like Charles Lindbergh — but on a Canadian scale — Barbara Ann Scott was a big deal. She was the talk of the country. Girls wanted to buy the dolls of her likeness that came out soon after her triumphs. The *Globe and Mail* wrote in a 1948 editorial that "by her charm as well as her skill she has made friends for Canada."[7] In balloting to name Canada's female athlete of the half-century in 1950, "Canada's Sweetheart" was second, narrowly losing out to Bobbie Rosenfeld, the great 1920s Olympic track star and all-round athlete.

King's evident affection for her and the time devoted to her is understandable: for any prime minister, proximity to an athletic champion is political gold. The fact that all of this was taking place in Ottawa also made it very easy for him to be a part of what was a national celebration. Today, prime ministers meeting Olympic athletes is as regular as the Games themselves. In January 2018, Prime Minister Justin Trudeau beamed alongside ice dancers Tessa Virtue and Scott Moir as he announced on Parliament Hill they would be Canada's flag-bearers at the Olympics in PyeongChang, South Korea, that winter. The athletes' message about "diversity and inclusion" could have been written by the PM himself.

The confluence of celebrities and prime ministers can occur unexpectedly as well, with both comic and unwanted consequences. Both remind us that occasionally the prime minister is at the mercy of circumstances beyond his control. Lester Pearson discovered this in a moment that seemed to foretell future encounters between politicians and stars, as well as the manipulation of the media. In 1963, fresh off his victory over John Diefenbaker's Tories, Pearson was singled out by master media manipulator and Hollywood bombshell Jayne Mansfield, a thirty-year-old actress known for her stunning looks and sex symbol status, which was almost as great as Marilyn Monroe's. She was Kim Kardashian before there was such a thing and knew how to get the media's attention.

Arriving in Hamilton, Ontario, Mansfield was asked what she thought about the new PM. "Very sexy," she was reported to have said. "I like his grim jaw, kind eyes, sugar-daddy hair and suave features. If he'd put his bow tie away forever, and have his wardrobe overhauled, he'd go places. Neither Marlon Brando nor John F. Kennedy could compete with him."[8] Two months later, on the CBC television program *Inquiry*, Mansfield was asked about her previous comments. She demurred. But only a little.

"I don't mean I've ever came out and said he has sex appeal," she cooed. "But I will say that he has a definite virility, masculinity, that attracts a woman and in fact attracts a person who likes to see a strong, dominant man. I think every person likes that, especially in the driver's seat of a country.

"As far as sex appeal is concerned," she continued, "I feel our number one boy is not doing too badly, Mr. Kennedy. But certainly Mr. Pearson wouldn't be put down by anybody."[9]

It was the kind of comment that would have been a social media firestorm in today's world but back then did not become a sensation.

Of course, Mansfield was likely playing with Canadians and doing a masterful job of getting media attention. Pearson had his charms, but it is unlikely the Hollywood starlet really felt the prime minister's masculinity and sex appeal eclipsed that of Jack Kennedy or Marlon Brando, two iconic sex symbols of the age.

Pearson laughed when he heard the comment — he was so self-deprecating — and said he had always wanted to be a matinee idol.

Pierre Trudeau's handlers in the PMO, on the other hand, were far less sanguine about his moment with another blond starlet. In 1971, Trudeau and his principal secretary, Marc Lalonde, had decided to get out of

Ottawa to refresh themselves after what had been a fairly dismal winter in terms of the economy and political fortunes. They went to Switzerland to ski. On the way back they were invited to a new ski resort, which happened to be hosting a film festival. French actress Brigitte Bardot was there and asked if she might be able to meet the prime minister. Trudeau accepted the request and met with Bardot outside as they were getting ready to hit the slopes. Two days later, Trudeau's press secretary telephoned Switzerland: "What the heck are you two guys doing over there with Brigitte Bardot?" he asked. "How stupid could you be?"

It turned out that a photograph of Bardot and the prime minister graced the cover of *Paris Match* magazine. There was the PM gallivanting with stars in the Swiss Alps while back in Canada the country was mired in depressing economic times. And it was winter. This was not the image the Trudeau entourage wanted seen back home — he was married at the time, as well — but it was the one that made it to the front of many of the nation's newspapers. Bardot would later be a thorn in Trudeau's side because of her lengthy campaign against the seal hunt. The incident shows that meeting celebrities can be a double-edged sword for a prime minister.

Two other encounters between prime ministers and celebrities highlight the unexpected elements inherent in these meetings, the power the celebrity holds, as well as the changing nature of fame. One incident is from 1931, the other from 2012, and both feature prime ministers known for their public reserve and desire to control: R.B. Bennett and Stephen Harper.

Few Canadians today would be able to tell you much about Emile St. Godard, but in the 1920s and early 1930s he was a world-renowned dogsled racer. He won the famous Pas Dog Derby in Manitoba five years running between 1925 and 1929. In 1932, he finished first in dogsled racing at the Lake Placid Olympics when it was a demonstration sport. He died at age forty-two in 1948. In 1956, St. Godard was inducted into Canada's Sports Hall of Fame where he remains the only dogsled racer to be so honoured.

In 1931, after St. Godard won the Ottawa derby, Prime Minister Bennett was asked to present the Château Laurier trophy to the famous musher outside the eponymous hotel. Bennett arrived at the appointed time of 4:00 p.m. on a cold and grey February day. "Crowds gathered, movie machines clicked, when discovery came that the hero, St. Godard, was missing." Where was the "monarch of mushers," as the *Globe* called him? He was resting in his hotel room. When officials arrived to tell him the prime minister was waiting, St. Godard told them the PM should come back at five o'clock. St. Godard needed to rest.

How did one of Canada's grumpiest and most controlling PMs handle this slight? "Well," he told the crowd, "I guess the affairs of State can wait. Go tell Mr. St. Godard I will come back here at five, as he has directed me."[10] And with that, Bennett returned to his East Block office, returning one hour later to complete the ceremony with the country's renowned athlete, who was feeling much more rested.

The circumstances for Prime Minister Stephen Harper were not so egregious in 2012 when he met Canadian pop sensation Justin Bieber, but the sartorial choice made by Bieber for the brief meeting got the Twittersphere going. As with Bennett before him, Harper handled the situation with a dash of humour — perhaps a prime minister's greatest and most underappreciated weapon.

The plan was for the PM to present Bieber with a Queen Elizabeth II Diamond Jubilee Medal for his contribution to Canada. These are the easiest of photo ops available for a prime minister, but nothing is simple when it comes to Justin Bieber. The unpredictable pop star showed up to get his medal from the PM wearing a T-shirt and overalls. Bieber was heavily criticized on social media. The Gawker website referred to him as the "White Trash Prince," while Harper did not fare much better. He was described as looking like "an extra from *The Office*."[11] The prime minister found his sense of humour, though, when he tweeted to his followers: "In fairness to @justinbieber, I told him I would be wearing my overalls, too."

So what is the benefit of meeting celebrities for a prime minister? Like in any relationship, there is often a symbiosis. John Lennon and Yoko Ono were in Canada to promote their peace festival to be held at Mosport Park Raceway the following spring. Meeting Pierre

Trudeau certainly helped the cause. As for the prime minister, after more than a year and a half in office and with his popularity on the wane, he and his handlers saw these types of endorsements as beneficial only for him. As Tim Porteous, Trudeau's speech writer at the time, recounted, "For the prime minister's staff, the principal object of the PM meeting John and Yoko was not the discussion of how to achieve world peace. The proposal was for fifteen minutes of conversation and — more importantly — fifteen minutes of photography."

Porteous and Trudeau got their money shot, partly by happenstance. Peter Bregg, the Canadian Press photographer who took the famous picture of the threesome, got his unique vantage point by being one of the last photographers to join the PM, Lennon, and Ono, in the prime minister's office.

"The rest of the media were already inside so I had to kneel in front so as not to get in the way," Bregg remembered. "This turned out to be a good thing. The problem when you have several reporters and photographers shouting questions and orders to look this way is you end up with three people looking in different directions. At one point Trudeau looked down at me and said, 'Watch out for this guy.'* All three looked at my camera and I had the shot I needed."[12]

While diplomacy and celebrity can go hand in hand, the latter can occasionally get in the way of the former. Prime Minister Stephen Harper found this out the hard way when he met former Soviet hockey star Vladislav Tretiak in 2007. The legendary goalie was in Ottawa as part of the thirty-fifth anniversary celebrations of the eight-game 1972 Summit Series defined by Paul Henderson's dramatic game-winning goal with thirty-four seconds left in the final game. Harper was asked by a reporter if meeting Tretiak was a perk of the office. "Yes," he replied with a wide smile on his face.

Unfortunately, for Harper, Liberian president Ellen Johnson Sirleaf — the first African woman elected as a head of state — was

---

* Pierre Trudeau liked Peter Bregg. As he once told him: "Peter, I like you because you don't carry a pencil."

also in town. The matter was raised in the House of Commons by Liberal MP Bryon Wilfert.

"The prime minister yesterday had an opportunity to meet with hockey players," he began. "That is very nice, but unfortunately the president of Liberia deserves better from the prime minister. As we celebrate the two-hundredth anniversary of the abolition of slavery in the British Empire, why will the prime minister not take time from his schedule today to meet with the president of Liberia? Does he not care?"

After the pressure from Question Period, Harper agreed to meet with Johnson Sirleaf, a get-together that apparently lasted for ten minutes. Mr. Tretiak got thirty-five minutes of the prime minister's time.

Diplomacy and celebrity certainly played a large role in the friendship that Prime Minister Paul Martin enjoyed with U2's lead singer, Bono. Both share a mutual interest in improving the life of those on the continent of Africa. They met when Martin was finance minister — a meeting after which Bono called Martin "a fucking great guy."* But the Irish singer was unable to get Martin to boost Canada's foreign aid to 0.7 percent of GDP. Nonetheless, the two were amicable and enjoyed a few beers together after the G8 summit at Gleneagles, Scotland — "more than one if I remember correctly," Martin recalled.

In similar fashion, Prime Minister Justin Trudeau crossed paths with the late Gord Downie, lead singer of the Tragically Hip, in 2016. Both Downie and Trudeau shared a desire to address Canada's ongoing reconciliation with the country's Indigenous Peoples. A tweeted photograph of the two men embracing before the band's final concert in Kingston, Ontario, contained added poignancy since Downie was dying of brain cancer. During the Tragically Hip's show, Downie took a moment to hail Trudeau for his work on the Indigenous file. "Prime Minister Trudeau's got me," he told the roaring crowd. "His work with First Nations ... he's got everybody! He's going to take us where we need to go! He's going to

---

* When Martin was first told he was having a meeting with Bono his response was: "Who?" After he was told that he was the lead singer of U2, he replied, "What?"

be looking good for about at least twelve more years. I don't know if they let you go beyond that. But he'll do it."

Trudeau, who wore a concert T-shirt like no prime minister before him ever could, did not address Downie's comments afterward. He didn't need to. With a television audience of more than ten million, Gord Downie had just given the prime minister the best publicity possible for one of his policy priorities, as well as a ringing endorsement from one of the country's most beloved rock stars. When Downie died in October 2017, an emotional prime minister — in tears — told the country about the pain he felt at his passing. "I thought I was going to make it through this but I'm not," he told reporters. "It hurts."

A meeting such as the Trudeau-Downie one had an emotional component as is sometimes the case with certain celebrity meetings. I asked Jean Chrétien if any of his encounters with the famous stuck out in his memory and he was quick to recall a 2001 introduction he made between iconic Canadian jazz pianist Oscar Peterson and South African president Nelson Mandela. "It was a very moving moment," the former prime minister recalled, his voice lowering as he recounted the story of two legends who overcame racism and other obstacles in becoming leaders in their respective fields.

Meeting celebrities can have more nuanced, diplomatic purposes, too, revealing the strategic instincts of the prime minister. Take Brian Mulroney's 1985 meeting with famous American entertainer Bob Hope. The thought of a visit from Hope was serious enough that Mulroney sought advice from the Clerk of the Privy Council, Gordon Osbaldeston, for an appropriate way to recognize Hope, who was the headliner for a fundraiser for the Royal Ottawa Hospital Foundation.

"The only case I am aware of in which the prime minister or government directly recognized an entertainer for charity work was in 1977," wrote the Clerk, "when the prime minister [Trudeau] awarded a citation to Mr. Harry Belafonte. In that instance, the circumstances were somewhat different, as Mr. Belafonte had undertaken a nine-city, cross-Canada tour in support of Canadian symphony orchestras. This involved an extensive commitment of time by Mr. Belafonte, who brought with him a five-piece band and took a full month to complete the tour."[13]

The memo to Mulroney noted that news reports suggested that Bob Hope was being paid a substantial sum for his Ottawa appearance and that he was spending all of one night in the capital. "I would not, therefore, recommend something as formal as a certificate," the Clerk advised, "and would suggest that any action you take be relatively low key."

A small reception or luncheon was suggested to the prime minister — nothing too fancy — but instead Mulroney decided to host a black-tie cocktail party at 24 Sussex. Why did Mulroney give Bob Hope the fancy treatment when the Clerk of the Privy Council was seemingly against it? Did Mulroney just want to glow in the light provided by a Hollywood legend? He had been PM for less than a year. Perhaps so. But another possibility is that Mulroney knew that a couple of good anecdotes from meeting Bob Hope could be pure gold in a subsequent meeting with U.S. President Ronald Reagan, himself a former Hollywood celebrity. Mulroney was always working an angle, so who knows?

Brian Mulroney, like all prime ministers, entertained a variety of celebrities. While the Clerk of the Privy Council advised Mulroney to host a low-key affair for Bob Hope in 1985, the PM opted for a black-tie cocktail party instead.

On the other hand, some celebrity encounters are merely private affairs, meetings that occur out of public view. Mulroney, for example, had long-time friendships with recording impresario David Foster, as well as hockey legend Bobby Orr, both of whom he entertained at Harrington Lake. Their friendships predated his time as prime minister.

In 1989, after President Ronald Reagan left office, Mulroney had dinner at Reagan's Bel Air, California, home where he met with Hollywood film legend James Stewart, famous for his role in *Mr. Smith Goes to Washington.* "A delightful dinner," he wrote in his personal journal.

Mulroney enjoyed meeting with celebrities, but this does not make him unique among prime ministers — it is perhaps true, though, that he enjoyed it more as the country's schmoozer-in-chief. Even when he did meet with celebrities in private, however, he frequently advertised such meetings in his speeches and in interviews he gave. He used to joke that people criticized him for his constant name-dropping. Mulroney said he was going to stop doing it. "The Queen Mother told me I had to," he once quipped. For Mulroney, whose Rolodex of contacts was unrivalled, meeting people with wealth, power, and fame was in large part because it could help him advance his agenda. In the end, relationships are vitally important to the success of all politicians, especially prime ministers.

It would be impossible to tell the story of every celebrity encounter by a prime minister — there are just so many — and some might say such meetings are just a perk of the job.

Prime Minister Justin Trudeau, however, made some insightful comments about celebrity in a December 2017 radio interview with his friend and radio host Terry DiMonte on Montreal's CHOM-FM. "It's interesting because you can tell quickly who is real and who is willing to be real with you." About meeting other famous people, he said:

> People who are celebrities build up this wall to try to
> keep themselves protected from all the energy people
> are trying to thrust at them both positive and nega-
> tive. Some will meet a fellow or peer or celebrity or

whatever it is and immediately drop the wall and others won't. So it's really interesting to see when people are willing to crack open a little bit and connect and to see what they're really like.

For outsiders, though, news of these liaisons feeds an interest in celebrity lives. The politicians may like to think it has a political payoff and perhaps it does. One 2005 study found that young people's beliefs can be strengthened by political endorsements from some famous people.[14] For that reason alone, prime ministers will continue to meet celebrities from the worlds of sports, music, or Hollywood. Looking behind the photo ops and speeches, though, we can learn a little bit about Canada at different times and the nature of those who held the office of prime minister. Consider the intimacy and unscripted nature of these visits for Mackenzie King, including a long-forgotten two-day visit with the most famous man in the world; the chaos of him chaperoning a young Shirley Temple; R.B. Bennett and the dog-sledder forcing him to wait — these are real encounters among many that put a human face on the job before it became so controlled and manufactured.

CHAPTER 7

"I AM NOT PUBLIC PROPERTY":
PRIME MINISTERS AND PRIVACY

I suppose some of you have different views on the life
of a prime minister than I do, but I want to make it
quite clear: as far as I am concerned, if I am a public
figure, I'm not public property.
— Pierre Trudeau, 1969

It is the summer of 1993 and Prime Minister Kim Campbell is sitting in a Toronto hotel restaurant enjoying dinner with her partner, Gregory Lekhtman. She has already paid the bill but Lekhtman does not know this, so they continue in dinner conversation as he waits for a bill that is not coming. The misunderstanding is finally sorted out, and as they rise to leave the prime minister notes that at least they aren't the last couple to leave the restaurant. But as she and Lekhtman look back, they see the other "couple" exit the restaurant, as well. It is the RCMP security detail. For Kim Campbell it is one more reminder that being prime minister is a job like no other. Even eating in a restaurant is not done without someone hovering nearby watching over her. Everything from "impromptu" walks in the woods to trips to the cinema is done with someone looking on. Ironically, she writes later in her memoirs about feeling lonely in the job. "It seems odd to say that I felt lonely that summer. I was seldom alone."

Since the days of Sir John A. Macdonald, Canadians have been interested in the private lives of prime ministers. This interest has only intensified with the ever-growing appetite in our culture for celebrity news and gossip. And social media has made it easy for politicians to share more and more of what they do, including curated — but supposedly "behind-the-scenes" shots — on Instagram or Twitter — of prime ministers at work or spending time with a pet.

A century and a half ago, John A. Macdonald's disappearances and drinking binges were covered by the newspapers of the day, but the press's exposure of his private life was unusual, a result of his extreme behaviour. Sir Wilfrid Laurier was much more successful at keeping his private life private. Not only did his behaviour not attract the attention that Macdonald's did, he, himself, was less inclined to share his personal affairs.

Not long after Laurier became prime minister in 1896, the editor of *La Patrie* had a request for him. He wanted information about Laurier's reading preferences for a feature he was to write about the interests and habits of public figures, something commonplace today. But Laurier refused. "I do not want my daily life to become public," he said.

Fast-forward a century and the most-recent incarnation of "Sunny Ways," Justin Trudeau, has very little about him that is private, as he uses social media accounts to publicly chronicle moments of each day like no prime minister before him.

It is difficult to imagine Wilfrid Laurier on Instagram or Twitter (#FollowMyWhitePlume?)*, but if there is one undeniable truth about being prime minister today, it is that you will lose your privacy more

---

* There are a surprising number of Twitter accounts in the names of former PMs. @pmlaurier is one of the most popular.

than you expected. Your life — even if you were a public figure before — takes a dramatic turn toward a position at the centre of Canada's political and celebrity vortex, and the consequences are not always pretty. A *Globe and Mail* editorial from 1970 still applies. "Any prime minister today — the day of television — loses almost all natural privacy the moment he assumes the office. He cannot walk down Bay Street, eat in a public restaurant, or climb aboard a commercial jet without attracting a mob."

This fact of life for a prime minister became maddeningly true for Stephen Harper before he was even sworn in as PM after the 2006 election. On January 26, just days before he assumed office, Harper dropped his children off at school in front of a gaggle of photographers. The picture that ran the next day was the infamous shot in which the PM-designate appeared to coolly say goodbye to his nine-year-old son, Ben, with a handshake. The result was one of those typical tempests in a teapot, as Canadians began moralizing about how to send your children off each morning. The *Globe and Mail* received more than forty letters to the editor, the most popular topic of any news story that month. "A handshake, for goodness sake? What kind of caring does that show?" berated one.

Harper was upset by the mischaracterization. By all accounts he is a devoted parent. "The notion that he might be a distant or uncaring father hurt him," one former aide told Paul Wells in his 2013 book *The Longer I'm Prime Minister*. "It's the only thing I ever saw that did." It was a quick lesson in the changes that occur to the lives of those who become prime minister.

A few days later, a story ran in the *Globe* with the headline: "Smile Mr. Harper, you're on candid camera: The Harpers are now the de facto first family of Canada and life in the fishbowl has begun." Indeed it had. A trip by Harper to the hospital earlier in the week to get antibiotics for an asthma condition ended up on the front page of the *Ottawa Citizen*.

As all prime ministers discover, holding that position means life will be different. Robert Borden and his wife, Laura, regretted the looming loss of privacy once he was to become PM — a fact driven home by the gaggle of reporters that gathered outside the gate to his home the morning after his election victory in 1911. The same sentiment was expressed near the end of the century. "We've never had so little privacy," Aline Chrétien remarked just a few months after she and Jean Chrétien moved into 24 Sussex Drive. But the Chrétiens at least had thirty years of experience in public life to draw upon. Not the same for the Harpers. "They are very down-to-earth people," one friend noted in 2006. "So, in the global sense, it is going to be somewhat of an adjustment because they are used to living like regular people and they try to live that type of family life with their kids."[1]

Raising children while being prime minister creates its own set of privacy issues. There is a general rule that the children of prime ministers are off limits to the media. On the other hand, convention permits that they can be photographed at public events, and prime ministers have not hesitated to use their children to political advantage by appearing with them. It is, to some degree, unavoidable for a PM with a family not to be seen with his children. It makes them seem like real people. Pierre Trudeau jealously guarded his privacy but often took at least one of his children with him on his foreign trips. Geoffrey Stevens once quipped in a 1973 *Globe and Mail* article that "it would not be denigrating the minister of external affairs to suggest that Justin Trudeau played a more prominent role than Mitchell Sharp at last summer's Commonwealth Conference."[2] Looking at the situation today and the attention paid to Justin Trudeau's son Hadrien on an official trip to Ireland, it seems that the situation is the same, with adorable children stealing the show.

While the children of prime ministers usually lead to feel-good stories in the press, that is not always the case. In 1991, when Brian Mulroney was prime minister, the satirical rag *Frank* magazine went too far in an episode involving his daughter, Caroline, who was sixteen years old at the time. It ran an infamous contest in its magazine. "Hey, Young Tories!" it began. "It's *Frank*'s Deflower Caroline Contest!" Inside was a coupon for readers to clip and send in. "Yes, I did it! I've enclosed proof of conquest. Rush me valuable prizes."[3] Mulroney exploded. Six months later he was still fuming. In an interview with the CBC's Hana Gartner, Mulroney said, "When a trash magazine puts on the cover an incitement to gang-rape my daughter, I wanted to take out a gun and go down there and do serious damage to these people." The interview made headlines across Canada. "If you ask me whether I lost my temper, you're bloody right I lost my temper," Mulroney continued. "If I had that little guy within striking distance I'd like to choke him.... That's the kind of thing that drives me bananas."[4]

That was perhaps the most blatant disregard for the privacy and dignity of a prime minister's family. But public life means anything unusual will get reported. In 2014, paramedics were called to 24 Sussex to attend to an eighteen-year-old woman suspected of having alcohol poisoning. This was at a birthday party for Stephen Harper's son, Ben. While the PM's son was not the one taken to the hospital, no family would want these types of occurrences splashed across the media. But the incident introduced once more the debate about what is in the public interest when reporting about a prime minister and what is not. Evan Solomon, then-host of CBC's *Power and Politics*, noted at the time: "One of the things this raises ... is that line between the private and the public, what is in the public interest, what if anything should we know about the activities of the prime minister's family and there's a culture where you just don't ask about it."[5] No prime minister faced the dynamics of this question more than Pierre Trudeau.

Trudeau rocketed on to the political scene as prime minister when he succeeded Lester Pearson in 1968, later winning his own mandate in the general election in June of that year. His status as Canada's first bachelor prime minister in twenty years, combined with the fact Trudeau was an exciting and engaging personality, meant that there was intense interest in his personal life. It was the late 1960s, too, so attitudes and desires were changing. Women swooned after the new prime minister as the country got caught up in Trudeaumania. And the PM played to his playboy image.* After winning that 1968 leadership contest he was asked by a reporter if he would be giving up his famous silver Mercedes.

---

* Christina McCall wrote of him in *Grits: An Intimate Portrait of the Liberal Party*: "My God, Trudeau seems to have slept with as many women as Norman Bethune."

"Are you talking about the car now, or the girl?" Trudeau asked.

"The car," said the reporter.

"I won't give up either," came the reply.[6]

There was intense interest in the prime minister's love life, some of it brought on by Trudeau's own flamboyance and by virtue of the office that he held. Some of it was media prurience. *Chatelaine* magazine ran many articles about the prime minister, including one titled "Whom Should Trudeau Marry?" The prime minister had a reputation as Canada's most eligible bachelor, but in fact Trudeau was also something of a loner. Despite that fact, though, and as John English wrote in his outstanding biography of Trudeau, "He often appeared at theatres, in restaurants, on ski hills, and in the driveway of 24 Sussex Drive with many different but always beautiful women." Harrington Lake, the prime minister's summer residence, was known as a "romantic retreat."

The women Trudeau dated were of interest to the media and Canadians. But the issue of his various romances blew up at the end of a January 1969 Commonwealth Conference in London. The British press followed Trudeau closely and one of his dates, Canadian Eva Rittinghausen, blabbed to the British press about her lunch with Trudeau at a Chelsea restaurant, creating a minor sensation for the Canadian reporters who covered the story. "There are more women than just me," Rittinghausen was quoted as saying. "But I don't know of any other female in London he's taking out…. Yes, he's the No 1 catch of the international jet set. Certainly he can catch me … but I don't want to be the one doing the catching." When asked why Trudeau liked her, she replied, "I think it is because I am, how do you say … *très sportif*?" The *Daily Mail* article went on to name other Trudeau dates, including Jennifer Rae (sister of former Ontario Premier Bob Rae) and Canadian actress Louise Marleau.

The news precipitated a confrontation between Trudeau and the Canadian media, with the question of what is public and what is private at the centre of the controversy. At a press conference with Canadian reporters that was all but over, Trudeau picked a fight with them when he said that he thought their behaviour had been "pretty crummy."

"I suppose some of you have different views on the life of a prime minister than I do," Trudeau began, "but I want to make it quite clear:

as far as I am concerned, if I am a public figure, I'm not public property." Showing his anger at the whole affair, he replied to one reporter who had asked if his comments were on the record, "You can stick that where you want, what I've said — on the record or off the record, or elsewhere — I frankly don't care."

"Perhaps we had better have some files on all of you," he went on. "And perhaps it would be useful if the police could go and question some of the women you have been seen with."[7]

Part of what is so incredible about this exchange is Trudeau's willingness to engage with reporters in an intense debate about privacy and the prime minister. This was a different era, when the press had greater, less scripted access to the PM. But it was also a mistake by Trudeau to pick a fight, one potent example of what Ivan Head called Trudeau's capacity to go from "intellectual tower down to a bar-room brawler very quickly."[8]

It certainly made for compelling reading. "I really don't see the role that the press has to play in my private affairs," Trudeau continued, laying out his case for privacy. "There may be contrary views to this; you may think, once again, that, being a public figure, it's important to you, what happens in my private home or in my private meetings.... I think you once agreed when I said that the state had no place in the bedrooms of the nation; I ... could say that the nation has [no] place in the bedrooms of the state, and certainly [neither does] the press...."

Then Trudeau turns the tables on the reporters: "I wouldn't venture to question your wives about how you behave with them, because I respect your wives and I respect you, and I don't see why you would not do the equivalent with any politician."[9]

While Trudeau was excoriating the press for their perceived intrusions, privately there was another view of this imbroglio. Charles Ritchie, who was high commissioner in London at the time, observed in his diary: "The press have largely concentrated on [Trudeau's] 'love life.' He attacked them for it at his press conference, but he is himself largely responsible. He trails his coat, he goes to conspicuous places with conspicuous women. If he really wants an affair, he could easily manage it discreetly. This is a kind of double bluff."[10] This is an interesting diary entry from a man known for having had several romantic affairs of his own, including one with the well-known British author Elizabeth

Bowen. This view once more points out the great contradiction of Pierre Trudeau as a man who valued his privacy very much but yet did not shy away from publicly delicious moments with captivating women.

Of all the women Pierre Trudeau dated while prime minister, none created the stir that Barbra Streisand did. Trudeau met her in London at the premiere of her hit film *Funny Girl* in January 1969, this coming on the heels of the Commonwealth conference for which he was already in town. Streisand's marriage to Elliott Gould had recently come to an end (although they were only separated, not divorced), and she and the PM hit it off. John English called their relationship "very romantic," writing that Trudeau and Streisand "possessed an intensity and electricity that attracted all around them." In 2009, when asked by Margaret Wente of the *Globe and Mail* if the two had actually slept together, he said, "The evidence is overwhelming that [they] did."[11] Streisand biographer Christopher Andersen described the affair as "white-hot."[12]

Not surprisingly, the relationship caught the interest of Canadians and the media. A November 1969 lovers' weekend in New York for Trudeau and Streisand was reported on the front page of the *Globe and Mail*. Friday night the two dined on the Upper East Side at Casa Brasil and then went to Raffles, a well-known, members-only nightclub at the Sherry-Netherland Hotel. Saturday, intriguingly, the prime minister and the film star spent the entire day in Streisand's Central Park West apartment. On Sunday, they went to the theatre.

While they were hounded to some degree by paparazzi in New York, for Trudeau it was a wonderful escape from the Ottawa bubble. "It's marvellous," he told reporters. "I can do anything — pick my nose if I want."[13]

Both Trudeau and Streisand were clearly smitten with each other, the latter saying that the prime minister "was everything my imagination had promised and more." She called him an enticing blend of "Marlon Brando and Napoleon." When a reporter asked Trudeau how long he had known Streisand, he answered by saying, "Not long enough." Soon after, they were "burning up the phone lines between Los Angeles and Ottawa."[14]

All of this was nothing compared to what was to come when the *Funny Girl* star came to Ottawa in January 1970. The cold Canadian capital was set ablaze by the glamour and star power of a charismatic

Pierre Trudeau resented the encroachment into his private life when he was prime minister. His relationship with American film and music star Barbra Streisand was a potent mix of glamour, power, and celebrity that lit up Ottawa during her 1970 visit. One Streisand biographer remarked that she looked "as if she had stepped out of the pages of *Dr. Zhivago*." Just over a year later, he married Margaret Sinclair.

prime minister with sex appeal and a Hollywood actress with looks and magnetism to match. Streisand was Trudeau's date at the National Arts Centre gala celebrating Manitoba's centennial as a province. Their appearance together was front-page news, with Trudeau and Streisand cutting a striking figure in photographs from the event. "Ms. Streisand was stunning in a floor-length gown of white wool with a plunging neckline,"[15] gushed the *Globe and Mail*, while the *Toronto Star* reported that the "vivacious" movie star brought "unexpected glamour" to the event.[16] Andersen probably captured it best when he wrote that Streisand, "emerged looking as if she had stepped out of the pages of *Dr. Zhivago*."[17]

There was no hesitation on Trudeau's part to benefit from his relationship with Streisand, and his top advisors had already concluded that the courtship was "political gold." So much for privacy. Streisand was flaunted the next day in an appearance in the visitors' gallery at the House of Commons. She looked as fetching in this daytime appearance as she had the night before, and her presence in the Green Chamber sent the MPs into a tizzy. "And all through the question period, [Trudeau] blushed and looked up at the gallery, waving occasionally and making little signals with his hands," reported the *Toronto Star*.[18] There was one reference to Streisand's presence. Conservative MP George Hees stood up and told the Speaker he would like to ask the PM a question, "if he can take his eyes and mind off the visitors' gallery long enough to answer it."[19]

Once Question Period was over, the prime minister retreated to his office, where he met up with Streisand, who ran the gauntlet of reporters, protected by Trudeau press aide and former B.C. Lions football player Vic Chapman. After a short meeting, Streisand left in a car, her destination unknown, but not before she and Trudeau exchanged intense glances. When the prime minister was ready to leave the office later that evening, he made his plea for privacy — this after bringing his date to the House of Commons.

"If I say I'm not going out to dinner tonight, will you go home?" he asked a crowd of reporters outside his office.

"Yes," someone said.

"Well, I'm not going out tonight," he said, holding a large case of briefing papers. "I've got all this work to do."[20]

The prime minister returned to 24 Sussex Drive but curious reporters still followed him. When he emerged later that evening wearing jogging pants and a windbreaker, he was annoyed when he addressed journalists who were staking out his home.

"What are you guys doing here? Now everyone will be coming to see me jog every night."[21] He picked up some snow and threw snowballs at the gathering before he ran off into the night and the grounds of the governor general.

Trudeau was not seen again that evening, so when or how the tryst continued is not known, though there was some speculation that Trudeau was in a red corvette that later pulled up to Sussex Drive. Regardless, this romance was in full bloom. Andersen wrote in his Streisand biography that the couple shared a candlelight dinner alone at Sussex Drive that night. In fact, the relationship was moving along so quickly, Trudeau proposed marriage to Streisand.[22] But there were many obstacles to such a union. Trudeau was Catholic, Streisand, Jewish. What would happen to her film career? "I'd have to learn how to speak French. I would do only movies made in Canada. I had it all figured out," the American actress said.[23]

As enticing as a marriage between a movie star and prime minister might be, *People* magazine nuptials were not to be. The Trudeau-Streisand relationship faded away, as it did in public memory, but they would meet again a couple of times, most publicly at a 1994 event honouring Hillary Clinton at the New York Public Library. Their appearance together was a minor *cause célèbre* and photographs appeared in the newspapers. As for Trudeau, it did not seem to occupy his mind much when he wrote his 1993 memoir. The only mention of Streisand is in a photo caption of the two of them at the celebrated National Arts Centre event.

There is one interesting point of contrast to be made when we consider all of the media attention paid to this bachelor prime minister in the late 1960s and early 1970s. Fast-forward to 1993 when Canada once more had an unmarried prime minister in Kim Campbell. Just a few weeks after that year's election loss Campbell was asked by *Maclean's* magazine "if [she] had found love." Her response tells us how little things had changed.

"I don't know why there is this prurient interest in my private life," she chafed, echoing Pierre Trudeau's comments twenty-four years earlier. "Yes, I have a social life and one of the compensations of not being prime minister is to have both the time and privacy to pursue it. It's just such an invasion of my privacy to be talking about that."[24] Any prime minister would agree.

Pierre Trudeau's relationship with Barbra Streisand, as well as his dalliances with a long list of other attractive women whom he dated, was only the beginning in terms of perceived violations of the privacy of a prime minister. His marriage to twenty-two-year-old Margaret Sinclair in 1971 would test the limits of what was fair game when reporting on the life of the county's most public politician. Trudeau had been dating Sinclair since August 1969 — so even while he was dating Streisand. When she learned of the hot romance in the newspapers, she was angry. After the movie star left town, Trudeau called Sinclair to ask her out once more.

"Go back to your American actress," she yelled into the telephone.

On another occasion she found a pile of photographs of various women in Trudeau's desk drawer. "Are you ranking us?" she asked.

"Maybe," came the reply.

It was to be a stormy, publicly documented marriage that would cause the prime minister a great deal of anguish.

Trudeau's nuptials with Margaret Sinclair were clandestine, and newspaper reports mentioned the prime minister's desire for privacy in their articles. The wedding was a secret so well kept that no one in his Cabinet even knew. "I thought he'd gone skiing," exclaimed External Affairs Minister Mitchell Sharp, who was the acting PM. That Trudeau got married at all was a major surprise and the extent of his courtship of Sinclair was not well known. The news of the union was cause for friendly congratulations as well as jibes in the House of Commons as members gently admonished Trudeau for being so secretive.

But the marriage was ultimately doomed and its breakdown luridly played out in the media. By 1977 the relationship was at its nadir. "Maggie" was hanging out with the Rolling Stones or taking off to party in New York, while Trudeau went to Disneyland in California, where he was accompanied by one RCMP officer and *Toronto Star* journalist Val Sears. "A terribly proud man, he'd been driven almost to his knees by Maggie," wrote Sears in 1984. "A woman radio reporter shoved a mike in his face at every exit and asked: 'Is it true, Mr. Trudeau, that you gave your wife a black eye? What really happened with Mick Jagger?' Trudeau had turned to stone or he would have killed her."[25]

On March 4, 1977, six years after their marriage, which included the birth of three children (Justin in 1971, Sasha in 1973, and Michel in 1975), Margaret and Pierre entered into a trial separation for which there was no public announcement.

Speculation about the state of the union continued and the press covered the ongoing story in an age when this type of journalism had growing appeal. It had become "the country's conversation piece, gossipy, sad, crass."[26] * Echoing this sentiment, the prime minister's press secretary, Patrick Gossage, wrote in his diary, "Has lust for personal knowledge of the great become the only common currency, the real edge of competition, which worries even the mighty *Toronto Star*, [and] esteemed *Globe and Mail*?"

Letters to the editor of publications such as *Maclean's* magazine or the *Toronto Star* took them to task for their sensational coverage of Margaret Trudeau's life and, by extension the PM's marriage. "Who appointed you watchdog over the PM's wife's morals? Non-gentlemen: consider yourselves slapped for bad taste," blasted one. There should be "some regard and consideration" for the prime minister "when his private life is on the line," wrote another.[27]

Throughout it all, Pierre Trudeau somehow kept his cool. On May 30, 1977, the PMO officially announced the separation in a statement and life went on as usual as much as was possible. Margaret Trudeau's 1979 tell-all book, *Beyond Reason*, was a publishing juggernaut that aired a number of salacious stories about her life and her

---

* Dick Beddoes, who wrote those lines, said in the same column that the Trudeaus had been like folk heroes. "It was a bit as though Bobby Orr had married Anne Murray."

thoughts about being the wife of a prime minister. Serialized in magazines and newspapers, the book came out during the 1979 election campaign. Trudeau's team informed all candidates that the personal life of the PM "was not an election issue" but secretly worried that the book could cost votes. But new ground was broken in the media coverage of the Trudeaus. Publishing "gossipy, sad, and crass" material would no longer be off limits for prime ministers. And Trudeau lost the election to the Progressive Conservatives led by Joe Clark.

Remarkably, during the period from 1976 to 1983, Trudeau was able to keep his intense romance with classical guitarist Liona Boyd out of the press. Boyd recounts her numerous and amorous rendezvouses with the prime minister in her memoir *In My Own Key*. In the book she writes about the lengths they went to in order to keep their affair quiet. "We still had to exercise extreme caution over the media and the public discovering our romance." Giving an example, she tells of one incident when she had to hide under a pile of coats in the back seat of the prime minister's chauffeur-driven car as she and Pierre headed for a romantic getaway at Harrington Lake.

John English writes that close associates of Trudeau — as well as his family — doubted the accuracy of the accounts in Boyd's book. The truth likely lies somewhere in between, but the lengths a prime minister needed to go to protect his privacy remains undeniable.

Being prime minister means being the subject of rampant media speculation and rumour mongering. Is R.B. Bennett getting married? Why *isn't* he married? Is Stephen Harper's wife having an affair? Is Brian Mulroney drinking again? All of these are questions raised at one time or another about those involved. Rumour and innuendo are just another part of being prime minister.

As for Bennett, he *was* thought to be getting married to Hazel Beatrice Colville of Montreal. She had told many friends a union was to take place with the prime minister. King, who had been ousted from office by Bennett in the 1930 election, relished the rumours in his diary. "It is Bennett's love of money which is being urged among other reasons as the occasion for the marriage to be," he wrote with rather more than a hint of pettiness and, perhaps, envy. The proposed marriage was something of a scandal in 1932 since Colville was a twice-divorced Catholic, a circumstance that was not to be overlooked. She was also connected to many previous romances. According to Bennett biographer John Boyko, the rumours fascinated Canadians because both the prime minister and the leader of the Opposition were bachelors. In fact, Bennett had been seeing Colville romantically, but by the spring of 1934 she put an end to the relationship after he asked her to quit smoking, quit drinking, and quit enjoying the nightlife of Montreal. Colville understandably declined.

But why did Bennett never marry? There have been a number of explanations over the years, some more salacious than others. One was a rumour that Bennett never tied the knot due to some issues with his honourable member — that is to say his penis. The story was that Bennett suffered from phimosis, a tightening of the foreskin around the penis that results in painful erections. Another theory was that he had Peyronie's disease, a condition that caused a curved penis, resulting in similar uncomfortable challenges to endure when sexually aroused. But Boyko concludes that "despite the popularity and persistence of these rumours, and another that he had had this problem dealt with through surgery in London, there is no evidence that Bennett ever mentioned either disease or that any of the women with whom he was romantically inclined discussed it with anyone." Not that they would.

Bennett asked his potential wife to quit drinking as he was not an imbiber himself. The same could not be said for Brian Mulroney. It was well-known that Mulroney was at one time a heavy drinker, but he gave up the bottle in 1980, and, as he writes in his memoir, has "never had another drop." But that did not stop spurious rumours of Mulroney hitting the bottle in 1993. "Ottawa is awash in queries about the PM's drinking habits and the state of his marriage," was the breathless secondary headline in the *Globe and Mail*. There were rumours Mulroney was drinking, that Mila was having an affair with Christopher Plummer, and, of course, none of it was true. But because *Frank* magazine, the racy tabloid, had written about it, journalists could get around any qualms they might have by writing *about* the rumours that were being written about.

"Besides being delicious and malicious," Charlotte Gray wrote of *Frank*, "it has also been oblivious to trivialities such as solid evidence." She later wrote that she had no substantiation of any of the rumours, but that did not stop the paper from running a front-of-section story about it. "Who knows?" she wrote. "Perhaps post-Meech depression, and the treachery of his buddy Lucien Bouchard, drove a devastated Brian Mulroney to a few Hemingway evenings up at Harrington Lake last July. But I don't believe any of the fascinating rumours now current in Toronto."

As for Mulroney, the rumours and innuendo must have angered him. But sometimes the best weapon is a little Irish charm and humour. At the Press Gallery dinner that year, the prime minister told the audience, "The last time I saw Mila, at the liquor store, she wasn't sure she was coming tonight. It's a long way from Montreal."[28]

Frank certainly changed the climate of reporting in the late 1980s and early 1990s. "The Press Gallery was less inclined to tear the veil of privacy in pre-*Frank* days," Gray wrote. "Today, no such inhibitions handcuff Hill-watchers."[29] One can only imagine the fun *Frank* would have had during the Trudeau years, or even with Mackenzie King.

Frank was not around during the Mackenzie King era and very little was known about the private lives of prime ministers from the days of Sir John A. Macdonald through to King. The prevailing sentiment was captured by one Ontario newspaper when it wrote in 1930: "We think a public man has a right to a decent degree of privacy in his private life, that even in his official life he should not be constantly badgered by reportorial surveillance.... We do not want to know and indeed have no right to know who has tea with the prime minister, or goes to his dinner parties, or if Mr. King has a new Fall coat."

Mackenzie King would have naturally agreed, but Canada's longest-serving PM could be said to have suffered the greatest violation of privacy in prime ministerial history — albeit posthumously — and we are lucky that it happened. King kept a diary that ran from his days as a student at the University of Toronto in the 1890s to a few days before his death in 1950. Running some thirty thousand pages and

7.5 million words, King's diary is one of the greatest historical resources in Canadian history and continues to fascinate readers. Take a dip anywhere in it and you will find something of interest. But if King had gotten his way, this remarkable document would never have seen the light of day.

In February 1950, King wrote in his final will that he wanted his diary destroyed "except those parts which I have indicated are and shall be available for publication or use."[30] But he never indicated what those parts were and died in July of that year. Further muddying the waters, some of his previous indications were contradictory.

For example, in an 1893 entry he wrote that his reason for keeping the diary was to allow "the reader ... to trace how the author has sought to improve his time." In 1902, he wrote, "This journal is strictly private, and none should look upon its pages save with reverent eyes...." And, when John D. Rockefeller Jr., whose foundation had contributed $100,000 to his memoirs project, wrote to him in 1950 saying the diary should not be destroyed, King bristled at the suggestion.

A long debate ensued over what to do about the diary, given King's wishes that it not become public. His long-time companion, Joan Patteson — who figured prominently in the diary — weighed in on the debate in a 1951 letter to another King friend, Violet Markham, writing, "Mr. McGregor (one of the literary executors) and I have not been at one over the diaries. Rex [King] made me promise to see that Mr. McG. burned them without reading — and while I saw the need perhaps of reading them, the dying request was very sacred to me — and that I think is what I have suffered most. I have no knowledge of their contents — but I have wished that his wishes could be carried out."

The other literary executors — who included Jack Pickersgill (former private secretary to King and Clerk of the Privy Council in 1952), Norman Robertson (diplomat and former Clerk), and W. Kaye Lamb (Dominion Archivist) — faced a problem in light of its clear historical significance. How could they honour the former prime minister's request without destroying one of the most valuable artifacts in Canadian history, the detailed diary of the country's longest-serving prime minister?

Eventually, after years of considerations, leaks, and partial releases, including a four-volume work titled *The Mackenzie King Record*, portions of the diary were made available to the public in 1971, but only writings up to 1931. Behind the scenes, there had been plenty of intrigue about the diary and intense debate about whether to release it. A malcontented employee at the Public Archives, as it was then known, had made photographed copies of the diary and had been attempting to sell parts of it to newspapers. The story of the existence of the boot-leg copy was not well known but, according to Trent University histor-ian Christopher Dummitt in his excellent book *Unbuttoned: A History of Mackenzie King's Secret Life*, its presence made King's literary exe-cutors far more reluctant to destroy the original and more apt to make it publicly available so as to not increase the value of the illegal copy.

By the end of the decade, the entire document was available in the national archives and other select research libraries, despite the fact that King never really wanted people to read it. But why the big deal?

As anyone who has read the diary can attest, there is some strange material in it. As historians began to delve into the secret world of Mackenzie King, they learned that there was a completely different side to him. King held seances during which he spoke to the dead, including Wilfrid Laurier, his grandfather, his mother, and other friends; he had an unusual fealty to his dog; he was obsessed with numbers; and he led what he referred to as "a very double life." These words provided the title for a sensational and controversial book by historian C.P. Stacey based on the diaries published in 1976. In it, Stacey chronicles all of King's weirdness and made an indelible contribution to developing King's reputation as something of an odd duck, a reputation richly deserved. Stacey wrote that King "was an inhabitant of two worlds. One was the very practical world of politics and public affairs.... The other was his private world, a world populated by his family (and his dogs), his innumerable women friends, and in his later years the spirits of the dear and the great departed." The book also noted that King, when a young man, cavorted with prostitutes and that the diary was replete with "an endless procession of females who glide through King's life."

"People did not think of the bachelor Prime Minister of later years as in any sense a ladies' man," wrote Stacey, "but this was one of the many matters in which people were wrong about him." Indeed, King had what appeared to be platonic relationships with women throughout his time as prime minister and it is beyond doubt that he would not have wanted his thoughts about them to become part of the historical record. But they are.

Not only that, there were notebooks King kept about some of his spiritual communications. These his literary executors burned page by page in Jack Pickersgill's fireplace, perhaps wisely. "Given some of the sensational nature of what the executors have been willing to unleash," wrote *Maclean's* in 1979, "the supressed notebooks written for King's eyes only, could well have contained material far more kinky than anything published in the steaming pages of *Psychopathia Sexualis*."[31]

King's diary was one of his greatest gifts to Canada. More valuable than Laurier House or his Kingsmere estate. In it we get an unprecedented and private view into the life of one of the country's greatest prime ministers. His diary added an inimitable texture to events and remains a fascinating resource. Robert Fulford once wrote that it would be the only Canadian historical document still read five hundred years from now. And yet, one of the things King valued most was his privacy. The debate over the release of the diary centred on what rights a prime minister has to privacy. Dummitt quotes a 1958 *Maclean's* magazine article that asks, "What right has a politician, a statesman or a military leader to keep his official and semi-official documents under lock and key while he's in office, pack them up when he leaves office, burn such of them as he'd like to have forgotten, and then turn the rest over to a chosen biographer or use them as material for a book or books of his own?"

King was fortunate that the press did not snoop around as it does today. In an anecdote told in Allan Levine's *Scrum Wars*, King dressed down a reporter when he wrote that the prime minister had taken a bath after his government delivered its 1930 budget. But as Levine notes, these kinds of transgressions were rare and King was lucky that there was not much prying by the press into his personal affairs nor was there rampant speculation about his relationship with his erstwhile companion Joan Patteson with whom he spent much time. "In those days you never covered a prime minister's private life," Levine quotes journalist Alex Hume as saying.

Ironically, for a public figure King abhorred spending a lot of time interacting with others and needed and liked his moments alone, perhaps more than any other PM. In fact, this was one of the reasons he bought the Kingsmere estate in Chelsea, Quebec — to get away from everyone.* But he also liked to be appreciated (probably even more than he liked to be alone). "Though King might roll over in his grave at the thought," wrote *Maclean's* magazine in 1979, "[the diary's] release means his memory will not soon be forgotten."[32] How right they were.

Mackenzie King is not the only prime minister about whom some private moments were revealed after his death. More recently this happened to John Diefenbaker, when questions arose about the paternity of George Dryden, who died in 2016 after injuries suffered during a suicide attempt. Dryden, who was born in 1968, had been trying to convince people that Diefenbaker was his father, and he certainly had a very strong resemblance to the former prime minster. DNA tests had proved that Dryden's presumed biological father, Gordon Dryden, was in fact not his father. George Dryden had always maintained that his mother, Mary Lou Dryden, admitted to him that she had had an affair with Diefenbaker in the late 1960s. Then there was a further revelation: Diefenbaker had supposedly sired a son with his housekeeper, Mary Rosa Lamarche, in the 1930s. That child was given up for adoption and took the name Edward Thorne. Two of Thorne's three sons conducted DNA tests with George Dryden, and the results showed a near-certain nephew-uncle relationship. Neither Edward Thorne, nor George Dryden, was conceived while Diefenbaker was prime minister, but the story is remarkable and cause for reflection on the Chief. Who knows what other dalliances Diefenbaker may have been up to while prime minister.

Diefenbaker would not be the only PM to have fathered a child out of wedlock after living at 24 Sussex. In 1991, constitutional lawyer Deborah Coyne gave birth to a daughter, Sarah. Pierre Trudeau, at the venerable (and yet virile) age of seventy-one, was the father. And rumours have persisted for more than a century about the paternity of a Liberal MP named Armand Lavergne, who had an uncanny

---

* In 1928, Mackenzie King went to New York City as part of a vacation. While there he bumped into two Cabinet ministers: Ernest Lapointe, on Fifth Avenue, and Fernand Rinfret, on the elevator at Macy's. Said King: It shows "how little one can get away unobserved, anywhere."

resemblance to Sir Wilfrid Laurier. Laurier maintained a fairly intimate and torrid epistolary relationship with Lavergne's mother, Émilie, who also happened to be the wife of Laurier's law partner. "I would wish for a long rest. Could I join you and spend a few days of sun and breeze in your company? I would come back as strong as Samson," Laurier wrote in one. But the relationship came to a quick end once Laurier became prime minister. André Pratte, a Laurier biographer, found no evidence of the affair, despite looking for some.

The same is true for the stories about Stephen Harper and his wife, Laureen. Ottawa was rife with rumours during his final years in office. Was Mrs. Harper seeing an RCMP officer? Was the marriage on the rocks? John Ibbitson, in his 2015 biography of Harper, wrote that he — along with innumerable other reporters in Ottawa — dug far and wide to try to substantiate the rumours but could find no corroborating evidence. "They are false," he wrote. "They spring from a bitter clash among those guarding the prime minister, and perhaps from something very dark in the psyche of the Laurentian elites."

All of this simply means that when you are prime minister, your private life will come under an uncommon scrutiny, some of it legitimate, much of it for titillation. We live in a society that seems bent on sharing everything, where gossip, rumour, and innuendo appear to have more interest than fact. The main difference now is that what once was just whispered among a few journalists or others inside a very tight Ottawa bubble, is now deemed to be fair game in mainstream media and anywhere online.

Being prime minister means that your life is at the centre of a public conversation. The focus on the PM has existed since Macdonald occupied the office and has only increased over time, as we dive deeper into the lives of the famous and powerful. When it comes to love lives, or anything that shows the human condition, whether that involves sex, booze, paternity, family, or spiritualism, there will be an avid readership. When we see that prime ministers, in many respects, experience some of the same joys and trials as we do, it gives us a chance to believe they might be like us — and in some ways they are — but there are few who would relish the idea of being permanently in the spotlight.

"When you're in politics — and you choose to be in politics," Lester Pearson once said, "you have to give some things up and one of them is privacy. It's irritating for the press to pry, but it's more irritating if they don't — if they just don't care."[33]

Pearson's comments did not mean that he failed to recognize the need for some semblance of a private life. Quite the opposite. He once lamented the constant demands on a prime minister's time and that he wished for a life with "more leisure, some privacy and no autographs."[34] He was only mildly protesting and said this at a time when he was already looking forward to retirement. But Pearson likely captures the secret wish of many of our PMs — quiet time away from it all.* For a prime minister there is no such thing as a day off, nor is there much private time. Even away from the office at "home" there are constantly people around you, whether it is to prepare for travel, provide security, serve you meals, or take you somewhere. "There is no space for non-performing," as one person close to a former PM once put it, and the result is pressure from always being "on."** The challenge to separate yourself from the job to any degree must be enormous, and perhaps even impossible. Pierre Trudeau said he had to take what he called a "schizophrenic" approach to separating his life as PM from his private life. Others such as Mackenzie King or R.B. Bennett never made the distinction — their work was their life. What is a prime minister to do? The answer lies in two words, the beauty of which only a PM will ever understand: Harrington Lake.

---

* Brian Mulroney dismissed the need for privacy. "Never bothered me," he replied when asked about the loss of it in our interview.
** One person close to a former PM told me the only real private place for a prime minister is in the bathroom.

CHAPTER 8

"MAYBE NOT YOUR GRANDMOTHER'S HOME": PRIME MINISTERS AT HOME

I have abandoned the idyllic charms of Harrington Lake
for the less idyllic burners of government — but not, I
hope, for long because that cottage, the peace, the water
and the co-operative fish, is going to be a life saver.
— Lester B. Pearson, 1963, writing about the prime
minister's official country retreat, Harrington Lake

Prime Minister Louis St. Laurent finishes with the business of
the day at the House of Commons and reluctantly heads into
his waiting car that will whisk him home to 24 Sussex Street, as it was
originally known, the new official residence of the prime minister of
Canada. Rushed, the PM is barely there in time to greet his first visitors,
Senator and Mrs. J.J. Kinley. They are the first of three hundred guests,
including MPs, their spouses, and the press gallery, attending three separate receptions to show off the new prime ministerial abode. In total,
nine hundred people will file through on this day in late May 1951.

As visitors arrive, they note the beds of red tulips and yellow snapdragons outside. Guest books are dutifully signed before a different member of the St. Laurent family shows guests around the home. Ever the gentleman, St. Laurent takes great care when touring with George Drew, the leader of the Opposition, pointing out to him the pros and cons of the residence. The house is "friendly and smoothly arranged" and has wonderful personal touches. There are vases of purple irises, red roses on a piano, photographs, and French- and English-language literature on the bookshelves. The rooms are warm in colour and inviting in their assembly. A plaque above one doorway reads, "God Bless our Home." One newspaper reporter describes it as "the sort of home Canadians might well be proud of providing their prime minister, even though he stubbornly insisted on paying $5,000 a year rent."[1] It is a mindset that will not last.

Since 1951, when Louis St. Laurent moved out of his Roxborough apartment in Ottawa, 24 Sussex Drive has been home to Canadian prime ministers. It was a decision about which the modest prime minister had to be convinced, reluctant as he was to be seen accepting something as grand as a mansion in which to live. Mrs. St. Laurent, who never loved Ottawa, was decidedly more upbeat about the move.

Legislation to make Sussex the official residence of the prime minister was introduced while St. Laurent was absent from the House, and it quickly gained all-party support. And while the house, situated along the Ottawa River about three kilometres from Parliament, was originally built in 1868 and christened "Gorffwysfa" — meaning "place of peace" in Welsh — it has often been anything but for prime ministers of Canada. As Brian Mulroney wrote in his memoirs: "But for me and those who preceded and followed me, the official residence was anything but restful."

In the decades since the St. Laurents unpacked their moving boxes, 24 Sussex has gone from being a "fairy place" in the words of John Diefenbaker, its second occupant, to a national embarrassment so toxic that Prime Minister Justin Trudeau refused to move in after his 2015 electoral victory. Kim Campbell is the only other PM since 1951 not to live at Sussex. Instead, she spent her time at Harrington Lake — "Mila warned me about the blackflies and mosquitoes," she noted.

Nonetheless, 24 Sussex and Harrington Lake — the principal residence and country estate available to all prime ministers since the 1950s — offers a prism through which to observe the domestic styles and sensibilities of Canada's prime ministers, and perhaps their spouses, over the last seventy years. They have been home to the country's leaders, who were variously fathers and grandfathers, bachelors and husbands. For significant periods during the past seven decades, they have also been the homes to ten children of four different prime ministers. As for 24 Sussex Drive in particular, unlike the White House in Washington, it is primarily a private family residence — not a place of work. This is an important distinction, but not one that has prevented it from becoming embroiled in politics. This chapter will explore the lives of prime ministers and their families at home, as well as while escaping Ottawa, but will focus on Sussex Drive and Harrington Lake. The only other residence that housed more than one prime minster was Laurier House, where Sir Wilfrid Laurier and Mackenzie King lived.

The importance of a place to call home is understood by all Canadians, and prime ministers and their families are no different. In looking at their lives at 24 Sussex and Harrington Lake, we see not only some of the same experiences but also the tribulations faced by those who are public figures. From plumbing and pools to closets and cooling — not to mention encounters with wildlife — life at home for prime ministers has rarely been far from the news.

Before Sussex, there was no official residence for the country's leaders, so they lived in their own private homes in various places across Ottawa. Sir John A. Macdonald's first abode was nothing to write home about, but he did so anyway. In one letter to his mother-in-law he complained about the awful smells in the house due to faulty drains. "The fact is," he wrote of the house he rented on Daly Street in Ottawa, "our drains stopped up and my study, where I do all my work, had so offensive a smell that it began to affect my health."

In 1883, Macdonald purchased Earnscliffe, a beautiful riverside three-storey home of grey limestone, located just down the street from 24 Sussex. The prime minister had rented the home on two separate occasions, in 1871 and 1882, before finally purchasing it for $10,400. It was actually Macdonald who had suggested the name Earnscliffe to the home's original owner, "Earn" being an old Scottish name for eagle. The Macdonalds made Earnscliffe into a wonderful family home, which included a second-floor viewing area for his daughter, Mary, who suffered from hydrocephalus, so that she could observe the goings-on in the house. It also contained an office for the PM. Today, the home serves as the residence of the British high commissioner, much to the chagrin of those who wish that such an important piece of history were still in the hands of Canadians.

Apart from Sussex Drive, the most famous residence of a Canadian prime minister is Laurier House. Sir Wilfrid and Lady Laurier lived there from 1897 (Laurier was PM from 1896 to 1911) until the prime minister's death in 1919. Two years later, after Lady Laurier died, the house was bequeathed to the new prime minister, William Lyon Mackenzie King, who conducted a series of renovations, including the installation of an elevator to the third floor. While the twenty-room house still carries the name of the country's first francophone PM, Laurier House today is far more associated with King than Sir Wilfrid. It was here that King began his day in his third-floor office. It was here that he held seances and rapped the table to speak to the dead. Laurier House was very much like an official residence for the bachelor prime minister, who worked long hours there before and after sittings of the House; it was also where he entertained numerous guests, both official and private. King's refuge from work took place at his country estate known as Kingsmere, located in the Gatineau Hills, just across the Ottawa River in Quebec. This was a beloved sanctuary for him, and as we shall soon see, escaping from Ottawa was a requirement for all who were prime minister.

King's long tenure in office was interrupted by a brief interregnum when R.B. Bennett held office. He was one of the wealthiest men ever to serve as PM, but he didn't own a home in Ottawa. Instead, he took out a seven-room, five-thousand-square-foot suite at the iconic Château Laurier. The hotel was once dubbed the "Third Parliament" because of the number of important decisions made there throughout Canadian history.[2] The hotel had always been home to a number of MPs and senators, but only one prime minister, though Pierre Trudeau lived there from 1965 to 1968 when he was a member of Lester Pearson's Cabinet. Bennett enjoyed hotel-prepared meals and the short walk to his Parliament Hill office, his only form of exercise.

King, on the other hand, was fortunate to have benefactors who helped him afford his home in Ottawa. "Had it not been for the generosity of friends who helped me to furnish Laurier House, I doubt very much whether I would have been in a position to occupy it," he told the House of Commons in 1948. It was in this final parliamentary speech of King's that he advocated for the establishment of a permanent residence for the prime minister. "Ours is one of the few countries in the world where that has not been done," he noted. "The obligations are very great indeed upon the individual who holds the high office of prime minister of his country," King said. He felt that relieving the prime minister of the financial obligation of finding suitable housing was necessary to allow him to do the job well. "The state should seek to make the leader of its government independent of considerations of the kind, that he may give his whole time and thought and energy to the discharge of his public duties in the largest way possible."

Few would disagree. The Canadian government had already expropriated the home that would become 24 Sussex Drive in 1943 as it bought up land on the shore of the Ottawa River to prevent it from being commercialized. But its future as the home of the country's leader was far from certain. In fact, Prime Minister Louis St. Laurent regularly received correspondence with offers of homes for sale that might serve as the official residence.

"I should consider it a great honour indeed to have my home, but twenty years old, occupied by Canada's prime ministers.... Government valuators would, I think, find my idea of price fair and reasonable," wrote the resident of 725 Acacia Avenue, in the posh neighbourhood of Rockcliffe Park. St. Laurent gave the offer some consideration, but like most prime ministers who succeeded him, he was not keen to get too involved. "I am very reluctant, however, to make the solution of my personal housing problem one of the first preoccupations of the prime minister and the government after the election," he wrote in his reply of August 5, 1949.

In 1950, the decision was made to turn 24 Sussex Street, as it was then known, into a permanent residence for Canada's prime ministers. At the time, the expropriated home belonged to Gordon Edwards, the nephew of the prominent lumbering family headed by William Cameron Edwards. The nephew had also been an MP from 1926 to 1930 and under the conditions of the expropriation was permitted to live in the home until he died. When Gordon Edwards passed away in 1946, the government was free to do what it wanted with the property. In 1946–47 it briefly served as the location of the Australian High Commission.

Extensive renovations began that dramatically changed the appearance of the home, both inside and out. Similar to the debates about what to do with 24 Sussex today, this was not without controversy. Speaking in the House in 1950, M.J. Coldwell, leader of the CCF (Co-operative Commonwealth Federation, now known as the NDP), said,

> [T]he government would be well advised to build a new house, with modern conveniences, and perhaps more suitable for the purpose in mind, instead of reconditioning or rebuilding the interior of an old house. I think a mistake was made in not demolishing the old house and building something more in keeping with the purse-strings of future prime ministers of this country and perhaps even the present prime minister of Canada.

With 24 Sussex slated to be the PM's new home, Canadians began writing to St. Laurent with suggestions for what the house should be called. "The name 'LAURENTIAN HOUSE' would be my choice," wrote Dorothy S. Sharpe from Toronto.

> With the beautiful Laurentian Mountains in the background of Parliament Hill, they being typically

Canadian, then part of your name being 'Laurent' and you belong to all the peoples of Canada (this was undoubtedly proven in the last election) what name would be more appropriate than 'LAURENTIAN HOUSE' for the first residence of the prime minister of Canada and his gracious Lady.

Another correspondent suggested "Premier House" for the name. "Premier is a prose word of poetical tone, one which is familiar alike to French and English. The combined words carry our traditional two languages.… Simple, easy of enunciation, easily understandable to Canadians and strangers to our country."

Of course, 24 Sussex already had a name: "Gorffwysfa." The original owner, lumber baron Joseph Merrill Currier, had the home built as a wedding gift for his third wife, Hannah, giving it the Welsh name for "place of peace." A 1949 letter to the editor of the *Edmonton Journal* extolled the virtues of the word. "Gorffwysfa" means more than haven of rest, it said. "It means supreme place of rest, a place of retreat for meditation, a sanctuary of the soul," and for our prime minister it would be a "respite from the soul-withering pains" of politics. "As Mr. St. Laurent goes into his inner sanctum for surcease from the commercialisms of the day," the letter continued, "I will suggest that he whisper 'Gorphwysfa' to himself several times, and it will raise him to the spiritual realm of peace and *gorfeledd* [exultation], and to the full realization of his position as prime minister of our great Canada. Heaven help him if he tries this with 24 Sussex Street."

No official name would end up being attached to 24 Sussex, though it has often gone simply by its number, "24," much as 10 Downing Street in London, the home of the British prime minister, gets called "Number 10."

Letters from the public, newspaper editorials, and remarks in the House of Commons all revealed a great deal of support for the idea of a prime minister having an official residence. The impeccable character and ordinary nature of the St. Laurents, the first occupants of "24," had something to do with the charitable reception. "There is much about life in the official home of the prime minister that suggests the head of the country and his wife live pretty much as do any other Canadian married couple," said one magazine article, which also noted the separate bedrooms for the prime minister and Mrs. St. Laurent. "Both like to read in bed and have lamps attached," it remarked in 1950s modesty.

The fact that St. Laurent insisted on paying $5,000 (approximately $50,000 in 2017) rent probably didn't hurt either, this at a time when the PM's salary was $15,000 (approximately $150,000 in 2017). This $5,000 rent was the law until 1971. Some scoffed at the idea of the country's leader having to pay any sum at all. "Are we that cheap that we must have our pound of flesh from the already inadequate salaries that we pay our prime ministers? I beg you, let us show a little generosity in this matter," intoned a 1951 letter to St. Laurent.

"When Parliament voted in 1950 to provide an official residence for Canadian prime ministers, it wanted them housed in suitable dignity," wrote John Bird in the *Toronto Star* in 1959. "That has been effected and Canada can be proud of No. 24 as it is now run. But we cannot be proud of the cheap-skate rider in the law by which our prime ministers are charged $5,000 for rent and food. Parliament should correct this cheap and silly business, forthwith."

The St. Laurents ruffled no feathers during their stay at 24 Sussex and their decorating was modest — what one journalist referred to as "eclectic blandness, much like a shop window at Eaton's College Street, circa 1948."[3] Perhaps the most exciting thing to happen there during their stay was the prime minister's seventieth birthday party, a surprise affair that moved the PM to tears.

The scene was not much different later in the decade when John and Olive Diefenbaker moved in. Some rooms changed colour, from red to Tory blue; Diefenbaker kept a stuffed moose head mounted on the wall in the basement; there were plenty of books about Winston Churchill in the library; and many of the fireplaces were plugged up to prevent drafts. Over the mantle in his bedroom hung a tartan blanket. Dief's bedroom featured piles of books and stacked reports, reflecting his somewhat disorganized approach to work. There was a large television and sun lamp. "It was here, with the prime minister reading as he leaned against the leather backboard of his bed while Olive sat nearby knitting or doing petit point, that the Diefenbakers spent some of their happiest hours," wrote Peter C. Newman in *Renegade in Power*.

John Diefenbaker did make one significant addition to the prime minister's residence, a change that involved much more than a new coat of paint, however. He had a bomb shelter constructed at 24 Sussex. It was no secret. "As prime minister, I occupy a house on Sussex Street," he told the House of Commons in 1961. "It was suggested to me that we should have a shelter there — a shelter really protective to the 'nth' degree. That is where I shall be when and if war should come."

It was the height of the Cold War and Canadians were encouraged to be prepared by the Emergency Measures Organization, a government agency established in 1959. The organization (now Public Safety Canada) was responsible for civil training in the case of an emergency and encouraged Canadians to build their own nuclear fallout shelters in their backyards. Not many did so, due to the costs, but the organization published a pamphlet called *11 Steps to Survival*. The threat of nuclear annihilation was a clear and present danger. In 1959 the Diefenbaker government also secretly approved the construction of a nuclear fallout bunker — later nicknamed the "Diefenbunker" — almost forty kilometres from Parliament Hill. It was built large enough to house key members of the government and military for thirty days. Decommissioned in 1994, it now operates as a Cold War museum.

Diefenbaker used the construction of the bomb shelter to further burnish his populist credibility: "That is where I shall stay, and we have there now a basement shelter identical with the one we have asked Canadians to put in their own homes. There is not one bit of difference between that and the one we suggest for others, excepting that this is to accommodate the staff as well as my wife and myself. It covers those in the building. That is where we shall be."

What was that shelter like? Kay Kritzwiser of the *Globe and Mail* found out when she visited Olive Diefenbaker for a tour of 24 Sussex in 1962.

And what after all does one say of fallout shelters? Admire? Enthuse? Or merely look …?

The shelter walls are pink. Cheerful at least. It has room for ten persons, the prime minister, his wife, and their staff; ledges to let down to hold air mattresses; an auxiliary light plant; a telephone; cartons filled with heavy soled rubber boots, and cupboards stocked with tins of meat balls and spaghetti, pork and beans. Instructions in the government handbook on shelters were followed and a minimum outlay of money was sanctioned by the Diefenbakers.

In one wall, a panel lifts off. It is wide enough for a man to crawl through. Inside the gloom, a timeless grey rock juts up, part of the foundation on which the house was built. There is room around the rock for hapless humans to crouch.

Seven months after the *Globe's* visit to the Sussex Drive bomb shelter, the world wondered just how much they might need one when the United States discovered missiles had been placed on Cuba. The resulting drama, known as the Cuban Missile Crisis, brought the world to the brink of nuclear war before President John F. Kennedy and Soviet leader Nikita Khrushchev were able to work out a back channel agreement.

Diefenbaker's successor as prime minister, Lester Pearson — along with his wife, Maryon — were the first occupants of Sussex Drive to make significant changes to the residence of a personal nature. The Pearsons lived there from 1963 to 1968. During that time they had a back porch winterized, allowing for year-round access to the magnificent views of the Ottawa River, often cited as the greatest feature of the house. This is the same porch that CBC comedian Rick Mercer famously insulated with plastic wrap in a do-it-yourself home repair with Prime Minister Paul Martin in 2004. "It gets a little drafty here in wintertime," Martin admitted before the two headed to Canadian Tire to get supplies.[4]

In 1966, Maryon Pearson earned much praise for her efforts to promote Canadian furnishings as the country's centennial year approached.

She spent two years looking for suitable and representative Canadian antique furniture and decorations to be on display at 24 Sussex in what would come to be known as the "Canadiana Room." The work of Mrs. Pearson earned plaudits from the *Globe and Mail* when it wrote in an editorial that the country was "well-served by Mrs. Pearson's enterprise and taste."[5] The rest of the house was dotted with paintings by Canadian artists such as Joseph Plaskett, David Milne, Emily Carr, Pegi Nichol MacLeod, Paul-Émile Borduas, and Lawren Harris. "I enjoy decorating very much," Pearson said in a television interview from 24 Sussex, "especially when I don't have to pay for it."[6] A slightly different philosophy from the St. Laurents, who insisted on paying rent, and Olive Diefenbaker, who made her own curtains for Sussex Drive.

Together, the St. Laurents, Diefenbakers, and Pearsons established a conservative and uncontroversial life for the official residence of the country's prime ministers.* As one reporter put it: "In brief, 24 Sussex and its inhabitants seemed a lot like home. Maybe not your grandmother's home in Owen Sound but the house of your mother's glamorous sister who'd married the naval commodore and learned a thing or two about quenelles and blanc de blanc[s]."[7]

That would all come to a flamboyant end when Prime Minister Pierre Trudeau moved into the official residence in 1968 after taking over the leadership of the Liberal party and winning the ensuing election. Not long after, reported the *Globe and Mail*, Trudeau "turned Mrs. Pearson's Canadiana room in the basement into a go-go palace with long-haired musicians and revolving lights." Trudeau was putting the "sex" in Sussex. Guests at one 1968 party "frugged" the night away.

"Let's shake it up," the PM said, when one visitor asked him to dance.[8]

Just as the age during which Pierre Trudeau governed changed the world, Trudeau would transform "24" like no other prime minister in

---

* John Diefenbaker once famously served coffee at a reception for two hundred MPs, senators, and members of the press gallery. "Dry receptions are almost unheard of in official and diplomatic circles here," groused the *Globe and Mail*. Cabinet minister George Hees knew better. He brought his own booze to spike the lemonade whenever he came to 24 Sussex.

Canadian history. Arriving with just two suitcases and a 1960 Mercedes 300 SL coupe, the bachelor PM had never owned a home in his life. "When I lose this job as prime minister, I have nowhere to move my goods and chattels to," he told one writer. The previous three occupants of Sussex had either been grandparents or the age of grandparents, but Trudeau would become the first prime minister to raise children at the official residence and truly make it into a family home. He — along with his wife, Margaret — would not only modernize and update the house, but would also engender considerable controversy as a result of their lavish spending. Ultimately, it was the beginning of a long, slow decline for "Gorffwysfa."*

After the 1972 election, Trudeau gave Margaret the green light for a major renovation of the official residence, a task she approached with "gusto." "Hideous" and "shabby" was how she described 24 Sussex in her sensational 1979 memoir *Beyond Reason*. "There was nothing to be proud of in this dim, gloomy establishment." The servants' quarters were redone, new china was purchased, new linens, furniture, and much more. Room by room, she redecorated the residence, introducing a great many changes, including an orange-red wallpaper in the dining room. Some of this was undone by Maureen McTeer when she and Joe Clark moved into 24 Sussex in 1979, changes Margaret Trudeau would later describe as the "rape and pillage" of the home.[9] But the expenses incurred during the Trudeau years caught attention. Between 1979 and 1983, when Trudeau had lived at both Stornoway, the official residence of the leader of the Opposition, and at Sussex, it was estimated that $365,000 was spent on the two homes. In 1984, just as the Mulroneys were moving in, Roy MacGregor wrote in the *Toronto Star* that "compared to Pierre and Margaret Trudeau and their whims, the Mulroneys seem like those strange people who save their empty milk bags."[10]

But the renovations carried out by Margaret would pale in comparison to the hullabaloo caused by Trudeau's decision that he needed a pool at 24 Sussex Drive. The issue took on a life of its own both in the press and in the House of Commons. The push for a private prime ministerial swimming hole began in 1972 when Trudeau told

---

* Margaret Trudeau chafed under the restrictions of life at Sussex and would later refer to it as "the crown jewel of the federal penitentiary system."

aides he needed a pool. Alarmed, they enlisted Keith Davey to try to talk the PM out of this, as it did not mesh with the message of austerity being preached to Canadians.* This was the early 1970s and the Canadian economy left many in difficult circumstances, a period marked by "stagflation" — a period of high unemployment and inflation. Building an expensive pool was bound to cause problems. "Keith, you have often told me I'm the meal ticket for this party," Trudeau told Davey when approached. "Well, what would you say if I told you that your meal ticket considered the swimming pool a biological necessity?"

Trudeau did like to swim and had been making do by taking his lengths in the pool of the Château Laurier. Since Davey could not talk the PM out of getting one for 24 Sussex, he decided to try to get a doctor who would provide political cover by declaring that a pool was necessary for the health and well-being of the prime minister. Famous Montreal neurologist Dr. Wilder Penfield was approached, but this got bogged down by the good doctor's discussions about what was meant by "biological necessity." Dr. W.H. Fader of Toronto stepped up to lead the cause for the pool and news stories from 1974 announcing the plan highlighted the physical fitness benefits for the PM, as well as for future prime ministers. Noting that President Gerald Ford had reinstalled the pool taken out by Richard Nixon at the White House, Dr. Fader said, "I thought the prime minister of this country should have this sort of thing."[11]

Initially, no one got too vexed over the pool. Costs were estimated to be anywhere from $30,000 to $45,000 (about $140,000 to $210,000 in 2017). The *Globe and Mail*, in a lighthearted editorial, noted that Trudeau "will probably make good use of this splendid new facility" and that "the swimming pool which is now being added to 24 Sussex Drive should help give Canada what it really needs: a fit leader." The double entendre was clearly intended. The editorial also alluded to the Ford-Nixon reversal, writing, "When we don't have Pierre Trudeau to kick around anymore (he has been known to go off at the deep end *without* a pool), we trust his successor will still have this way of keeping in shape."[12]

---

* Historian Michael Bliss once wrote: "If Mackenzie King had been a swimmer, he too might have appreciated such a favour. Robert Borden, I think, would have turned it down."

The construction of an indoor pool for the prime minister during an era of fiscal restraint was too powerful a symbol for opposition MPs to ignore. The cause was taken up with zeal by noted parliamentary disruptor Tom Cossitt, a former Liberal MP turned Tory. He regularly raised the issue of the pool. Trudeau dismissed the critiques with typical disdain, telling the House, "I feel the Hon. Member for Leeds especially will be proud when I win a gold medal for swimming."

Cossitt took issue and retorted that, "I am sure that all Hon. Members of the House will wish the prime minister well in his quest for a gold medal because it at least shows that he is trying to do something as prime minister."

Debate only degenerated from there, as Cossitt continued to press the issue about making public the list of people who donated funds toward the construction of the pool. "The prime minister has now shown the reason for his haste in acquiring the pool, and surely the House can expect similar haste in making clear the list of donors, the amounts donated. "

> **Trudeau:** Mr. Speaker, I do understand the interest of the Hon. Member, and I can understand his interest in investigating the matter. Perhaps the best way to reassure him is to say that if I am interested in a medal for swimming, he might be interested in a medal for diving, and I would invite him over to be the first to dive. He could even come before the water is in the pool.
> **Some Hon. Members:** Oh, oh!
> **Some Hon. Members:** Hear, hear!
> **Mr. Cossitt:** On a point of order, may I just say this: I would like to assure the prime minister that I could never equal his feat of walking on the water.

Trudeau's infamous pool would open five months later and, evidently, without too much concern for public approbation since the media was invited for a pre-splash inspection. Or perhaps this was an attempt to show that this was the people's pool. The costs had soared to more than $200,000, (more than $860,000 in 2017), largely as a result of having to blast through rock on the property to build both the fifty-foot carpeted tunnel from the residence and a cedar pool house, which included a small kitchenette, sauna, and a glassed-in lounge looking out to the backyard. This was more than a pool.

Despite the controversy over the funding and the price tag, the addition was a big hit. When Prime Minister Joe Clark hosted a reception after the funeral of John Diefenbaker in 1979, no one cared about the decor in 24 Sussex itself; the guests all wanted to see the pool.[13] Clark was not a swimmer and did not make much use of it, but subsequent prime ministers and their children enjoyed the space.* The Trudeau children spent many moments having swim time with "Daddy," which was to take place precisely after the prime minister finished the last of his forty-four lengths in the pool. Princess Diana also used it to get some private exercise during a 1983 royal visit.

Indeed, the Trudeau years transformed 24 Sussex from an official residence into what was really a family home. For twenty-two years, beginning with the birth of Justin Trudeau in 1971, until the Mulroneys and their four children moved out in 1993, Sussex was filled with birthday parties, Halloween trick-or-treating, and epic games of hide-and-go-seek. Jean Chrétien often had his young grandchildren over for important dinners, many of which featured such delicacies as hot dogs. Maintaining that sense of family was essential for the young children who grew up at 24, as well as for the mental health of the PM who was juggling his demanding job as a father along with the duties of being prime minister. The children of Pierre Trudeau, Joe Clark, Brian Mulroney, and, later, Stephen Harper were all very young (all of Trudeau's children, plus one of Mulroney's, were born while they were in office) and that made a tangible difference at the official residence.** "I do actually think that there is something about the youthfulness of children in a house like 24 Sussex or at Harrington [Lake] where they actually change the atmosphere," said Bonnie Brownlee, who worked for Mila Mulroney during the years the family lived there.[14]

---

* On the campaign trail in 1984, Brian Mulroney teased crowds about coming for a swim at the pool after the election. "All you need is a towel," he'd tell the party faithful.
** It was said that there was no meeting — whether it was with the President of the United States or with a member of the Royal Family — in which Mark Mulroney would not find some way of entering.

If life was fun and family oriented inside Sussex Drive under the Trudeaus and Mulroneys, it was quite the opposite outside the home, as the media continued to have a field day with the ongoing drama of the costs associated with renovations, upkeep, living expenses, and decorating. Access to information requests (David Vienneau of the *Toronto Star* and public information advocate Ken Rubin were particularly irksome to the Mulroney PMO) became a staple for some reporters who seemed simply to be looking to satisfy what Brian Mulroney described as the media's "well-known proclivity for items of titillation."[15] The Mulroneys were victimized by this more than any others, as the media wrote petty stories about the size of their shoe closets, the cost of the wallpaper (well, it was $100 per roll) and the prime minister's preference for Gucci loafers. It all seems a bit excessive looking back.*

The tendency of the media to publicize any spending on Sussex meant prime ministers were afraid to be seen as agreeing to the expenditure. When John Turner moved into 24 Sussex Drive in 1984, he was so concerned about its state that he commissioned a report to examine what needed to be done. The engineering firm that reviewed Sussex found that it needed $600,000 worth of repairs, saying that the home was in a "grave state of disrepair." With the political climate against any kind of large spending on prime ministerial perquisites, Mulroney would assent to only $100,000 of essential repairs. "We just couldn't go along with it," Mulroney said, "so the repairs have been kept to a minimum."[16] The media were more fascinated to know if a satellite dish purchased for Harrington Lake or a hot tub for Sussex Drive were paid for out the of the public purse than they were concerned about the withering official residence of the prime minister.

The issue became a concern at the highest level of Mulroney's PMO. In 1987, Jean Pigott, head of the National Capital Commission, overseeing the official residences, sent a confidential memo to Mulroney's chief of staff, Derek Burney, with the outline of a proposed op-ed titled "Perks or Prerequisites?" in which she planned to defend the expenditures on Sussex and official residences. Pigott wrote to Burney, saying, "Any suggestions, comments, or ideas as to the handling of this from your office would be much appreciated."[17]

---

* Mulroney was a favoured target. Journalist Val Ross was once told the PM was drinking club soda. "It'll be Perrier in my piece," he retorted.

The response from Mulroney's director of communications, Bruce Phillips, reveals how sensitive the issue was. He wrote back to Pigott, saying that the language needed to be toned down. "I feel it needs to be written to make it a more factual, less argumentative document. The document should be as flat and unemotional as possible."[18]

Given all of that, it's no wonder prime ministers have been shy about spending to keep Sussex in good shape. Successive prime ministers simply kicked the can down the road. Jean Chrétien agreed to get the roof redone in 1998 — largely because that year's ice storm made the repairs not only understandable but also impossible to avoid — but that was it. Paul Martin was afraid to do anything, telling *Maclean's* magazine in 2004, "Basically my life is, I come home at night, I go to bed, I get up in the morning and go to work. The house has a lot of character, and I don't notice anything else about it."[19] Stephen Harper took a similar tack. He was asked to delay his move in to Sussex in 2006 so essential repairs could be done, but he refused.

The house continued to deteriorate and was becoming a national joke. A 2008 auditor general's report indicated that 24 Sussex needed at least $10 million worth of repairs. No extensive work had been conducted on the house since it was originally renovated by the government before Louis St. Laurent moved in. "It is therefore not surprising to note that a number of the residence's systems are reaching the end of their useful lives, are in poor condition, and will have to be replaced in the near future."[20]

How bad was it?

> The house was wired for electricity some fifty years ago, and the electrical system is operating at nearly maximum capacity. It cannot meet increases in demand or new operational requirements. The plumbing system is deficient. This building, which functions as a reception area for distinguished national and international guests, does not have universal access for persons with reduced mobility. The service elevator dates back to the 1950s and cannot accommodate modern wheelchairs. Service areas such as the kitchen and the

basement laundry are not functional.... The only element of the exterior at 24 Sussex that is in good condition is the roof, which was re-done in 1998. The
other elements are in poor or fair condition.[21]

But did this finally get the prime minister to move out so the official residence could be fixed? No. "The Prime Minister and his family
find the home adequate to their needs," said Stephen Harper's spokes-
man Andrew MacDougall.[22]

Prime ministers from Pierre Trudeau to Stephen Harper all share
responsibility for allowing 24 Sussex to degenerate to its current state.
"We all made mistakes," Jean Chrétien admitted to me in a 2017 interview in his Ottawa office. In a misguided attempt to appear prudent
with taxpayers' money, or in an effort to look like ordinary folk, the
house has been allowed "to become a home only a raccoon could love,"
as a 2018 *Globe and Mail* editorial noted. "Meanwhile, an important
and historic Canadian public building continues to moulder."

But the media's picayune reporting must also bear much of the
responsibility; afterall, it was their "gotcha" journalism, writing about
expenses as though high crimes were being committed, that skewed the
debate. "I should have let the media come in to take pictures of the buck-
ets filled with water from the leaking roof," Chrétien recounted.[23] These
stories boxed the prime ministers into very difficult positions. Sussex
Drive was in such bad condition that when Justin Trudeau became
prime minster in 2015 he decided not to move in to the home in which
he grew up (though his family has made use of the infamous pool).
Instead, his family moved into Rideau Cottage, located on the grounds
of Rideau Hall, the home of the governor general. Sussex had become
uninhabitable. Anne Kingston of *Maclean's* magazine put it well: "24
Sussex has become Canada's *The Picture of Dorian Gray* — invisibly fall-
ing into disrepair while the facade never changes in photo ops."

The future of the home remains unclear. In the Byzantine world
of bureaucratic Ottawa, the RCMP, the NCC, and the federal

government all have a role to play in determining what happens. Without clear leadership from the top, nothing will. But a 2017 report from the National Capital Commission, *The Plan for Canada's Capital, 2017–2067*, called 24 Sussex Drive a first priority and indicated that the NCC would "renew and transform the prime minister of Canada's official residence." At the time of the publication of this book the home was still occupied to staff RCMP who are securing the home. Just keeping the lights on costs money. From November 2015 to March 2016 — a five-month span — $180,000 was spent to keep 24 Sussex operational.

If 24 Sussex Drive seems to have been far from a "place of peace" or rest, Canada's prime ministers could always escape to take solace in what Brian Mulroney called "the only real perk of being prime minister": Harrington Lake. The cottage was built in 1925. During the late 1950s, Major General Howard Kennedy, who was chairman of what was then known as the Federal District Commission, supported the idea of making Harrington a prime ministerial retreat. The problem was that John Diefenbaker had to be convinced of the merits of such an idea. Kennedy knew the best way to do this was to take the Chief fishing, engaging him in his favourite pastime. History shows that Diefenbaker caught one, and as Maureen McTeer, the wife of Prime Minister Joe Clark, wrote in her history of Canada's official residences, "I will be forever grateful to that unknowing trout on the end of Mr. Diefenbaker's fishing line."[24]

Diefenbaker and his wife, Olive, quickly came to love Harrington, as have all subsequent prime ministers. He was aware, however, as St. Laurent was about 24 Sussex, that people might object to the country retreat. "I suppose there will be some criticisms, but as it is not being used to any extent and was to be the prime minister's summer home I cannot see how there can any objection," he noted in a letter to his mother. "The only reason it was not used by Mr. St. Laurent was that he preferred to be close to his home in Quebec City."

Diefenbaker spent some of his most relaxing moments at Harrington Lake (the lake is also known as Lac Mousseau) throughout his time as prime minister, and, for someone who loved to fish, as he did, it was an idyllic spot. After his first visit there in 1958, he called it "the most restful day and a half that I have spent in over a year and a half." He continued in his letter to his mother: "I went fishing and caught four speckled trout. I have never tasted anything better than those trout. They weighed from 1 ¼ to well over 2 lbs. and you may be sure I will be out fishing a great deal during the summer." Even the blackflies were forgotten. "I didn't feel [them] because I was so interested in the fish!"

Two decades later, in 1975, Harrington Lake and those fish would cause a significant row between Prime Minister Pierre Trudeau and Diefenbaker, ending up on the front pages. In a House of Commons speech, Trudeau accused the Chief of making "the largest land grab when he was in office that was ever made by a private citizen of Canada. He did so when he decided that Harrington Lake and the building on it should be the country residence of the prime minister.... He was adding thousands of acres of land for his private enjoyment."

None of this was true. But Trudeau went on: "The Right Hon. gentleman for Prince Albert liked fishing and had Harrington Lake stocked at public expense with fish for his enjoyment.... That was a shameful incident." It was also a classic example of the pot calling the kettle black.

Diefenbaker was not amused and raised the matter as a point of privilege in the House. In his defence, he noted that while *he* did not stock Harrington Lake, in 1967 it was populated with eight thousand speckled trout, five hundred Atlantic salmon, and, a year later, three thousand rainbow trout. Trudeau finally withdrew his remarks accusing Diefenbaker of stocking the lake, but not before needling the thin-skinned Chief: "I certainly understand now why the right honourable gentleman was not such a great fisherman when he did not have the number of fish I thought he had in the lake."

Country retreats for the prime minister did not begin with Harrington Lake. Not surprisingly, previous heads of government knew the value of getting away from the intensity of political life in Ottawa. Robert

Borden loved to escape to Echo Beach in Muskoka to fish; between 1873 and 1890, John A. Macdonald regularly went to Rivière du Loup, Quebec, on the south shore of the St. Lawrence River to relax in an area popular at the time among the Anglo elite. It was the same place Louis St. Laurent used to escape to fish and relax with his extended family and served the same purpose as Harrington Lake would for future prime ministers.

The best-known pre–Harrington Lake retreat was the one built by Mackenzie King, beginning in 1901, when he purchased three acres of land near Kingsmere Lake, the body of water that gave the property its name. Located in Chelsea, Quebec, about twenty kilometres north of Ottawa, Kingsmere was King's pride and joy, his sacred escape from the stress of being prime minister. "I view it as insurance against fatigue and impaired health. I really need some place to come to at week-ends, and when I want to be absolutely free of interruptions." Eventually, his property would grow to five hundred acres as King slowly accumulated more land when it became available, looking upon it as his principal investment and something to bequeath to Canada as a "thank offering."[25]

Like prime ministers after him, King was weary of being accused of living a life of luxury — he disliked references to Kingsmere as an "estate" — and felt his place was modest. "There is no air of royal magnificence here, no Hollywood swimming pools, no mahogany bars, no model barns filled with prize-winning Holsteins," wrote *Maclean's* magazine in a profile of the property in 1951, following King's death the previous year.[26]

What the property became known for, however, was King's accumulation of "ruins," his collection of cast-off pieces from various historic homes and buildings, including one from Westminster Hall in London. After the May 10, 1940, bombing of London — part of the German Blitz — Lester B. Pearson, the first secretary at the High Commission, received a telegram marked, "Secret and Most Immediate." Inside was a request from the prime minister for a stone or two from the rubble of Westminster. Pearson understandably worried about the insensitive request, figuring the Office of Works in London "might take a jaundiced view of a suggestion to find, pack, and ship some shattered stones to gratify a prime minister across the Atlantic."

But the request was honoured and King had his treasures sent across the ocean, safely skirting the fleet of German submarines in the Atlantic.

These became the focal point for his walks around the property, which he particularly enjoyed at night when they reflected a ghost-like quality. It was here, as well, where King buried Pat, the first of his beloved Irish terriers. The ruins remain a popular spot for pictures when tourists come to visit the estate, which is now part of the federally administered Gatineau Park.

When in Gatineau, King spent most of his time at two cottages he owned: Moorside and The Farm, the latter of which is now the home to the Speaker of the House of Commons. The cabins are situated in a heavily wooded area, and the prime minister occasionally had visits from bears, especially those who became interested in the honey produced by King's bees. Making matters worse, in 1946 some members of the Soviet embassy rented a cottage not far from his property. Its occupants regularly fed the bears. With the animals making more visits for honey and destroying his apiary, King feared that eventually someone might get mauled by one of the bears, so he had his beekeeper set a trap. Later, he heard a gunshot. "Pat and I looked out of the window together. Sure enough, down near the beehives, I saw the cars of men who had come out evidently to finish Mr. Bruin for his thievery. He had come back for the third time. In the meantime, the trap had effectively been set and his days were ended." King was fascinated by the kill and wanted to see it up close. "The men said it was about one year old. Would weigh I should think between 100 and 150 lbs. A beautiful young black bear. I patted his fur, which was as clear and clean as if brushed this morning. I felt … sorry to see the little fellow deprived of his life, but felt the act was justified when he entered on his path of aggression. He has succeeded in destroying one hive." King seems to have overreacted, which is a little strange given his love of his own dog. Attitudes toward wildlife were not what they are today, and without a prying media, there was little to worry about.

Bears and bees aside, there was a tranquility to Kingsmere. It provided King moments of reflection, solitude, and opportunities to be around nature, essential ingredients to recharging the batteries of a prime minister, a point not lost on the man who helped King get those ruins.

Pearson was a life-long lover of the area and had his own cottage in Burnett, eleven kilometres down the highway from Wakefield, Quebec, where his final resting place is. Given his family history in the region, it is not surprising that Harrington Lake became a significant and treasured part of his life while prime minister. He spent a great deal of time there, relaxing, having occasional Cabinet meetings, fishing, or recovering from illness. Less than a month after he became PM in 1963, he and his wife, Maryon, were already up at the cottage. His comments about the retreat speak to its importance: "I have abandoned the idyllic charms of Harrington Lake for the less idyllic burners of government," he wrote after his first visit in 1963, "but not, I hope, for long because that cottage, the peace, the water and the co-operative fish, is going to be a life saver."

The cottage became central to bringing together the extended Pearson family, including his grandchildren.* He was "a veritable pied-piper," recalled his daughter-in-law, Landon Pearson. "He would gather however many of them happened to be there in the morning, and, clutching his walking stick, march them off into the woods.... Or else he would take them fishing." Out on the lake with his grandchildren, the prime minister named different bays after them. "Grand-daddy had this remarkable ability to make me feel so special,"[27] recalled one grandchild years later.

The extended Pearson family skated on the frozen lake in winter, tobogganed, screamed around on a snowmobile, or were entertained by the PM who, on one New Year's Eve at Harrington, wearing his maple leaf tartan jacket, danced around with a stuffed sealskin Ookpik (a type of owl toy crafted by Inuit) to the delight of everyone. The unguarded and amiable side of Pearson — perhaps something found in all prime ministers — was permitted to shine in the relaxing setting provided by the official country residence.

Harrington Lake was also the place where Pearson gave various flag designs their first test run as he worked toward giving the country a new, distinctive banner. Doing so angered Diefenbaker, the prime

---

* An added bonus for kids about the Harrington Lake cottage is that its size made it an ideal hide-and-seek venue, according to Landon Pearson, the prime minister's daughter-in-law.

minister's nemesis, who raised the issue in the House of Commons. "I am not asking the prime minister about the aesthetic properties of this flag," Diefenbaker thundered, referring to the so-called Pearson pennant, which featured three maple leaves in the centre, bordered by two blue bars. "What possible business of the prime minister of Canada is it to use a flag that has not been designated, and fly it over a home bought and paid for by the people of Canada as an official residence?"

Pearson, in his various answers about flying the flags at Harrington Lake, poked the bear, telling Dief that the flag "looked wonderful." Continuing, he said, "Mr. Speaker, I have received a great many models, some on nylon and some on textile, and I had the pleasure of flying some of them to see how they looked on a flag pole. I would tell my honourable friend that, in addition to looking at the flag yesterday, I also went fishing."

Harrington meant the world to every PM who retreated there. For Pierre Trudeau, Pearson's successor, it was no different, and the cottage was one of his favourite places to be. There the Trudeau family hiked, swam, snowshoed, cross-country skied, and explored as young families do. "Harrington Lake in those days was like the setting for a Hardy Boys novel, a place that begged for adventure," wrote Justin Trudeau in *Common Ground*, his memoir of his early life. "My father, to our delight, always seemed to encourage the idea."[28]

When the younger Trudeau became prime minister in 2015, he was asked about his childhood, and it was memories of time at this fabulous cottage that were paramount, touching on themes that will resonate with many Canadians.

As a kid, I used to wait all year for the summer. Like for so many Canadians, the summer meant getting out of the city and into the wilderness. It's where some of my earliest family memories were formed. It's where I got my first sense of how wild and wonderful Canada's environment can be. And more than any other place, it deepened my love of this country.…

Mom and Dad were never far away. Harrington Lake was one of their favourite places to spend time together. I cherish the memory of my brothers and I scrambling to keep up with my parents as they climbed confidently through the Gatineau Hills. Or the countless nights sitting out under the stars, gathered around the campfire, listening to my father tell us stories.

Harrington Lake is the home of many of my fondest childhood memories, and as summer finally comes around, I hope that it will become a special place for my children, too.[29]

Brian Mulroney knew the value of Harrington as well. It "brought us sanctuary in the storms and joy and freedom as a family." Every summer, the Mulroneys — like the Trudeaus before them and the Harpers after — moved the family (and their two dogs) out of Ottawa to the Gatineau Hills, where they would stay until school began again in September. Hiking, swimming, and other water sports, along with quality family time were the essential components to life at Harrington. At Christmas, the family went there again, where skating and shinny were the favoured activities (the Trudeaus enjoyed broomball). The Mulroneys entertained friends such as hockey legend Bobby Orr and music impresario David Foster at the cottage, along with political visitors such as French president Jacques Chirac. Occasionally, high-level meetings were held out there, but for the most part this was the private family escape of the prime minister. Whatever the occasion, when you walked into the Harrington Lake property it felt like a warm, family cottage because of the work Mila Mulroney put into renovating it.

Jean Chrétien made good use of Harrington Lake as a private retreat and enjoyed fishing or going out on the boat or other personal watercraft, often attempting to elude his security detail. For him, as with other prime ministers, time at the retreat provided him with a period of reflection — a walk in the woods, a casual chat with RCMP security detail — an essential component of being prime minister. In 1999, Chrétien completed a cottage of his own at Lac des Piles,

Brian Mulroney wrote that Harrington Lake, the prime minister's country retreat, "brought us sanctuary in the storms and joy and freedom as a family." He is pictured here with his son Nicholas in 1987.

Even at the relaxed surroundings of Harrington Lake, work inevitably must get done by a prime minister. Here Brian Mulroney engages in one of his favourite activities, talking on the telephone, while reviewing some documents.

Prime Minister Justin Trudeau, who grew up at 24 Sussex Drive as the son of Pierre Trudeau, chose not to move into the official residence after his 2015 election victory. Instead, he and his family live at Rideau Cottage. They have made occasional use of the pool at 24 Sussex, however.

Quebec (just over two hours northwest of Montreal), and spent more time there. His successor, Paul Martin, was more interested in spending time relaxing at his farm in Knowlton, Quebec, in the Eastern Townships, though Martin wisely approved some key repairs to spruce up the Harrington property.

When Stephen Harper took office in 2006, his family also fell in love with the cottage at Harrington and spent every summer there. "If I could retire here, this is where I would retire," he once told CTV.[30]

One of Harper's first visits to the retreat led to a funny anecdote about the power of a prime minister's words. Harper's former chief of staff, Ian Brodie, recounts the story.

> At one point Mr. Harper is sitting by the lake, [his daughter] Rachel is playing by the lake, and the lake is surrounded by big pieces of Canadian Shield rock, and [Harper] looks around and says, 'Geeze, this would be a beautiful place for a beach, if the beach was sandier, this would be a beautiful place for a beach.' One of the National Capital Commission guys was puttering around and fixing something up, and the next day the rock is gone and sand has been carted in to create a beach! I think it was the first time Mr. Harper understood that if he mused about these type of things."[31]

Maureen McTeer loved Harrington Lake and wrote about it. She and Joe Clark relaxed there with their young daughter, Catherine, when he was briefly prime minister from 1979 to 1980. So perhaps the last anecdote should involve her and her family. Once, when McTeer came across a raccoon in the kitchen at Harrington, she advised the RCMP security detail there to kill any of the annoying animals should they come across them. "About five minutes later she heard about five shotgun shots; the RCMP had taken her to heart," recounted Catherine Clark, who noted that her mother never thought the Mounties would actually do it.[32]

Today, the Trudeaus are back as Justin Trudeau and his family retrace the joys of his childhood at Harrington. Perhaps because it is outside of Ottawa and out of public view, the prime minister's country escape has rarely been criticized. Sussex Drive is a different story. It has always been in view of passersby and, as the principle residence of the prime minister, it has captured a lot more attention. Wherever a

PM spends time — whether at Sussex Drive or another residence, or out at Harrington Lake — the details of the life lived there, the view through the domestic prism, allows the emergence of a more personal and intimate portrait, one in which the guard of the prime minister is lowered, allowing us to see glimpses of our leaders usually hidden from public. It is never easy being prime minister, but looking at life at home reminds us of the human side of the job that is too often obscured by activities in the House or elsewhere.

CHAPTER 9

"THE TRUEST FRIEND I EVER HAD": PRIME MINISTERS AND THEIR PETS

I had said to Joan, 'Little Pat is all that I have of my own.' It is so true, and strange that having all in the eyes of the world as prime minister, Pat alone seems to be the one life I truly possess, the one and only real possession.
— Mackenzie King in his diary, writing about his first Irish terrier, Pat, July 12, 1941

It is July 12, 1941, and Prime Minister Mackenzie King's train has pulled into the downtown Ottawa station, completing his journey back to the nation's capital from a trip out to western Canada. In no rush, he meets a few people in the stateroom of his private railcar and enjoys his breakfast before eventually heading to Laurier House, his residence. Once there, he deals with some routine matters, such as his correspondence. He then places a telephone call to Kingsmere, his country home, where he gets a report from his butler, MacLeod, that his dog, Pat, is not doing well. King's pet of seventeen years "ha[d] been quite confused in a way, had lost his regular habits and in the last day or two had been whining quite a bit when left alone. He thought he was older and weaker." The prime minister is concerned but carries on with his day's work in Ottawa, including a visit to Rideau Hall to meet with the governor general and, later, a lunch with Malcolm MacDonald, Britain's high commissioner.

"I returned from luncheon to Laurier House, gathered papers, etc. and reached Kingsmere at 4 p.m. Just before starting, MacLeod told me that he was glad I was back. He was afraid I would be shocked by Pat's appearance, his having become considerably worse today. I wish I had not sat up so late last night and had come out to Kingsmere before beginning the morning's duties in the city." The prime minister was about to begin a two-day vigil over his "one and only real possession" that would ultimately conclude with the death of his beloved canine.

In a discussion of Canadian prime ministers and their pets, one can only begin with William Lyon Mackenzie King. From 1924, when he was given his first beloved Irish terrier, Pat, until his death in 1950, King was a steadfast dog owner, one whose love and devotion to his pets would surprise — perhaps shock — even the most ardent dog lovers in the country today. It is not every pet owner who will write more than twenty single-spaced pages chronicling the final hours of his dog. King may have been exceptional in his devotion to his dogs, but a brief look at prime ministers and their pets shows he was not alone in his attachment. Even when the connection was not so strong, the relationships between PMs and their pets not only offer us insight into the owners but also remind us that the country's prime ministers have a human side not always visible to the public.

These stories also reveal the joys and sadness that all pet owners share. Like many Canadians, prime ministers have had to euthanize loyal companions and deal with lost and disobedient dogs, but they have also shared in the pleasure provided by the unconditional love of animals. Whatever their pet — dog or cat, chinchilla or bat — our prime ministers have not faced the burdens of office completely alone. And this is an essential point — particularly for someone such as William Lyon Mackenzie King, who was a bachelor. It has been said that "it's lonely at the top"; having a pet at home brought some measure of faithful companionship.

Stories about Mackenzie King and his canines are as much a part of his image as are those of Pierre Trudeau and his canoe. When King's diaries became public, newspaper stories invariably concentrated on what was most unusual or sensational — what King wrote about his mother and his interest in spirituality. The many long and emotional entries about his dogs also attracted a lot of attention, because everyone loves a pet story. But, as we shall see, what King wrote about his pets was a little strange. A 1978 *Globe and Mail* story on the release of new diary entries referred to the contents' "painful detail" regarding King's dog.[1]

King actually had three dogs during his time as prime minister, and each of them received the same name: Pat. Pat I was given to him by his Kingsmere estate neighbours and friends the Pattesons, who had acquired an Irish terrier of their own from the same litter. Pat and the prime minister were instant friends, and King's diary is filled with references to the trials and tribulations of his "little friend, Pat." Trials and tribulations there would be.

A case in point: in 1924 there occurred an incident to which virtually all dog owners can relate. Pat went missing after not being properly supervised by his minder. King was furious — and intensely worried. "My heart aches for the little lad, poor little thing, so timid and alone," he wrote in his diary. "It has saddened me beyond words, and with my fatigue made everything seem unreal to me."

King travelled to Port Arthur and Fort William (now Thunder Bay) the next day but Pat was very much still on his mind. Thankfully, good news arrived by telegram two days after the dog first disappeared:

> I was delighted to receive a wire about 10:30 telling me little Pat had been found, all night I thought of him and was very sad and lonely because of his loss, indeed he has filled my mind and thoughts to the

exclusion of all else, even now that I know he has been found I cannot throw off the feeling of sadness which settled over me when I thought he was gone. I prayed earnestly for his recovery or being recovered last night, fearing my faith was not what I was [as] a child.

This was not the only time Pat went missing — and sometimes these wayward wanderings of the prime ministerial dog made it into the newspaper. In 1930, the *Globe* ran a small story, "Pat Back at Laurier House Before Return of Master":

> The Irish terrier was reported to have taken "French leave" of his comfy quarters at Laurier House.... Many Ottawans were keeping a sharp weather eye for the wandering canine, some prompted by the knowledge that the dog was a strong favorite with the prime minister and others by the fact a generous reward was offered for his return, when there came a scratching at the main door of Laurier House that was familiar to the servants' ears. Pat had come home.

King's concern went beyond his own dog, revealing a humanity rarely, if ever, seen in public. Blair Fraser, the legendary *Maclean's* political reporter, told a story about the time his own Irish terrier went missing. He placed an advertisement in the local paper stating the breed, dog name, and gave a telephone number.

"About 10:30 that evening," Fraser wrote, "the phone rang."

"Fraser? This is Mackenzie King speaking. Have you found your dog?"

Fraser was not 100 percent convinced it had been the PM, so he kept the story to himself. Finally, he worked up the courage and mentioned the story to one of King's secretaries, who told him, "Oh, that was the PM alright. He does that kind of thing all the time."

"Mr. King wasn't the hermit he was painted," Fraser concluded.[2]

While it may seem odd by today's cynical standards, there was no political calculation to King's dog ownership. Pat simply came into his life when the Pattesons gave the animal to him, filling a void for a lonely man who had no children and no spouse. Pat became "the truest friend [he] ever had" and that relationship lasted seventeen years. Indeed, a dog was the best kind of companion for a bachelor prime minister who enjoyed his solitude.

The pet also served as a barometer of how well King might like a visitor. Pat was present for virtually all interviews for staff that the PM conducted at home "from Cabinet ministers on down. If Pat showed any indication of wagging his tail and being friendly," recalled one aide who worked for King, "it was an indication that you were alright."

When Pat's life eventually came to an end, virtually everything stopped for the prime minister. Indeed, King actually requested the postponement of a meeting of the War Cabinet, a revelation of how important Pat was to him but something to which C.P. Stacey took issue, writing that "the most extraordinary thing about this maudlin and, I fear one must say, rather repulsive record is that it was set down by the prime minister of a country engaged in a desperate war."

The dog was, essentially, his family. All of this transpired in July 1941, and the diary entries in which King chronicled the final two days of Pat's life are head-scratching in their detail and expressions of devotion to a pet that he said "saved his soul." A quick look at a sampling of what one might call King's "dog diaries" is revealing. The PM referred to this recording of events as "one of the most significant and valuable of all I have."

Monday & Tuesday, July 14 & 15, 1941

I sang more hymns, held him to me, his little body warm, legs not cold, his little heart got very weak, almost imperceptible.... When I turned on the light he lay there like a dog that had just taken a great leap — forefeet together outward, hind legs together, stretched back as far as they would go, his body in a straight line — a noble creature. He had bounded in one long leap across the chasm which all men call death. My little friend, the truest friend I ever had — or man ever had — had gone to be with Derry [the dog from his litter owned by King's neighbours] and the other loved ones. I had given him messages of love to

William Lyon Mackenzie King was a devoted dog owner. All three of his Irish terriers were named Pat. The bachelor–prime minister said of the first Pat that he was "the truest friend I ever had." The dog died at age seventeen.

> take to father, mother, Bell, Max, Sir Wilfrid & Lady
> Laurier, Mr. and Mrs. Larkin, & the grand-parents.

When Pat passed away, journalist and early King biographer Bruce Hutchison filed a story in the *Victoria Times*, writing that the canine pet "was a more familiar figure in Ottawa than many politicians and, I fancy, knew a great deal more. He had better opportunities, of course.

When you sat at Mr. King's table in Laurier House, with candles throwing shadows on the portrait of Sir Wilfrid and his lady, old Pat always lay under the table, on your foot, one eye open." Laurier House would be a "lonely, gloomy place without him," Hutchison wrote.[3]

In politics, pets have a well-known ability to soften the image of a person, and with King, when you get past the rather strange devotion he had to his dog, as noted in his diary, this was certainly the case. One illustration of this occurred in a speech he gave to the Canadian Association of Broadcasters in 1944. In recognition of his twenty-fifth anniversary as Liberal party leader, the CAB presented the prime minister with a small bronze statue of himself with Pat. In his speech after accepting the honour, King let his guard down and spoke personally, intimately, and emotionally about his dog. "If I have been true to some of the great causes that I have sought to remain true to, it's been the example of that little fellow that has helped in many, many ways," he said to an audience giving him its rapt attention. With a voice soft and reflective, King continued, "What it has meant after coming home from the House of Commons to have him at the front door, waiting, waiting, just to greet one when one came in. And he seemed to have an instinct for politics. He always knew when there had been a fight on! And I, I could tell if everything had gone well or if it hadn't by the rapid movement of his tail and by the extent to which he would jump up and down on those occasions."[4]

The way people talk about their pets can be revealing. The candour, emotion, and pride with which King spoke about Pat in this public forum is startling, given the privacy King valued and given the fact that the remarks came in an era not noted for personal revelations. "Well, that must be the best political speech that Mackenzie King ever made because it shows the man," said Don Harron after playing the recording on CBC Radio's *Morningside* program in 1978.[5]

Despite King's well-known status as a pet owner, dogs and prime ministers have never taken on the same mythical proportions as have dogs and presidents of the United States. "You want a friend in Washington?" Harry Truman once said. "Get a dog." For most of the history of the

U.S., notes *First Dogs: American Presidents and Their Best Friends*, "there have been two top dogs at 1600 Pennsylvania Avenue — one with two legs, one with four." While some Canadians of a certain age might be able to tell you that Richard Nixon had a dog named Checkers (who died before Nixon became president) or that Bill Clinton had a well-known chocolate Labrador named Buddy, Mackenzie King's Pat is likely the only canine to register in the Canadian historical consciousness. And Pat's notoriety rests entirely on the eccentricities of his owner, rather than any great public affection developed for the dog during King's life.* In fact, there were two more Pats.

The health of King's second Irish terrier generated considerably more angst for the prime minister than even the overwrought death of his first dog in 1941. Later that year, King acquired Pat II, again from his friends the Pattesons, who had given him his first pet. The prime minister and this second dog soon became fast friends, but just six years later, Pat II was diagnosed with cancer. During a surgery to remove a tumour, it was discovered that the disease was too far advanced and that the dog had to be euthanized. The death of his beloved pet sent King into paroxysms of grief, and when the contents of his diary from 1947 became public in 1978, his comments about the dog took top billing in newspapers. And it is not hard to see why. "King felt his dog deserved Order of Merit, diary says," reported the *Globe and Mail* on its front page. The prime minister called the death watch over Pat II "a purifying and spiritual experience."[6] He chronicled Pat's final days.

> **August 6, 1947**
> [The dog] came and looked into my face, his little sad dark eyes looking pathetically into mine. It was a sort of farewell — tho' it may not prove to be such. I patted and talked and prayed with him then

---

* King recorded in his diary Pat's age in human years. "I should think the truth that Pat is about 100, or over." His vet also told him, "it is remarkable about famous dogs and horses that they live to a great age."

involuntarily found myself pronouncing a blessing on his little head. "May God bless you and keep, lift up his countenance upon you, cause his face to shine upon you and give you peace."

As with any pet owner, King found the whole ordeal a challenge. He listened to the dog's rapid breathing: "The continual breaking and loss of sleep is telling a little on me, but I feel it is all a discipline and I pray God good may come of it, in the love that grows between Little Pat and myself which will continue 'beyond the veil' and in a purification through suffering of my own heart." King was desperate and that day he phoned the Ottawa Research Laboratories so he could get Pat, who was no longer eating, in to see a vet. "I did not know whether we would return with little Pat alive. He sat up awhile on the front seat and then lay with my arm around him all the way in."

King wrote of his visit to veterinarians who were employed by the government. In his diary he noted that he felt the country "would not blame him or begrudge [him] what good offices they could lend after my years of service and the problems with which as PM I was still faced — I needed this help if I were to get my sleep. They were only too ready to help."

King continued to monitor the hour-by-hour health of Pat during the next few days. Matters of state intruded, including death of Fisheries Minister Frank Bridges, who passed away on August 10, but the dog was the prime minister's chief occupation.

On August 11, Pat II's final day, King's car was pulled around at his Kingsmere estate, and he grabbed Pat's little green cushion for the ride in to the vet:

> I kept touching his little body on the way in all so clean, and beautiful in colour, lovely tan, hair short and smooth. He had no trouble breathing ... I was glad again I still have the heart of a child. I thought of where little Pat's last resting place might be ... I sang ever the little hymn "Safe in the arms of Jesus — sweetly our souls shall rest" (especially the little hymn "Jesus, tender

shepherd hear me / Bless my little dog tonight.") It was hard to utter those words without deep emotion. It was our last ride together our last journey I kept thinking to myself, we were taking it in state, as it were, the best that I possessed for my little hero, my little chivalrous knight, my little spirit of love.

Mackenzie King consulted with the veterinarians in Ottawa. They seemed to be preparing him for the inevitable when he asked for a final moment alone with his loyal friend:

> Then came the moment of parting. The little fellow tried twice to come with me, to follow me out of the door with Dr. Mitchell who came with me to the car. I went back and patted him once. I told him I was leaving him in the care of these good kind physicians who knew what was best. As I came away I could just see his little tail, in the shape that indicated he did not like being left alone, but Dr. Chute was with him.

The prime minister, overcome with emotion, drove back to Kingsmere in the cool August air.

King's writing about his dogs still comes as a shock. It is hard to imagine a prime minister devoting such time and emotion to a pet, and it is also unlikely King ever expected his grieving to become part of the public record. But pet stories capture the imagination of the public and the press made the most of it. King and his dogs have become a part of the narrative of King's life away from politics and policy, but at the same time it should be remembered that his diary was his main outlet for his emotions. It was not as though King had a spouse with whom to share his grief.

There was some sympathy for him when these intimate thoughts were revealed in 1978. Writing in the *Globe and Mail*, Bruce West was understanding: "They gave a rather pathetic insight into what must have been the terribly lonely private world of an aging bachelor who had for so long carried upon his shoulders the great burdens of leadership of his country in severely troubled times." Speaking of when his own dog died, West continued, "I'm now glad I wasn't keeping a diary at the time in which to record my own feeling on that dismal day."[7]

Later on the evening of August 11, 1947, King telephoned the vet who gave the prime minister the news that Pat had been euthanized. There was no chance of pulling off a successful surgery. The next day, the dog's body arrived at Kingsmere in an oak-finished box with brass screws. The PM, a spiritual man with strong religious beliefs, opened the box to touch his pet one last time:

> I stroked his little head and back, so cold — a touch of moisture tho' and the heat of the day where he lay, his little head reaching forward, his ears up, his little tail stretched out, clear he had gone to the very end. I felt as though he had died for me, that my sins might be forgiven me. I broke down for the first time. As I took my last look at Pat and closed the lid of the box down I could find no words to equal what I felt save the words "lamb of God." That indeed he was — that taketh away the sins of the world — may that be what my little Pat may yet have done for me.

There would be a third Pat for Mackenzie King, an event that found its way into the August 14, 1948, *Globe and Mail*. "He steps into an important niche in dogland," the newspaper noted, "for Mr. King's affection for his two previous Pats is well known. A bachelor who has a few intimate friends, the prime minister made each dog his companion and his pal as far back as the 20s."[8]

The third Pat was a retirement gift from his private secretary, Edouard Handy. This dog, too, became a constant companion to King, who wrote about him regularly, expressing concern for his health, which he felt was not that good. The pet was important enough in the prime minister's life to accompany him on his visit to Governor General Field Marshal Viscount Alexander when he submitted his resignation as PM on November 15, 1948; he "was glad to have Pat in the car."

On July 15, 1950, King, no longer prime minister, had a visit to Kingsmere from his long-time friend Joan Patteson. She placed three roses on the graves of the first Pat and his sibling Derry. King noted that it was the ninth anniversary of Pat's death, and clearly this truest friend King ever had still meant much to him. The former prime minister was too weak himself to climb up the hill to place those flowers. One week later he was dead and Pat III was given away to friends.

While King was the best known of prime ministers to own a dog, he was not the only one. John Diefenbaker got his first canine while prime minister when his wife, Olive, gave him a yellow Labrador retriever for a Christmas present in 1961. There was considerable discussion about what to name the pet, as Diefenbaker rejected the first thirty or so names he was given. But this is not a real surprise given what we know about the Conservative PM and his decision-making habits. His inability to be decisive even affected his domestic life as he tried to name his dog. In any case, the prime minister finally said he would name the dog Tory, at which point all of his advisors got more than a little skittish as they imagined the field day political cartoonists might have with a dog so named. One Diefenbaker aide, Gilbert Champagne, was there for the discussion and told the PM, "Tory" meant "George Drew, striped pants ... stuffy. I would not be happy with that word." Dief turned to him and laughed, saying, "That's it. Happy."[9]

Happy was the first dog to live at the prime minister's official residence at 24 Sussex Drive. Upon his arrival, the pup was kept in the recreation room in a brightly painted kennel that had a little picket fence around it. At Christmas, a little stocking with treats in it hung from the roof. Eventually, the dog graduated to be able to move around the house and spent much time outdoors on a leash on the grounds of 24. The prime minister enjoyed taking Happy for walks, and people in the neighbourhood got to know both the pet and the owner through these regular constitutionals. Reporters enjoyed throwing sticks to "Canada's most-written about dog," as they killed time when covering the PM.[10] For Olive Diefenbaker, it was easy to know when her husband had come home after work because of Happy's barking. Whereas she used to get a telephone call about his pending entrance, "Since

Christmas and the arrival of the pup with a coat like blond plush, her status had been pre-empted."[11]

One of John Diefenbaker's favourite stories about Happy — and every dog owner has his or her favourite pet stories — was about the time he was out taking him for a leisurely Sunday walk. Happy spotted a cat, and, as was his wont, he took off after it. The PM gave chase as well. A passerby in a car slammed on the breaks when he noticed the prime minister chasing a dog chasing a cat — not an everyday occurrence. The driver offered to help Dief get his wayward canine. But the Chief — who had more than just a touch of pride — took a look at the man behind the wheel, who was described as having "an ample build," and replied, "I can run harder than you, anytime."[12]

Happy would not live up to his name, however. The pet bit Olive Diefenbaker on the wrist — quite badly according to reports — so in 1963, not long after the Conservatives lost power to Lester Pearson's Liberals, Happy was euthanized. An earlier operation had revealed that he had a strangulated hernia and this made the dog prone to being vicious.[13]

The Diefenbakers were understandably crestfallen at having to put down Happy. But like Mackenzie King, Diefenbaker — who was no longer prime minister by then — would not be without a dog for long. Later that fall, Olive gave her husband another canine gift, a dog who came to be known as "Happy II." Like his predecessor, though, Happy II also caused no end of trouble. The dog often disappeared. "Happy's gone," became a familiar cry in the Opposition leader's office and Dief's staff knew exactly what that statement meant. Dief's driver, Jim Macmillan, would go out in his car to look for him, and staff would notify the police that the dog was missing. Inevitably, Happy II would be found by a neighbour or another citizen, and occasionally Dief's missing dog would make it into the newspaper as an announcement. He once thought about taking Happy II to a dog show he was attending to present an award, but ultimately changed his mind. "My dog has the ancestry and distinguished pedigree, but no training at all," he admitted.[14]

Happy II, unfortunately, would meet an untimely and tragic end. In 1968, Diefenbaker was out with his pet when it was struck

John Diefenbaker owned two dogs named Happy, though he had wanted to name the first pup Tory. Happy, pictured here, was the first dog to live at 24 Sussex Drive but was eventually euthanized after biting Olive Diefenbaker.

and killed by a car. Newspaper reports presented the death as a hit-and-run accident.[15] In a letter to the Chief from his brother, Elmer, he wrote, "In the case of Happy, this thing seemed to be inevitable. He was a very fine dog, but he was not amenable to discipline and I was afraid this would happen."

But there would be a silver lining yet. When news of Dief's loss became known, Randy Kleckner, a fourteen-year-old boy in Saskatchewan (Dief's home province) wrote to Diefenbaker to offer him one of his poodles he was raising at home. "It's seven weeks old, miniature, and registered," he wrote. The young boy, who suffered from cerebral palsy, said he was offering the dog to Diefenbaker for free but "hoped he could pay for the shipping."

Diefenbaker — who at this time was leader of the Opposition — was understandably moved. He replied to Kleckner, writing, "Your letter to me offering your French poodle, Cheeko, is one of the most, if not the most, inspiring letter that I have ever received. My wife and I will be happy and honoured to accept your gift, as I so advised your mother a short while ago when I talked to her on the telephone." The story ended up on the front page of the *Gazette* featuring a picture of Kleckner at his desk with the pup and framed shot of Dief. As Diefenbaker noted in his letter, the dog's name was Cheeko. In fact, Kleckner had two dogs. The other was named "Trudeau."*

John Diefenbaker's successor as prime minister, Lester B. Pearson, was not known for being a dog owner, perhaps because neither of the dogs he had stayed very long. The first was a beautiful black poodle named Pepi. Unlike his diplomatic owner, Pepi displayed a much more aggressive character (it seems Pepi may have been more like the leader of the Opposition than the prime minister). Pepi snapped at visitors and was "too excitable" for 24 Sussex Drive, so he spent more time out at Harrington Lake before he was eventually farmed out to friends.[16]

When Pearson retired as leader of the Liberal party and prime minister in 1968, he was given another dog, this time a West Highland terrier named Toby. The idea belonged to Liberal party president John Nichol, himself an owner of a rather spirited terrier. He and his

---

* There was also a dog named "Diefenbaker" in the 1990s television show *Due South*, starring Paul Gross as an RCMP officer working in Chicago. In the show the dog was "half wolf and half dog." Dief the dog was deaf but could lip-read English and Inuktitut.

wife, Liz, thought a pet would bring some energy to Pearson's retirement. But they had not accounted for the reaction of Pearson's wife, Maryon, who was dead set against the idea because of how much the Pearsons travelled. So Toby, who barked a lot, particularly at postmen, ended up with Pearson's son, Geoffrey, and his wife, Landon.[17] Toby would eventually end up in London with Christopher Young (who was Maryon's nephew) and his wife, Ann, when the former was posted there with Southam News.*

Many Canadians would be surprised to learn that both Pierre Trudeau and Brian Mulroney were dog owners while prime minister. Like virtually every dog-owning PM before him, Trudeau's dog came to him as a gift — his from noted Canadian author Farley Mowat and his wife, Claire, though the circumstances of the present came about quite serendipitously in 1971. Pierre and Margaret Trudeau were travelling on a government icebreaker between Prince Edward Island and Newfoundland when they decided, quite literally, to drop in by helicopter on the Mowats' property on the Magdalen Islands in the Gulf of St. Lawrence. I wrote to Claire Mowat about the dogs and she vividly recalled the day in a letter to me:

> At the time, Margaret T was pregnant. Our two dogs, Albert and Victoria, were about to have puppies. Vicki was about 8 weeks along. Farley suggested that if the T's were going to have a baby they should also have a puppy. We would happily save one for them. We did.[18]

The puppy was subsequently delivered to the Trudeaus at 24 Sussex Drive and Margaret christened the black Labrador/St. John's water dog cross Farley. The dog's parents were named Victoria and Albert, the father "a magnificent swimmer and retriever," recalled Mrs. Mowat,

---

* Patricia Pearson, the PM's granddaughter, recalled trying to ride Toby like a pony when she was a little girl. Toby bit her as a result.

"and I think that was why Pierre T was impressed with him and agreed to get one of his dog offspring."

In spring 1972, the Mowats were invited out to the prime minister's official cottage at Harrington Lake ("just [the Trudeaus] and baby Justin. There was no staff, Margaret did all the cooking. The RCMP were nearby but not intrusive," Mowat recalled). The Mowats brought with them a second puppy, which the Trudeaus had requested. Margaret named this dog Fiona but, as Mrs. Mowat noted, while Fiona had the same mother as Farley — Victoria — "she had a different father this time — some fellow unknown to us. Fiona, sorry to say, turned to be a bit of mongrel."

Many Canadians may not see Pierre Trudeau as a typical dog owner — one Cabinet minister recalled that his pet was "*accepted* perhaps more than loved by the prime minister" — but Mowat remembered the prime minister as being very good with Farley. Trudeau told her that he had "patiently ... taught him many things," adding, "Farley the dog was a great swimmer — like his father Albert. We all swam that weekend except the five-month-old baby, Justin," she wrote.[19]

Fiona and Farley were sent to Vancouver later that year to live with Margaret Trudeau's parents after being caught chasing deer in Gatineau Park, an apparent no-no. The story did not end well for Farley, however. He was hit by a car and died.

Trudeau's successors as prime minister, Joe Clark and Brian Mulroney, both owned dogs. Clark's was a Great Dane named Taffy, whom he described as "gentle but huge, a formidable guardian of then-tiny Catherine on her sled or cart on walks around the neighbourhood."[20] Mulroney's dog ownership was also decidedly low-key. He and his family owned two rather rambunctious standard poodles named Oscar and Clover. In one memorable incident in 1984, when the Mulroneys were at Harrington Lake for one of their first visits there since he had become prime minister, Oscar got into a tussle with a porcupine. "It was a short encounter," Mulroney recalled in his memoirs. "Oscar was soon at the door, his snout and face full of quills that were painful even to look at. We whisked the dog inside, and that night the prime minister of Canada, his wife, and their children spent many hours on the floor of the kitchen removing the quills from poor Oscar."*

Neither Mulroney nor Trudeau ever attempted to make political gain from their status as pet owners. In fact, one *Ottawa Citizen* columnist drew attention to the absence of a prime ministerial dog from Mulroney's Christmas card, the usual place where pets appear. "Oscar Mulroney may be the prime minister's secret weapon," wrote Don McGillivray. "If the polls keep going against Mulroney, he may one day need to make an 'Oscar' speech along the lines of Roosevelt's 'Fala' speech and Nixon's 'Checkers' speech."[21] Little did McGillivray know Oscar needed to be sent to obedience school, so it was unlikely the dog would even have sat for the photograph for the card.

This non-political approach to pet ownership stands in stark contrast to the situation in the United States, where the absence of a presidential pet for Donald Trump sparked articles in the *New York Times*. "Of all the stains besmirching the Trump presidency — the ethical lacunae, the spasmodic 'policy' fits, the *Golf Digest* aesthetic — none looms so large as the absence of a White House pet," the article noted with a heavy dose of hyperbole.[22] Trump would be the first president not to own a dog since William McKinley in 1901.

There is an argument that one of our more recent prime ministers, Stephen Harper, *did* try to use the presence of pets to political advantage, in this case to soften his image. Harper, along with his wife, Laureen, were cat lovers. They sheltered cats throughout their stay at 24 Sussex, and the PM's website had links about how to adopt or foster pets. The only other prime minister who appears to have had cats around the house was Sir Wilfrid Laurier, who, along with his wife, Zoé, enjoyed pets of all kinds in their home, including birds. They also

---

* In 1943, King's second Pat also tangled with a porcupine and was taken to the vet. "The porcupine was no respecter of persons," reported the *Globe and Mail*, as "Pat encountered a walking pincushion."

had two dogs, one a King Charles spaniel with the original name of King Charles and the other a Pomeranian named Mme Topsey.

The introduction of the topic of cats and prime ministers does invoke the debate about cats versus dogs, however. For Harper's part, he once offered that politicians who like dogs want to be loved, while those who are cat lovers want to serve. Research by Sam Gosling of the University of Texas at Austin concluded that dog lovers were more agreeable, conscientious, and extroverted, while cat people were found to be "neurotic" but more "open minded."[23] What would King or Mulroney say?

In any case, after Harper's 2011 election victory, which secured him a majority government, *Maclean's* magazine wrote, "the image of [Harper] as a cat lover is taking on a certain iconic status. And his feline fixation is being pushed more proudly than ever."[24] The article noted that the day after the 2011 Throne Speech, the prime minister's Facebook page ran a poll to provide a name for his latest cat acquisition. Choices included Smokie, Stanley, Vingt-quatre, Earl Grey, Griffin, and Gandolf. Among the eleven thousand votes cast, Stanley was the winner. He joined resident cats Cartier and Gypsy at 24 Sussex. In 2013, Stanley, along with a pet never before owned by a prime minister — a chinchilla named Charlie — stole the show when Harper live-tweeted a day in the life of the prime minister. The tweet featured frankly adorable pictures of the two animals. The Harper Christmas card later that year featured Charlie once more, so great was his popularity.

Canadians seemed smitten by the Harpers' cats and even sent treats for them. Laureen Harper recalled in 2013 the time she received a package of "Bud For Your Best Bud."

> They said it was catnip, but who knows what it was. The police [looked] at it and [said] it's safe. Somebody said it could be pot. Who knows. So we left it on the desk and we thought, we'll have to figure out what this is. The next morning, someone went into the office and the cat had ripped with her teeth into the box and there was catnip all over. So we did not

have to send it to a laboratory. My cat was just laying there on her back drooling.[25]

After the 2015 election loss, Stanley and Gypsy, and Charlie the chinchilla, were packed up from 24 Sussex and shipped back to Calgary. But the Harpers left some other animals behind at Sussex.

The same year, Laureen Harper had installed a bat house to shelter the flying, furry creatures, and it remained after the Harpers moved out. This was not the only time flying animals lived at the official residence, though. The St. Laurents enjoyed the company of their budgie, Vicky, who was allowed to fly around the house occasionally and ate from Mrs. St. Laurent's lips or hand.[26]

A 1992 Australian study noted that pet owners had lower levels of accepted risk factors for heart disease.[27] From Pat the dog to Charlie the chinchilla, pets have not only provided love and companionship to Canada's prime ministers, they have also helped them in other ways. Those prime ministers who have had a pet have made a smart decision. The presence of the animals improved both their health and in some cases, their images.

But pet ownership also reveals to us that sometimes elusive side of prime ministers, the part rarely seen in public. Who knew just how much joy and companionship the bachelor prime minister Mackenzie King took from Pat? It was significant enough that it once meant the postponement of government business. The paroxysms of grief he suffered remind us that those who appear austere and unemotional may be quite different in the privacy of their own home. The same could be said for the often-criticized Stephen Harper. Being prime minister is a job like no other, but at home the "Right Honourable" title, the entourage, the security, the phone calls from the president of the United States — they impress neither cat nor dog. And it must have been good to know there was always an accepting friend waiting at the end of a long day.

CHAPTER 10

"OPEN AIR LIFE": PRIME MINISTERS AND SPORTS

There's a good reason why so many politicians like to play golf. Even more than the exercise, it gives them a rare opportunity to put down their briefing books, get away from their telephones, and have some quiet time in which to think.

— Jean Chrétien, *My Years As Prime Minister*

It is July 23, 1914, and Prime Minister Robert Borden climbs aboard a train as he leaves for a much-needed vacation in Muskoka, the beautiful cottage-country region located about four hundred kilometres west of Ottawa. The just-completed session of Parliament has been particularly stressful for Borden, who was also suffering from a breakout of blisters. "Thus, I looked forward with joyful anticipation to four restful weeks at Muskoka," the prime minister writes in his memoirs. Once there, Borden enjoys swimming, boating with Mrs. T. Eaton ("a bright, happy, and shrewd old body"), playing bridge, and lots of golf — a game he loves and plays regularly.

The weather is ideal and he takes his clubs out for several rounds with different friends, as well as his wife, Laura, who also favours the game. Throughout the vacation, Borden is kept abreast of worrisome events breaking out in Europe. "Prospects still very threatening for general European war," he writes in his diary. The next day he plays another round, but his vacation is about to come to an early end: A telegram from Ottawa informs him that the situation is "serious" and ministers should be prepared to come back to the capital. "Decided to go at once, despatched several telegrams," he writes. The following day, the prime minister takes a boat across Lake Joseph to the local train station and heads to Toronto to attend to the emerging crisis. His golf vacation is over and the world is headed to war.

Golf is just one of many sports and recreational activities that have been enjoyed by Canada's prime ministers. While the country's leaders, taken as a group, cannot be said to have been a particularly athletic bunch — with a few notable exceptions — a number of them have enjoyed sports, and many have enjoyed such pastimes as fishing. But prime ministers have also enjoyed swimming, skiing, canoeing, jogging, boxing, and playing tennis. Their participation in activities commonly pursued by many Canadians gives some insight into their personalities. Take Alexander Mackenzie, for example: John A. Macdonald's successor as prime minister had no time for sport or play. Speaking of Canada's champion rower, Ned Hanlan, he said that his latest victories were an "utterly useless trial of strength." On the other hand, had the task been "cutting and splitting wood, hoeing corn, ploughing or any other useful occupation which would be of general benefit to mankind, I could have some sympathy with the excitement."[1]

Mackenzie was a product of his time. For subsequent prime ministers, activities such as golfing, fishing, and swimming served as an important way to decompress from what is a very stressful job.

Unfortunately, for some, being prime minister meant the end of exercise regimes as it was too difficult to find the time.

Golf and fishing were dominant activities for prime ministers. This was likely due to two reasons. First, both can be highly social pursuits and prime ministers who participated in these pastimes delighted in the camaraderie that went with enjoying them. Second, both can be enjoyed by people of any age. They also happen to be popular sports across Canada.

Now that this chapter is teed up, let's take a look at the sport some have called "a good walk spoiled" — golf. A number of the country's prime ministers have been enthusiastic participants: Robert Borden, Louis St. Laurent, Jean Chrétien, and Paul Martin chief among them. The attraction of the game seems obvious to those who play and enjoy it: It's a wonderful respite from the quotidian stresses of life.

The country's most passionate golfer was Sir Robert Borden. His love for the links was rivalled only by Jean Chrétien's. He played the game his whole life, and by all accounts was a very good player — he took the game seriously, reflecting his own disposition. In Robert Craig Brown's two-volume biography of Borden, he wrote that the Conservative prime minister was "competent enough to enjoy the challenge of a good course and often chose his vacation hotel in Virginia or the Carolinas with an eye to the quality of its fairway and greens. Like all golfers, he was forever concerned about his technique." Borden would often "growl, in mock seriousness as he addressed the ball 'Dammit, Borden, hit it straight.'"

Golf was beginning its rise in popularity around the time of Borden's prime ministership. When the Canadian Golf Association was formed in 1895 (it received its "Royal" designation from Queen Victoria the following year), its membership comprised ten clubs. By 1914, when Borden was golfing in Muskoka, it had ballooned to thirty-four and by 1936 the RCGA boasted 128 member clubs. Borden played at the

Royal Ottawa, which was founded in 1891, getting its "Royal" designation in 1912. But Borden would golf anywhere and in all conditions. In 1913, when he was on vacation in Hot Springs, Virginia, despite an early fall snowstorm he simply put on his "rubbers" (boots) and played thirteen holes. "There are some banks of snow," he noted in his diary, "which makes it difficult to find the ball." A few years later, on a fishing trip in Ontario, he took the time to mark out an impromptu five-hole course, on which he and his companions played after fishing was done. And on one transatlantic crossing, Borden made use of a golf machine that was set up on the upper deck of the ship. He modestly noted in his diary that he won the prize for the three best drives.

Borden's passion for the game is beyond doubt. But he was also well suited to its rules and gentlemanly aspects. His interior sense of duty that was a hallmark of his personality is captured in one golf story that tells us as much about the times as it does about the personalities involved.

In 1919, the Prince of Wales, the future Edward VIII, was on a royal tour of Canada when he inquired of the prime minister about the possibility of playing golf on a Sunday. In those days, playing golf on the Sabbath created something of a conundrum. For example, at the turn of the century a foursome from Toronto challenged the prohibition against playing "ball games" on Sundays as decreed by the Lord's Day Act. The judge agreed with their petition and declared they could play on Sundays, saying, "This game of golf is not a game within the meaning of the law. It is not noisy. It attracts no crowds. It is not gambling. It is on a parallel, it seems to me, with a gentleman going out for a walk on Sunday and as he walks, switching off the head of weeds with his walking stick."

The issue for the prince was whether a game could be pulled off without attracting any public disapproval. Borden felt "any public criticism was improbable." Indeed, he felt much like the judge: "So far as I was concerned I could see no difference between playing golf or walking."

But this was Canada and it was 1919. As the prime minister insightfully recalled in his memoirs, "There were in Canada many earnest people who thought otherwise and they would be sincerely grieved and disappointed if the prince should play golf on Sunday. Thus, I had always refrained from playing on Sunday while prime minister, as I thought the convictions of such earnest and loyal people were entitled to respect."

Many prime ministers enjoyed sports and golf was one of the most popular. Robert Borden played whenever he could, even if it meant playing in snow. He golfed more than any other PM.

The prince — obviously keen to play — raised the request once more with Sir Robert. But Borden, ever the man to cling to duty and honour, begged to speak frankly and advised him, "It would be undesirable and unwise for him to play golf on Sunday." But that was not the end of the matter for HRH Prince of Wales.

Four days later, the question of a Sunday on the links once more occupied the prime minister, this time because the prince was heading out west on his royal tour where, he told Borden, they might not be so strict. He hoped to squeeze in a round. "Expressing my regret at disappointing him, I begged him to realize my duty to speak frankly. He put his hand on my arm and said to me with much earnestness: 'I solemnly promise that I will not play golf on Sundays unless you say that I may.' Finally, I agreed to send him a telegram in case I thought he might play. His boyish and earnest manner was most attractive and charming."

In addition to the leisurely appeal of golf for prime ministers, it also served as a diplomatic channel, one employed successfully by both Louis St. Laurent and Jean Chrétien, who used the time on the links to build relationships with other leaders. While Jean Chrétien and President Bill Clinton had a well-known fairway friendship, established during the 1990s, the template for golf and diplomacy was struck earlier by St. Laurent and President Dwight D. Eisenhower during the 1950s. Both men were noted for their love of the game, and while the two leaders were not fast friends in the mould of their more recent successors, they shared what has been described as "a distant respect."[2] So it was not too much of a surprise when, in 1956, "Ike" provided St. Laurent with an invitation all golfers dream about: A round at Augusta, Georgia, home of the famed Masters tournament.

It was a warm and sunny day in December 1956 when St. Laurent teamed up with Augusta's pro, Ed Dudley, while the president joined the prime minister's daughter, Madeleine O'Donnell, for a nine-hole "best ball" that ended in a draw. Newsreels of the event show the president and prime minister zipping about in an electric cart, with St. Laurent wearing a sweater vest and tie. Each player, apart from Dudley, was given one stroke per hole, which St. Laurent may have needed since it was said he rarely broke one hundred. He was not the golfer Eisenhower was. As *Maclean's* magazine put it in 1955: "He loves golf but plays poorly."

A golf match for Louis St. Laurent was a natural activity and one he enjoyed immensely. He was a member of the Royal Quebec Golf Club. He served as the club's president in the early 1940s before he became prime minister in 1948. Whether on holiday in New

Brunswick, Quebec, Florida, or Bermuda, the Liberal prime minister usually included the game as part of his vacation time. As with Jean Chrétien, though, he was no stickler for the rules. "Unlike President Eisenhower," wrote Dale C. Thomson in his biography of St. Laurent, "he did not take the game seriously, keeping no score, moving the ball out of the rough for a more convenient shot, using any club that was at hand, and displaying an amateurish style* that won him the somewhat disrespectful but affectionate nickname among caddies of 'Wiggles.'"[3]

For St. Laurent, though, time on the fairways was a time for diplomacy. As he told gathered MPs in the House of Commons after his match with the president: "I found … that the game of golf, with one of those electric go-carts, was about the best way to have an international conference, because you are getting off the go-cart quite frequently for only a couple of minutes but for time enough to reflect on what has been said up to that moment and what is *going* to be said when you get back on the seat of the go-cart."

Raising the issue in Parliament may not have been the smartest idea. St. Laurent's golfing exploits with the U.S. president opened himself up to criticism for being too cozy with his American counterpart. One MP told the Speaker that St. Laurent "seemed to be able to improve his golf score and his social relations with the President of the United States but apparently he was not able to reduce the [$1 billion] trade deficit by any appreciable degree."

"Ike took him for a ride," heckled another. Opposition members characterized the match as the "humpty-dumpty ride over the golf course" and the "rickshaw ride" with the president. This would not be the last time a prime minister endured Opposition opprobrium for spending time with an American golf buddy.

While Louis St. Laurent was well known for his golfing and set an example for grabbing the clubs with the president, it was Jean Chrétien

---

* Prime Minister Paul Martin was similarly challenged. As he told me in an interview: "I am an avid but lousy golfer." Journalist Lawrence Martin agreed, telling the CBC's Anna Maria Tremonti in 2003 that Martin "hasn't got what you would call a classic stroke."

who embraced the game and its friendship-building abilities. Chrétien was fortunate to serve in office at the same time as a president who loved the game as much as he did. Bill Clinton referred to the prime minister in his memoirs as "a strong ally, confidant, and frequent golfing partner."

In opposition, Chrétien made a point of saying he would not be caught fishing with the president. Golfing was another matter entirely, though. The two men met on the fairways at least a dozen times during their overlapping years in office between 1993 and 2001. In fact, during a 1997 joint news conference in Washington, Clinton — who had earlier fallen on the porch of famed Australian golfer Greg Norman (an accident that resulted in Clinton having to undergo knee surgery) — told the assembled media that "the biggest threat to our friendship is this injury of mine because it has precluded our indulging our mutual passion for golf. I don't think that — I don't know if any two world leaders have played golf together more than we have, but we meant to break a record, and I've had to take a six-month respite. But I'll be back in the arena before long."[4]

Despite the fact that Chrétien would have liked to keep his matches with Clinton quiet, his rounds of golf caught the attention of the media, as well as members of Parliament. A 1997 story in the *Globe and Mail* appeared under the headline "On the fairway to foreign policy." It drew comparisons between the styles of the prime minister and president.

"Clinton is the bigger hitter, likes to putter around the course, kibitzing with his partners and offering up tips. Chrétien is strictly business. He likes to play fast, waiting impatiently through Mr. Clinton's endless practice swings. He isn't crazy about unsolicited advice." James Blanchard, who was the American ambassador at the time, said "Clinton's game is more flamboyant and could be considered in some respects more exciting but also more dangerous. The prime minister is more focused and disciplined."[5]

It was true that Chrétien did not take kindly to advice — what golfer does? — and in one of their early rounds together, in 1995 during the Halifax G7 summit, the president continued to advise Chrétien about aspects of his game. Lawrence Martin recounts the story in his book *Iron Man*. "The president kept pointing out how Chrétien should stand, how he should grip the club, and Chrétien was becoming quite distracted. For the back nine, Chrétien asked that they play a straight game — no extra shots, no tips. 'You're the big guy from Little Rock. I'm the little guy from Shawinigan. Let's go!' The PM won the back nine."[6]

Martin, the author of a two-volume biography of Jean Chrétien, was no stranger to the PM's game, having once golfed a round with him. In a 2003 interview with CBC Radio's *The Current*, Martin described Chrétien as an "avid" and "serious" golfer who despised being interrupted while playing. During a match with the prime minister, Chrétien got a call he had to take from Mitchell Sharp, the former Liberal Cabinet minister and then-advisor in the PMO, disturbing a "great back nine he had going." Once the pressing business had been dealt with, he returned to the game. "He teed up the ball and shanked it away off into the trees," Martin recalled. "He was just furious. He said 'Goddamn Mitchell,' you know, cursing away, for interrupting his game. He threw him right off his concentration mode, and he was really ticked off."[7]

Cursing a poor shot is a part of the game, and in Chrétien's case, a sign of his competitive nature. Much like the average player at the local course, Chrétien has played in all conditions. He played with Bill Clinton, whether it was in six degrees and high winds or in a "monsoon-like storm" in Vancouver (during which the president was still able to keep his cigar lit). In 1999, after Clinton gave his highly touted speech on federalism at a conference in Mont Tremblant, Quebec, he cut short a meeting with Quebec premier Lucien Bouchard so he could squeeze in a round of golf with Chrétien. They played the final two holes with the course lit by flashlights and the high beams of security vehicles.

A prime minister who loves golf is still just a player, like you and me, trying to figure the game out. Being the most powerful person in the country does not render you immune from the tips or protect you from a lousy game. Chrétien found out the hard way when he played a round with Tiger Woods in 2001 at Royal Montreal Golf Club. He got rattled when he teed off in front of a huge crowd. "Nothing in the game of politics had ever been as nerve-racking as that game of golf," he remembered.

While Chrétien's initial tee shot was down the middle, his game fell apart the rest of the way and no rapport developed between him and Woods. Neither had much good to say at the end of play. "The pressure was excruciating, and so was the humiliation," Chrétien recalled in his memoirs. "Even when I had a good shot, Tiger's was always a lot better."

No doubt this bothered Chrétien, who hated to lose, even in a casual game. Journalist Roy MacGregor, who once golfed with Chrétien shortly before he became PM, recounted how delighted the latter was when he finally beat MacGregor with a longer tee shot. "He was like a little kid with happiness. Down the back nine it appeared we would be close. I remember splitting the branches of a big dead tree with an approach and he groaned and laughed about my bullshit luck. I honestly do not recall our scores."*

MacGregor and Chrétien spent the nineteenth hole at the Royal Ottawa on a patio. "We had two drafts each and he regaled me with stories and the usual veiled and not-so-veiled attacks on [John] Turner. [He is] a wonderful golfing companion. Plays fast, serious, and has lots of laughs."[8]

Like St. Laurent, Chrétien knew the pleasures golf could bring to a job that had incredible demands. "There's a good reason why so many politicians like to play golf," he wrote in his memoirs. "Even more than the exercise, it gives them a rare opportunity to put down their briefing books, get away from their telephones, and have some quiet time in which to think. It's also a relaxing walk in a park with people who probably don't hate them, and a comfortable way to get to know what's on people's minds. In fact, I played more frequently when I was prime minister than after my retirement, not because I had more idle hours on my hands, but because I had more need of peace."

Perhaps the ultimate question to ask when it comes to Canada's prime ministers and the game of golf is this: Which PM would you most want to join you for a round of eighteen? A clubhouse sketch:

> **Borden:** A serious player; highly experienced. Wants to play a lot. Follows the rules. Erudite, but capable of a laugh once in a while on the course. May quote Greek verse to you. Unlikely to buy a round on the nineteenth hole.

---

* Chrétien might recall the scores. He was notorious for watching everyone's scorecard very closely — an aspect of his competitiveness.

St. Laurent: Older player, erratic swing. Enjoys the game. Amiable personality who will enjoy pleasant conversation. Watch where you stand when he tees off. Natty dresser. You'll need a cart.

Chrétien: Highly competitive. Focused player. Known to take a few mulligans. Claims to hit ball "straight down the middle" all the time. Will tell great stories during round, likely peppered with a few swear words. Happy to play with anyone but may delight in outdriving you.

Martin: Enjoys the game but knows his limitations. A younger, more charismatic St. Laurent. Chatty and friendly, you may end up asking others to play through you so you don't hold them up. Bonus: He has his own six-hole course in the Eastern Townships of Quebec.

The attraction of fishing as a leisure pursuit of prime ministers was not much different from golf. The ability to get away from the office and enjoy a period of relaxation was paramount. The day after John Diefenbaker won the 1957 election, he went on a fishing trip to his treasured spot near the small town of Lac La Ronge, Saskatchewan, 265 kilometres north of his Prince Albert home. "For me, there were no ringing telephones, no hurried consultations, no meetings with the press," he recalled of that post-election piscatorial trip. "I was fishing on Lac La Ronge. And, for a trout fisherman, the northern and eastern portions of the lake are in a class by themselves." Diefenbaker was then called by outgoing prime minster Louis St. Laurent to meet him in Ottawa and the Chief noted that the "halcyon days" were coming to an end.

Few would dispute the rank of fishing among all the summertime pursuits enjoyed by Canadians.[*] A number of prime ministers turned to this leisure activity during their time in office and the results often made their way into the newspapers of the day or into

---

[*] Justin Trudeau showed prime ministers can fish in the winter, too. In January 2018, at the First Nation reserve in Pikangikum, Ontario, Trudeau hauled in a sizeable northern pike on fishing lines set up by students there.

the correspondence of the country's leaders. From Robert Borden to Stephen Harper, Canada's prime ministers have indulged in fishing, making the activity a constant in prime ministerial history — and sometimes because of fish *not* caught.

Robert Borden loved fishing, particularly fly-fishing. He fished at various spots in central Ontario, such as Deer Lake, Bear Point, and Pickwick Lake, but favoured Echo Beach, about two and half hours north of Toronto in the Muskoka region. His diary is filled with references to the number of fish he caught, the lures he used, and the relaxation he felt. "Am feeling great benefit from open air life and respite from work," he noted on May 17, 1915. He also sent a box of his catch to his wife, Laura, and on another occasion he sent eight of his best fish to Government House for the Duke of Connaught, the governor general.

Borden's successor, Arthur Meighen, fished occasionally but he was nowhere near the angler Borden was. Mackenzie King did not enjoy the rod and reel, but Louis St. Laurent, who followed him as prime minister, certainly did. He enjoyed the sport and spent part of his summer vacations fly-fishing. As with other prime ministers, he knew the value of a vacation, and throughout his tenure as PM he found time to do so on his annual summer holidays to St. Patrice, Quebec. News reports usually cited his fishing, swimming, and golf activities.

Of all Canadian prime ministers, though, John Diefenbaker was the most enthusiastic angler. He fished in all parts of the country and the stories of his "piscatorial pursuits" (his description) appeared regularly in the press. In 1976 he was named one of the six inaugural inductees to the Canadian Fishing Hall of Fame along with Joe Clark. Diefenbaker was cited for "his leadership in conservation," as well as for his commitment to the sport.[9] Tom Van Dusen, who was a ministerial assistant in Diefenbaker's government, wrote, "It only gradually grew on the public that for John Diefenbaker fishing was a serious sport into which he put all of the energy and devotion that he gave politics." Canadians from across the country would send him flies and lures, as well as numerous invitations to fish at coveted spots (the same was true for Lester Pearson). Some of these invitations were even accepted by him. "He was and is no amateur," Van Dusen recalled.

Back to that day in 1957. That spring's election campaign had exposed a tired Liberal government led by Louis St. Laurent. The Conservatives capitalized, leading to a minority victory and the end of twenty-two years of rule by the Grits. As noted, Diefenbaker grabbed his tackle and went north to Lac La Ronge. Getting away to fish was one opportunity he knew might not come as often now that he was about to become prime minister, and Dief noted the beauty of Lac La Ronge, as well as the coming responsibilities of office in his memoirs.

That day on the lake, the prime minister–designate lamented the "terrible luck" he had with rod and reel. His comment is hard to fathom since he caught some seven fish that day, including five northern pike and two pickerel. Perhaps by Saskatchewan standards, this was small fry. When one of his fishing mates joked with him about the size of his catch, Diefenbaker, tanned and wearing his thick Cowichan sweater and faded baseball cap, replied, "No. I caught the big one yesterday." The story seems to have assured for Diefenbaker his place among prime ministers in the piscatorial pantheon since Brian Mulroney also recounted it in his own memoirs.

Not surprisingly, Diefenbaker's fishing also occasionally served to develop bilateral relationships. The Chief preferred one-on-one meetings as much as possible when dealing with foreign leaders, so he was keen to get President Dwight Eisenhower, another noted angler, out on to Harrington Lake when the president visited in July 1958. The president's suggestion of using a "popper," a lure favoured by the prime minister, led to some excellent results, but Dief later admitted that the large bass of Harrington were "snapping his line consistently." Despite Diefenbaker's attempt at one-upmanship, the fact that Ike and Dief could fish together was a good indicator of the strength of their personal relationship.

On the other hand, fishing had a role to play in souring relations between Diefenbaker and Eisenhower's successor, John F. Kennedy. On February 20, 1961, Diefenbaker took a quick flight to Washington to meet with the recently inaugurated American president. The meeting lasted three hours, including a working lunch, during which the prime minister and president got to know each other in their first bilateral meeting. As the prime minister had noted earlier in the House of Commons when he accepted Kennedy's invitation to the White House, "the president said this morning that it was a good thing internationally for old friends to get together." Privately, Diefenbaker was quite upset with the way Kennedy had mispronounced his name as 'Diefen-*bawker*.' It proved to be an omen for the way their relationship would unfold.

By all public accounts, the visit between Diefenbaker and Kennedy was a success, but history tells us that the Chief and JFK never really got along, and a story about a fish did not help matters. During the working lunch at the White House, Kennedy and Diefenbaker engaged in the sort of small talk that most politicians love. The president began "sparring facetiously" with the prime minister and pointed to a large sailfish mounted on the wall — a souvenir from Kennedy's honeymoon.

"Caught anything better?" he asked Diefenbaker.

The prime minister responded by telling Kennedy about the 140-pound marlin he landed the previous month in Jamaica. It was his proudest catch. "I've always wanted to get a marlin," he had told reporters in Montreal upon his return from that trip. The fish was eight-and-half-feet long, and Dief felt that he had reason to be boastful of a fish that took more than three hours to land.

But Kennedy mocked the story. "You didn't catch it!" he teased.

Diefenbaker was not amused by Kennedy's comment, meant light-heartedly. But such was the nature of John Diefenbaker. When President Kennedy returned to Ottawa in May of the same year, the prime minister had something in store for him in his East Block parliamentary office. When Kennedy entered the room, Diefenbaker proudly pointed out the mounted marlin he had placed on the wall for all to see.

John Diefenbaker was clearly Canada's greatest prime ministerial angler — he even once caught a thirty-pound shark — and he understood the benefits of the sport for a PM. "Fishing is the only time you can forget everything," he once said. And perhaps that is a most-telling comment about fishing from a prime minister. It provided an escape from a job that places demands on time and energy that most of us can only wonder about from a distance.[*]

Lester B. Pearson, Diefenbaker's successor as PM — and his jousting partner in numerous House of Commons debates — was a

---

[*] Another way Diefenbaker enjoyed decompressing from a tough day at the office was by watching wrestling on television.

Another favourite pastime of prime ministers was fishing. There was none more enthusiastic than John Diefenbaker, pictured here with a 140-pound marlin he caught in 1961. The fish led to a small flap with U.S. president John Kennedy later that year.

John Diefenbaker with a large haul of fish. He referred to the sport as his "piscatorial pursuits." Lac La Ronge, Saskatchewan, was his favourite spot.

considerable fisherman himself. In one sense, that rivalry carried over from Parliament to the lake. When Pearson became prime minister and settled in at Harrington, he was told the Chief had caught a four-and-a-half-pound trout, which dismayed Pearson because he doubted he would ever be able to best that record. As Peter C. Newman tells the story, Pearson "tracked down a local farmer who assured him that Diefenbaker had indeed hooked a fish that size. The farmer added, though, that Dief had never managed to land it in his boat. That allowed Pearson to enjoy life at the cottage."

Pearson certainly knew the value of fishing as relaxation. He was a member of the famed Five Lakes Fishing Club, formed in 1940 by Deputy Minister of Finance Clifford Clark. The philosophy behind the club was to provide an escape from the demands of work in Ottawa for a collection of top civil servants who would come to be known as "mandarins." So, as PM he was well acquainted with the value of getting out on the lake.

Not surprisingly, Pearson both began and ended his tenure as prime minister by fishing. After his April 8, 1963, electoral victory, he retreated to Harrington Lake, where he spoke of "co-operative fish."

Five years later, when Pierre Trudeau replaced him as Liberal Party leader and PM, Pearson headed for the lake once more.* "After lunch, I'm going up to Harrington Lake," he told a collection of reporters in 1968. "If all goes well this afternoon I may be out on the lake catching a trout." A reporter then asked the new prime minister, Pierre Trudeau, if he would allow Pearson to continue fishing at Harrington. "I have told him I'm not much of a fisherman myself and he's welcome to take as many (fish) out of the lake as he wants."[10]

A final fishing story involving Pearson revolves around a 1965 trip he made to British Columbia. The visit included a stop at the twenty-fifth annual salmon derby organized by the *Vancouver Sun*, at the time a Liberal newspaper. Pearson was said to be "turning his

---

* Brian Mulroney also said he was going to do a little fishing with his son Nicholas after he officially resigned in 1993. Before he drove away from Rideau Hall, Mulroney was asked by reporters to show his driver's licence. They wanted to see if he really had one.

attention from votes to salmon" and caught a two-pound coho, which was more than a little on the small side for a B.C. salmon.

The fish were not biting well that day and the *Sun* noted, perhaps with tongue in cheek, that there had been "malicious suggestions" the newspaper itself had arranged for "frogmen" to ensure that the prime minister ended up with something on his line. For Pearson, though, the little salmon was just enough, and later he made the most of it with reporters. Returning to HMCS *Saskatchewan*, which was to whisk him back to Vancouver Island, the prime minister told reporters the fish would make a perfect wedding anniversary gift. This was vintage Pearson, at his self-deprecating best, hamming it up with journalists.

"My wife thinks the fortieth is the ruby anniversary," he joked. "But I say it's the fish anniversary. My wife says it has been forty years of bliss," he said, before adding, "My wife has a good sense of humour." It's not clear how Maryon Pearson felt about the nuptial gift or whether the size mattered.

Most prime ministers, when given the opportunity of catching fish, have wanted to land as many as they can. Except one. Jean Chrétien. During the 1993 election campaign, Chrétien, then leader of the Opposition, vowed that he would never go fishing with the American president, a not-so-veiled barb directed at Brian Mulroney, who was well-known for his fishing trips with President George H.W. Bush. "While Canadians don't want their leaders to pick unnecessary fights with the U.S. president," Chrétien recalled in his memoirs, "they also don't want them to get too chummy either. 'My ambition is not to go fishing with the president of the United States,' I had joked on the campaign trail, 'because I don't want to be the fish.'"

After a visit to Washington as Opposition leader, Chrétien's intentional distance from the president was labelled as "The Doctrine of No Fishing" by University of Toronto professor John Kirton. Chrétien had reason to be concerned. A number of Canadians had grown weary of Mulroney's close relationship with both presidents Ronald Reagan and George H.W. Bush, the latter of whom Mulroney visited often at Kennebunkport, Maine, where they fished together.

During President Bush's first summer in office in 1989, the entire Mulroney clan went to the Bush summer home. The *Globe and Mail* reported that the Mulroneys arrived "with broad smiles, fishing banter — and only a hint of serious talk later." The prime minister was asked what would be on the agenda, and he replied, "Probably fish and tennis." Over eggs, bacon, coffee, and time fishing, the prime minister and the president discussed a variety of bilateral and international issues as they continued to build a rapport and friendship that would last well after the end of their political careers.[11]

But this intimacy grew tiresome for Canadians, who seemed to resent Mulroney's closeness. As a result, many of them felt that they had had enough of the Mulroney years. Jean Chrétien tapped into this during the 1993 election campaign. (Of course, Chrétien's relationship with American presidents would be equally close, only golf was his sport of choice.) His purposeful distance from American presidents was part of a platform that won his Liberal Party its first of three consecutive majority governments. The fishing trips were over.

Prime Minister Stephen Harper also grabbed the tackle and hit the lake to catch a few fish on occasion, although, looking back now, he may have regrets about his chosen partner. In the summer of 2012, Harper went bass fishing with Toronto mayor Rob Ford. The prime minister is not on record about this excursion, but the garrulous chief magistrate of Canada's largest city had lots to say.

"We were pulling in, I would say — and I'm not exaggerating — four-, five-pound bass. Oh, it's beautiful," Ford told CFRB talk show host Jim Richards. "There (are) tons of fish up there." According to Ford, Harper "likes fishing" but he was not too keen — perhaps a result of Ford's girth — to see Ford standing up and casting from the boat.

"I stand up in the boat all the time. He says, 'Sit down.' I say, 'No, no.' I stand up, I cast, you know, I get right into it."

In typical Harper fashion, there was no comment or photograph from his office detailing the day spent on the lake. If truth be known, Harper has never been a fishing aficionado, eschewing the outdoor pursuits of the members of the famed "Calgary School" that helped to shape his political philosophy. It is difficult to imagine Stephen Harper relaxed enough to be on the lake enjoying such a lazy pursuit. It does not seem to be part of his DNA, unlike many of his predecessors.

While fishing and golf have been the primary leisure activities for Canada's prime ministers, another way of looking at the subject is to wonder which of our leaders was the sportiest? The answer depends on how you interpret the question.

If you are asking about PMs at any time in their lives, then Lester Pearson and John Turner would take the laurels. Pearson was a star athlete as a young man, excelling particularly at baseball, a sport for which he played at the semi-professional level. He was also a star rugby player during his Royal Air Force days of the First World War. He even played hockey and lacrosse for Oxford University when he was a student there in the early 1920s. Indeed, Pearson was a superb athlete and loved sports. He once quipped that he sometimes thought he would rather have been captain of the Toronto Maple Leafs than be prime minister.

John Turner was also a gifted sportsman, a sprinter who, while a student at the University of British Columbia in 1947, held the Canadian record in the one-hundred-yard dash. He qualified for the 1948 Olympics but a car accident prevented him from attending.

But if the question applies only to the time a prime minister was in office, the candidates for most athletic prime minister narrow considerably to Pierre and Justin Trudeau and perhaps Jean Chrétien. Pearson played the occasional game of tennis; Stephen Harper was known to drop into the Rockcliffe Lawn Tennis Club to hit balls with his son, Ben. In addition to golfing and fishing, Louis St. Laurent swam. John A. Macdonald? He appreciated the value of sports for young Canadians but was not an athlete himself. Wilfrid Laurier? Weak lungs as a youth prevented him from doing much about sports. Mackenzie King? He swam at his Kingsmere estate and, if you count dancing as a sport, he quite enjoyed that activity, but no one ever thought of King as an athlete.

Brian Mulroney? "He likes to talk on the telephone," one close friend replied when asked what outdoor activities the PM enjoyed.[12]

Pierre Trudeau was very much an outdoorsman and a very athletic man as prime minister. He fit in with the times, as the 1970s witnessed the dawn of the personal fitness craze. In 1972, his government created the famed ParticipACTION agency to promote physical fitness among an increasingly sedentary Canadian population. As befitted his personality, Trudeau favoured individual sports such as diving, swimming, skiing, and canoeing. "In contrast to a social life that was hopelessly public," wrote Michael Farber in the Montreal *Gazette* in 1984, "his sporting life was asocial — no golf or tennis — and as solitary as any prime minister's could be."[13]

Solitary and adventurous, Trudeau loved to get thrills from his participation in sports. In 1969, he skied at the Bugaboo Lodge in British Columbia, an outfit that still today specializes in heli-skiing. Trudeau was an expert skier — "You have to be better than good on skis before the Bugaboo people will even consider taking your money," noted one news report — and was attracted by the opportunity to race down untraced powder on the mountain.[14] He took numerous ski vacations while PM, both in North America and Europe.

Trudeau sought more thrills in 1974 when he raced down the bobsled track in St. Moritz, Switzerland, known as the "Cresta," a chute travelled face-first on a sled, as with the winter Olympic event known as skeleton. Ever the competitor, Trudeau challenged his foreign policy advisor Ivan Head to a race on the dangerous track. "I told [the prime minister] that with the Cresta, he didn't know what he was getting into," Head later wrote. "This, as I should have known, only encouraged him."[15] Head admitted to being scared by the prospects of hurtling face-first down the track but the two men did it — twice — and lived to tell the tale.

The canoe is what many Canadians who remember Trudeau will still associate him with. The photos of him canoeing in his famous buckskin jacket provide what many consider the signature symbol of the man — they certainly capture an integral part of his life. "The canoe connection was a welcome personal brand," wrote Roy MacGregor in his 2015 book *Canoe Country*. "Paddling had political currency in this country so dependent on the native means of travel for its very being."[16] Trudeau canoed throughout his life, but when he became prime minister the number of extensive trips he could do dropped dramatically due to the demands of being prime minister. His excursions were much closer to home in Ottawa as opposed to heading the Nahanni River in the Yukon.* Nonetheless, the importance of canoeing didn't diminish. Its importance to him as an activity was in the way it drew him closer to nature and to his soul. The meditative nature of the pursuit appealed to Trudeau. "You discover a sort of simplifying of your values, a distinction between values artificially created and those that are necessary to your spiritual and human development," he wrote in his memoirs. "That's why, from my youthful expeditions right up to the present day, canoeing has always been such an important activity in my life." Canoeing was also a favoured activity through which he could spend time with his children, allowing him to pass on to them his passion for the outdoors and its related activities.

Justin Trudeau, not surprisingly, picked up the inclination toward athletics from his father. During the 2015 election campaign he was photographed canoeing in the Bow River near Calgary. Since becoming prime minister, he has appeared in numerous photographs skiing, snowboarding, kayaking, jogging, and, most famously for him, boxing. It was boxing, after all, that changed the narrative for Trudeau from backbench Liberal MP to ballsy tough guy on the rise as a result of his convincing win over Conservative senator Patrick Brazeau in a March 2012 charity bout. Trudeau said it helped him become prime minister.**

"If I was going to embark on a high-risk endeavour like that (fight) without knowing to a very high degree of confidence that I was going to be able to pull it off, then probably I wouldn't be suitable to be PM, because I would have made a very serious miscalculation and I would not know myself as much as someone who aspires to lead the country should know themselves."[17] In 2016, Trudeau did a photo op at the famous Gleason's gym in Brooklyn, an event that allowed him to further strengthen his ties to the sport, now part of his brand, and

---

* John Turner was also an expert and experienced canoeist, but he was only PM for just over three months. He paddled many of the country's great rivers throughout his life.
** Actor Matthew Perry, of *Friends* fame, bragged to one late-night talk show host in 2017 that he "beat up" Trudeau in grade 5 when they attended the same public school.

something that has allowed him to shed the image of being the spoiled son of a rich and famous former prime minister. One University of Toronto study came to the same conclusion: "By engaging in performances of traditional masculinity, he created a new brand for himself, and that was done through the media's construction of him."[18] Young and fit, Justin Trudeau is the most athletic person to serve as prime minister in the history of the country. In 2018, his famous abdominal muscles even made an appearance on Showtime's animated series *Our Cartoon President*, which lampoons U.S. president Donald Trump.

After the Trudeaus, Jean Chrétien is the only PM who can reasonably make the claim to have been athletic while in office. His golf exploits are well chronicled, but he also skied regularly, on both snow and water. He made good use of the pool at 24 Sussex and his eagerness to participate in almost any sport, whether it was cycling in China or playing basketball in Kosovo, got him in the newspaper many times. (In Kosovo, he took a nasty slip and fell flat on the ground, the resulting photograph gaining wide circulation. There is a risk and reward to many of these unscripted moments.)

Chrétien's well-known competitive spirit was not limited to the links. He competed with himself. On his sixty-sixth birthday in 1990, the prime minister told Bruce Hartley, his executive assistant, that he wanted to lift weights in the hotel gym as part of his celebrations. Why did he want to do this? He wanted to show everyone that even at age sixty-six this senior citizen could still pump the iron. Chrétien was not a weight trainer. He was more than a little sore the next day.

Being athletic and fit takes time. So does being prime minister. It is a challenge to be both, and more than a few prime ministers lamented the end of exercise regimes once they took up residence at 24 Sussex Drive. Prime Minister Kim Campbell was upset when her campaign manager, John Tory, presented her with a schedule with no time put aside for exercise. She knew, as we all do, that a healthy body is a healthy mind.

EPILOGUE

Near the end of my interview for this project with the Right Honourable Jean Chrétien, he had a question for me. "So, what have you discovered?" he asked. "What have you found out about prime ministers?" It was a great question for someone who was writing a book about them, and Chrétien was interested in the answer. He had a copy of Robert Borden's *Letters to Limbo*, a collection of his writings composed in the years after he served as PM but not published until 1971. Chrétien, like other prime ministers, had a keen awareness of those in whose steps he followed.

Going behind the scenes into the lives of the country's prime ministers reveals to us the human element of the job, something often overlooked in political coverage of the country's leaders. Canadians — and the media — tend to see our prime ministers only as political actors. As I pointed out in the introduction to this book, quoting Bruce Hutchison, the prime minister, who stands at the centre of our political institutions, is a human being. When we forget that, we fail to understand the nature of the office. While Stephen Harper was often trotted out as example of a cold political calculator (which he and many others were), he was also the prime minister, as I noted earlier, who gave an emotional apology in 2008 for the country's role in residential schools and crossed the aisle in 2014 to hug NDP Opposition leader Tom Mulcair and Liberal party leader Justin Trudeau. Prime ministers are human.

There is an artifice to being in politics — there always has been — and that prevents Canadians from really getting to know politicians who operate at the highest levels of power, such as the prime minister. Our PMs are tightly packaged by their handlers, so glimpses of them as real people are fleeting. If we can view them doing things as we mortals do — travelling, living with family, or playing recreational sports, to name just a few — then we can consider them with a "human lens" rather than a critical or media lens. We also get insight into the job of being prime minister.

These stories are important because they are revealing. "In studying the great characters of history," wrote E.B. Biggar in his 1891 book about our first prime minister, *Anecdotal Life of Sir John A. Macdonald*, "we can learn more about their natures by a single anecdote than by pages of subtle analysis or airy speculation." Focusing on Wilfrid Laurier's gentleness, Mackenzie King's observant life, or Lester Pearson's disarming manner allows us to see prime ministers through a non-political perspective, something that is not only instructive but is also part of what gives history and biography its appeal.

There is something about our perception of authority, too. "When your colleague becomes prime minister, overnight he assumes a different persona, or perhaps it is us who see him differently," wrote Donald Savoie in *Governing from the Centre: The Concentration of Power in Canadian Politics*. "We respect the fact that he has an impossible agenda, that he now has to deal with world leaders, and that we can no longer walk in his office for a relaxed chat. We quickly come to terms with the fact he can no longer be one of us." In that respect, prime ministers are different. They make sacrifices along the way to get there, and perhaps even more so once they have become prime minister. Anyone who has had the privilege of meeting a sitting PM will tell you about the aura of the office as much as the content of the conversation, something that continues even after being prime minister.

In my interviews with six of the seven former PMs (Stephen Harper declined to be interviewed for this book), there was noticeable correlation between years in office and the level of personal rapport that I established with them. The longer a prime minister was in power, the greater the distance was between former PM and interlocutor. Brian Mulroney and Jean Chrétien were gracious and thoughtful in my interviews but there was an aura about them. On the other hand, John Turner, Joe Clark, Kim Campbell, and Paul Martin all seemed more accessible on a human level than their longer-serving counterparts. Martin even gave me some advice for the book. "You give your book to your enemies so they know your thinking," he told me, "but make your friends buy a copy. And I will buy a copy of your book."

On another note, I thought it would be insightful if I asked each former PM for the names of two deceased prime ministers with whom they would most like to have dinner. Not surprisingly, Sir John A. Macdonald and Sir Wilfrid Laurier topped the list. All of them mentioned at least one of these two legends. "Many of us got to reshape the country," mentioned Joe Clark, regarding his choice of Macdonald and Laurier, "but they actually had to shape it, often through force of personality."

"In my judgment there was only one truly great prime minister," Brian Mulroney told me, "and that was Sir Wilfrid. Together at dinner [Laurier and Macdonald] could totally fascinate everyone by telling how they did it." John Turner agreed, saying Macdonald and Laurier would be outstanding dinner companions.

Jean Chrétien was interested to dine with several former prime ministers. He was naturally drawn to Laurier, with whom he shared a similar background, coming from rural Quebec. Both he and Laurier were francophone PMs who served at the turn of a century. But Chrétien said he would "always be happy to have another dinner with

Pierre Trudeau," before he also mentioned Mackenzie King and Robert Borden (*Letters to Limbo* was on his mind) for good measure.

Paul Martin wanted to dine with Macdonald and Laurier, as well, but gave reasons more related to his policy and diplomatic interests. He wanted to hear from Macdonald not only about Confederation and how he managed the British, but also, he said, he would "like to see if I could convince him to change his mind about his approach to Indigenous Canada."

He saw Laurier as the father of Canadian liberalism. "I would like to talk to him about his thought process in this area from beginning to end," Martin said.

Kim Campbell immediately mentioned John A. in her response. "I would love to be exposed to the Macdonald charm," she said. After some deliberation, her second choice was Lester B. Pearson. "I would be interested to meet him because he was sort of the 'unpolitician,'" she offered. "He certainly was ambitious. He was an interesting man and there was more to him than meets the eye."

Being prime minister is a demanding and difficult job. It is all consuming and can be physically draining. It can be a lonely one, too. But we are fortunate to have had good people give it their best shot in Canada, and mostly they have made the country better. Despite its challenges, prime ministers love the job. Setting the agenda for the country, being able to make a difference each day, is a special responsibility and, quite frankly, a privilege. While most prime ministers have at one point or another commented on the frustrations and seeming unfairness of the criticisms that come with it (hence that need for the "hide of a rhinoceros," as Pearson put it), it is worth noting once more that none ever said that there was a better job than being prime minister.

ACKNOWLEDGEMENTS

No book ever comes together by the author alone, and I am indebted to a number of people who have assisted me with this project. I would first like to thank my agent, Michael Levine, who met me serendipitously several years ago but recognized in me a passion for Canada and a desire to see the country's stories told to a wider audience. I appreciated Michael's patience and encouragement before this project was even conceived. As someone who had never before published a book, having someone of Michael's calibre and expertise in my corner was important. Without Michael, this book would not have ended up in your hands.

A number of wonderful people — some of whom I have never met personally — were enormously helpful in bringing this book to fruition. I would like to thank Roy MacGregor of the *Globe and Mail*, who was always very encouraging of this project and read several chapters, offering useful feedback and anecdotes. Roy and I have been correspondents by email (and a few pieces of snail mail) for more than fifteen years, and his willingness to engage, share stories, and encourage has been a source of motivation for me — and I suspect many other writers across the country. Lawrence Martin, also of the *Globe and Mail*, patiently read early drafts of the entire manuscript, offering encouragement and insight to make the book better. I thank him for all of the time and advice he gave me.

Anthony Wilson-Smith, the former editor of *Maclean's* magazine, now CEO of Historica Canada, gave so much of his time to me and read every chapter of this book. His speedy replies, suggestions, extra tidbits, enthusiasm, and leads to other people with knowledge of events, was instrumental to me during this process. I am greatly indebted to Anthony.

Other people helped with this project, as well. My cousin Greg Beatty was superb at clearing away some of the clutter and lazy prose from my first drafts. His initial feedback was frank and indispensable, and I thank him for it. I am grateful to editor Dominic Farrell of Dundurn Press for his advice throughout the various stages of writing this book. Dominic read early chapters and gave useful suggestions. His steady, patient, and meticulous editing hand helped to make this book into the professional product it is. I am also thankful to Carrie Gleason and Margaret Bryant, both formerly of Dundurn, who took a flyer by agreeing to publish this book. It's not everyone who will give an opportunity to a previously unpublished author, but Carrie and Margaret liked what they saw and gave me a chance to make a dream come true. Thanks as well to Laura Boyle for the striking cover and elegant design of the text inside. Her work exceeded my expectations and is an aesthetic home run. Additionally, Kirk Howard, founder and owner of Dundurn, has been a steadfast supporter of Canadian history throughout his life, and I appreciate the role he has played to keep our stories in the hands of Canadian readers.

Navigating the archives can be daunting for a first-time writer and researcher, so I thank my former student Joanne Archibald — herself working in the field of Canadian history now — who initiated me into how the whole archival research process works. At Library and Archives Canada, I was most fortunate to be assisted by Catherine Butler, who answered numerous questions, sought out documents, and generally advised me on the myriad aspects of finding useful sources at LAC. Arthur Milnes, a wonderful historian of prime ministers, was gracious with his time and supplied me with some highly interesting and useful archival material from the papers of Brian Mulroney, including private photographs that appear in this book. Many thanks. Thanks to the Diefenbaker Centre for the photographs of John Diefenbaker that they provided.

I would like to thank my colleagues at Bishop Strachan School, who listened to my various stories of prime ministers — as they have done for years, quite frankly — and who were supportive of this project, either with words of encouragement, questions about the process, or reading a chapter. My students, as well, to whom this book is dedicated, have been a source of motivation for me as a teacher and have made my job fun and rewarding. Thank you for your interest and enthusiasm for all that is Canadian history.

I would also like to express my sincere gratitude to six of Canada's former prime ministers. The Right Honourable Joe Clark, the Right Honourable John Turner, the Right Honourable Brian Mulroney, the Right Honourable Kim Campbell, the Right Honourable Jean Chrétien, and the Right Honourable Paul Martin were all gracious with their time in agreeing to interview with me as part of my research for *Being Prime Minister*. For that I am eternally grateful. What a country. For those wondering, I did ask Stephen Harper for an interview (three times) but he declined. Some may also wonder about Justin Trudeau. His office was asked, but after initially agreeing to an interview, actually securing one proved to be elusive.

I thank everyone else who agreed to interview with me for this project, including the Honourable Carolyn Bennett, Ian Brodie, Bonnie Brownlee, Pamela Divinsky, Peter Donolo, Bill Fox, Allan Gregg, Bruce Hartley, Scott Munnoch, Terrie O'Leary, the Honourable David Smith, and the Honourable Lyle Vanclief. Faithful correspondents Peter Bregg, Claire Mowat, and the Honorable Landon Pearson were also very helpful with details about the prime ministers they knew.

A book cannot be written without the support of the author's family. I thank Julia, William, and Madeleine for allowing me the time and space to complete this book and for putting up with what I will call occasional grumpiness. I could not have done this without them; they have all probably heard enough about prime ministers for a while. Thank you for your unwavering support of this project. The same goes for my siblings, parents, and in-laws.

Finally, my biggest and most sincere thanks go to University of Ottawa historian Serge Durflinger. Serge has been a friend and mentor for more than twenty-five years, since my days at McGill University, and I could not have completed this book without his advice and support since its inception. Serge's keen, demanding editing eye and exhortations to revise and rework the manuscript were instrumental during the writing process and made this book much better than it otherwise would have been. His guidance and friendship meant everything.

Mistakes, there will be a few. There always are. I am responsible for them.

A NOTE ON SOURCES

I n researching this book I relied on a great many sources, including primary source material from Library and Archives Canada, online diaries, debates from the House of Commons, newspaper and magazine reports, interviews, and email and postal correspondence, as well as numerous books and memoirs published by and about prime ministers. To limit the number of endnotes and streamline the reading experience, I have listed below the sources that were highly useful to me in the writing of this book rather than citing them individually with each reference in the text.

The sources that were regularly useful to me included the following:

BOOKS

Biggar, E.B. *Anecdotal Life of Sir John Macdonald*. Montreal: John Lovell and Son, 1891.

Borden, Robert Laird. *His Memoirs*. 2 vols. London: Macmillan, 1938.

Boyko, John. *Bennett: The Rebel Who Challenged and Changed a Nation*. Toronto: Key Porter Books, 2010.

Brown, Robert Craig. *Robert Laird Borden: A Biography.* Vol. 2, *1914–1937.* Toronto: Macmillan, 1980.

Campbell, Kim. *Time and Chance: The Political Memoirs of Canada's First Woman Prime Minister.* New York: Doubleday, 1996.

Chrétien, Jean. *My Years As Prime Minister.* Toronto: Knopf Canada, 2007.

Diefenbaker, John. *One Canada: Memoirs of the Right Honourable John G. Diefenbaker: The Tumultuous Years, 1962–1967.* Toronto: Macmillan of Canada, 1977.

Donaldson, Gordon. *Eighteen Men: The Prime Ministers of Canada.* Toronto: Doubleday Canada, 1985.

Dummitt, Christopher. *Unbuttoned: A History of Mackenzie King's Secret Life.* Montreal and Kingston: McGill-Queen's University Press, 2017.

English, John. *Just Watch Me: The Life of Pierre Elliott Trudeau, 1968–2000.* Toronto: Vintage Canada, 2009.

Goldenberg, Eddie. *The Way It Works: Inside Ottawa.* Toronto: McClelland and Stewart, 2006.

Graham, Roger. *Arthur Meighen.* Vol. 2, *And Fortune Fled.* Toronto: Clarke, Irwin, 1963.

Gwyn, Richard. *Nation Maker: Sir John A. Macdonald: His Life, Our Times.* Vol. 2, *1867–1891.* Toronto: Random House, 2011.

Hutchison, Bruce. *Mr. Prime Minister: 1867–1964.* London: Longmans, 1965.

Ibbitson, John. *Stephen Harper.* Toronto: McClelland and Stewart, 2015.

Levine, Allan. *Scrum Wars: The Prime Ministers and the Media.* Toronto: Dundurn Press, 1993.

Martin, Paul. *Hell or Highwater: My Life In and Out of Politics.* Toronto: McClelland and Stewart, 2008.

McIlroy, Thad, ed. *Personal Letters of a Public Man: The Family Letters of John G. Diefenbaker.* Toronto: Doubleday Canada, 1985.

Mulroney, Brian. *Memoirs: 1939–1993.* Toronto: McClelland and Stewart, 2007.

Neatby, H. Blair. *William Lyon Mackenzie King, 1924–1932: The Lonely Heights.* Toronto: University of Toronto Press, 1963.

Newman, Peter C. *Renegade In Power: The Diefenbaker Years.* Toronto: McClelland and Stewart, 1963.

_____ . *The Secret Mulroney Tapes: Unguarded Confessions of a Prime Minister.* Toronto: Random House, 2006.

Pearson, Lester B. *Mike: The Memoirs of the Right Honourable Lester. B. Pearson.* Vol. 3, *1957–1968.* Toronto: University of Toronto Press, 1976.

Pickersgill, J.W. *The Mackenzie King Record.* Vol. 1, *1939–1944.* Toronto: University of Toronto Press, 1960.

_____ . *My Years With Louis St. Laurent: A Political Memoir.* Toronto: University of Toronto Press, 1975.

Pickersgill, J.W., and D.F. Forster. *The Mackenzie King Record.* Vol. 2, *1944–1945.* Toronto: University of Toronto Press, 1968.

_____ . *The Mackenzie King Record.* Vol. 4, *1947–1948.* Toronto: University of Toronto Press, 1970.

Radwanski, George. *Trudeau.* Toronto: Macmillan and Company, 1978.

Robertston, Gordon. *Memoirs of a Very Civil Servant: Mackenzie King to Pierre Trudeau.* Toronto: University of Toronto Press, 2000.

Savoie, Donald J. *Governing from the Centre: The Concentration of Power in Canadian Politics.* Toronto: University of Toronto Press, 1999.

Smith, Denis. *Rogue Tory: The Life and Legend of John G. Diefenbaker.* Toronto: Macfarlane Walter and Ross, 1995.

Southam, Nancy, ed. *Pierre: Colleagues and Friends Talk About the Trudeau They Knew.* Toronto: McClelland and Stewart, 2005.

Stacey, C.P. *A Very Double Life: The Private World of Mackenzie King.* Toronto: Macmillan of Canada, 1976.

Trudeau, Pierre. *Memoirs.* Toronto: McClelland and Stewart, 1993.

NEWSPAPERS AND MAGAZINES

Globe

Globe and Mail

National Post

Ottawa Citizen

Maclean's

Toronto Star

LIBRARY AND ARCHIVES CANADA

Robert Borden papers
Tom Earle Fond
Wilfrid Laurier papers
John A. Macdonald papers
Brian Mulroney papers
Lester B. Pearson papers
Privy Council Fond
Basil Robinson papers
Louis St. Laurent papers
Pierre Trudeau papers

INTERNET

CBC Digital Archives
Diaries of William Lyon Mackenzie King

INTERVIEWS

Honourable Carolyn Bennett
Ian Brodie
Bonnie Brownlee
Right Honourable Kim Campbell
Right Honourable Jean Chrétien
Right Honourable Joe Clark
Pamela Divinsky
Peter Donolo
Bill Fox
Allan Gregg
Bruce Hartley
Right Honourable Paul Martin
Right Honourable Brian Mulroney
Scott Munnoch
Terrie O'Leary

Honourable David Smith
Right Honourable John Turner
Honourable Lyle Vanclief

DEBATES

Debates of the House of Commons were accessed through the Library of Parliament's Canadian Parliamentary Historical Resources at http://parl.canadiana.ca.

NOTES

INTRODUCTION

1. Brian Mulroney, "William A. Howard Memorial Lecture" (lecture, University of Calgary, Calgary, AB, September 13, 2016).
2. Paul Martin, telephone interview by author, December 14, 2016.

CHAPTER 1

1. Patrice Dutil, *Prime Ministerial Power in Canada: Its Origins under Macdonald, Laurier, and Borden* (Vancouver: UBC Press, 2017), 286.
2. J.D.M. Stewart, "The Machine Sends Its Thanks," *Toronto Star*, September 24, 2006.
3. Van Blaricom, "A Day with Canada's Premier," *Maclean's,* June 1909.
4. Klaus Neumann, "Backstage with the PM's Mail," *Maclean's,* November, 22, 1958.
5. Stuart MacKay, letter to Lester B. Pearson, April 11, 1965, MG 26 N8, Vol. 13, Library and Archives Canada.
6. Jules Pelletier, response on behalf of Lester B. Pearson, April 15, 1965, MG 26 N8, Vol. 13, LAC.

7. Stewart, "The Machine Sends Its Thanks."

8. Dan Beeby, "Dear Mr. Martin, Can You Cut Down the Gas Price?," *Toronto Star*, November 7, 2005.

9. Julie Hirschfeld Davis, "Obama Often Depends on Mail to Tell His Story," *New York Times*, March 13, 2016, www.nytimes.com/2016/03/14/us/politics/obama-often-depends-on-mail-to-tell-his-story.html.

10. Van Blaricom, "A Day with Canada's Premier."

11. Anthony Wilson-Smith, "The Private Prime Minister," *Maclean's*, January 24, 1994.

12. "Canada: Père de famille," *Time*, September 12, 1949.

13. "Justin Speaks One-on-One with CBC's Matt Galloway," CBC News, November 24, 2015, www.cbc.ca/news/canada/toronto/programs/metromorning/justin-trudeau-matt-galloway-full-interview-1.3334133.

14. M. Grattan O'Leary, "What It Means to Be Secretary to the Prime Minister," *Maclean's*, June 1, 1931.

15. O'Leary.

16. Michael Valpy, "The Final Day," *Globe and Mail*, June 19, 1993.

17. Peter C. Newman, "The Powerful Gifts and Glaring Flaws of John Diefenbaker," *Maclean's*, March 23, 1963.

18. Thomas Van Dusen, *The Chief* (Toronto: McGraw-Hill, 1968), 101.

19. Haydn Watters, "Fries with That, Mr. Trudeau? PM Stops In for Surprise McDonald's Lunch," CBC News, June 18, 2016, www.cbc.ca/news/trending/mcdonalds-trudeau-whitby-1.3642207.

20. Walter Gray, "Private Wire: Party Line Questions About PM," *Globe and Mail*, August 11, 1958.

21. Richard. S. Conley, "The Transformation of Question Period," *Canadian Parliamentary Review* 34, no. 3 (2011): 47.

22. Van Blaricom, "A Day with Canada's Premier."

23. Kim Campbell, interview by author, June 30, 2016.

24. Harry Anderson, "Bennett Is Eager to Return," *Globe*, April 17, 1935.

25. Blair Fraser, "Mackenzie King as I Knew Him," *Maclean's*, September 1, 1950.

26. "John Diefenbaker: He Recalls Buffalo Skulls and Riel's Lieutenant," *Maclean's*, March 29, 1958.

CHAPTER 2

1. "Sir Wilfrid in the West," *Globe*, August 20, 1910.
2. Ian Brodie, interview by author, June 29, 2016.
3. Gloria Galloway, "Common Touch Is Top Trait Valued in PM, Poll Finds," *Globe and Mail*, February 3, 2006.
4. Charles Power, *A Party Politician: The Memoirs of Chubby Power* (Toronto: Macmillan of Canada, 1965), 73.
5. Donald Creighton, *John A. Macdonald: The Old Chieftain* (Toronto: Macmillan of Canada, 1955), 252.
6. Power, *A Party Politician*, 73.
7. Cairine Wilson, radio address, November 20, 1941, MG 26, Vol. 810-812, LAC.
8. Quoted in Arthur Milnes, ed., *Canada Always: The Defining Speeches of Sir Wilfrid Laurier* (Toronto: McClelland and Stewart, 2016), 7.
9. Milnes, *Canada Always*, 461.
10. Marjory LeBreton, interview, April 3, 1985, R1026, Vol. 2574, LAC.
11. Anthony Wilson-Smith, "Mulroney Up Close," *Maclean's*, June 10, 1991.
12. LeBreton, interview.
13. Wilson-Smith, "Mulroney Up Close."
14. Alastair Fraser, interview, October–November 1983, R1026, Vol. 2562, LAC.
15. Fraser, interview.
16. Ian Sclanders, "How the Prime Minister Became Uncle Louis," *Maclean's*, January 1, 1955.
17. Jean Chrétien, interview by author, Ottawa, September 26, 2017.
18. Scott Young, "The Peaceful Prime Minister," *Globe and Mail*, February 1, 1965.
19. Dick Beddoes, "Gentleman Jock of Parliament Hill Tops in Hot Stove League," *Globe and Mail*, December 28, 1972. Dick Beddoes said this happened in 1963 but Gerry Ehman was not on the Leafs' playoff roster that year. The anecdote must be from 1964.
20. Mary Macdonald, interview, April 1984, R1026, Volume 2563, LAC.

21. Alexander Ross, "The Long Happy Life Of Lester Pearson," *Maclean's*, July 1, 1967.

22. "The Real Premier," *Toronto Star Weekly*, August 1, 1914.

23. Tim Cook, *Warlords: Borden, Mackenzie King and Canada's World Wars* (Toronto: Allen Lane, 2012.), 67.

24. "Canada's War Premier," *Globe and Mail*, June 11, 1937.

25. Fraser, "Mackenzie King as I Knew Him."

26. "Pearson speaks at King's statue unveiling," CBC Digital Archives video, 8:43, from a CBC Television News Special on July 1, 1968, www.cbc.ca/archives/entry./pearson-speaks-at-kings-statue-unveiling.

27. Bruce Hutchison, *Mr. Prime Minister* (London: Longmans, 1964), 243.

28. Michael Kesterton, "Canadian PM Ate Six Meals a Day to Bulk Up: R.B. (Bonfire) Bennett," *Globe and Mail*, July 1, 2000.

29. L.M. Grayson and Michael Bliss, eds., *The Wretched of Canada: Letters to R.B. Bennett, 1930–1935* (Toronto: University of Toronto Press, 1971), xxiii.

30. Conrad Black, "The Liberals' Tax Reforms Will Be a National Disaster," *National Post*, September 15, 2017, http://nationalpost.com/opinion/conrad-black-the-liberal-tax-reform-proposals-will-be-a-national-disaster.

31. Ishmael N. Daro, "With a Little Help from the Piano: How Stephen Harper Uses Pop Music to Soften His Public Image Among Voters," *National Post*, June 6, 2015, http://nationalpost.com/news/canada/pop-music-and-politics-787126.

32. Paul Wells, *The Longer I'm Prime Minister: Stephen Harper and Canada, 2006–* (Toronto: Random House Canada, 2013), 284.

33. Wells, 286.

34. George Hees, interview, September 20, 1983, R1026, Vol. 2562, LAC.

35. Tom Earle, interview, April–May 1994, R1026, Vol. 2574, LAC.

36. Basil Robinson, letter to Denis Smith, March 10, 1996, MG 31, E83 R3964, LAC.

37. Denis Smith, letter to Basil Robinson, April 14, 1996, MG 31, E83 R3964, LAC.

38. Michael Bliss, "Guarding a Most Famous Stream: Trudeau and the Canadian Political Tradition," in *Trudeau's Shadow: The Life and Legacy of Pierre Trudeau*, ed. Andrew Cohen and J.L. Granatstein (Toronto: Random House, 1998), 12.

39. Chrétien, interview by author.

40. Donald S. Macdonald, "The Trudeau Cabinet: A Memoir," in Cohen and Granatstein, *Trudeau's Shadow*.

41. Ivan Head, interview with Tom Earle, September–November 1989, R1026, Vol. 2570, LAC.

42. Peter Donolo, interview by author, Toronto, May 30, 2017.

43. Lyle Vanclief, interview by author, Toronto, September 22, 2017.

44. Eddie Goldenberg, *The Way It Works: Inside Ottawa* (Toronto: McClelland and Stewart, 2011), 72.

45. Lawrence Martin, *Iron Man: The Defiant Reign of Jean Chrétien* (Toronto: Viking Press, 2003), 1.

46. Carman Miller, "Abbott, Sir John Joseph Caldwell," in *Dictionary of Canadian Biography*, vol. 12, University of Toronto/Université Laval, 2003–, accessed July 21, 2017, www.biographi.ca/en/bio/abbott_john_joseph_caldwell_12E.html.

47. "Canada's Next Premier?" *Maclean's*, November 15, 1921.

48. Power, *A Party Politician*, 73.

49. W.R. Graham, "Meighen in Debate," *Queen's Quarterly* 62 (January 1955): 24.

50. "Joe Clark's Unexpected Cachet," *Globe and Mail*, June 14, 2001.

51. J.L. Granatstein and Norman Hillmer, *Prime Ministers: Ranking Canada's Leaders* (Toronto: HarperCollins, 1999), 166.

52. Stephen Rodrick, "Justin Trudeau: The North Star," *Rolling Stone*, July 26, 2017, www.rollingstone.com/politics/features/justin-trudeau-canadian-prime-minister-free-worlds-best-hope-w494098.

53. Peter Mansbridge, "Behind the Scenes with Justin Trudeau on His 1st Day as PM," *CBC News*, November 4, 2015, www.cbc.ca/news/politics/behind-the-scenes-with-justin-trudeau-on-his-1st-day-as-pm-1.3304860.

CHAPTER 3

1. Frank Jones, "How Trudeaumania Flamed Again," *Toronto Star*, May 20, 1969.

2. Ronald Lebel, "Trudeau Crosses Sound Barrier in Plane and Poverty Line on Train," *Globe and Mail*, May 19, 1969.

3. Maurice Pope, ed., *Public Servant: The Memoirs of Sir Joseph Pope* (Toronto, Oxford University Press, 1960), 57.

4. "Taunts, Tomatoes, Mar PM's Holiday in Posh Rail Car," *Globe and Mail*, August 10, 1982.

5. Geoffrey Stevens, *The Player: The Life and Times of Dalton Camp* (Toronto: Key Porter Books, 2003), 135.

6. Val Sears, "Travels with Pierre Fun Only for Luggage," *Toronto Star*, March 1, 1984.

7. Van Blaricom, "A Day with Canada's Premier."

8. "Quebec's Royal Welcome to Sir Wilfrid Laurier," *Globe*, October 18, 1902.

9. Scott Munnoch, interview by author, July 2016.

10. "Canada's First 'Air Force One': Prime Minister Mackenzie King's Silver Saloon," *Ottawa Rewind*, January 12, 2014, https://ottawarewind.com/2014/01/12/canadas-first-air-force-one-prime-minister-mackenzie-kings-silver-saloon/.

11. Robert Borden, *Letters to Limbo* (Toronto: University of Toronto Press, 1971), 33.

12. Mulroney, interview by author, August 23, 2016.

13. John Burns, "How the PM Gets Around and Who Pays," *Globe and Mail*, January 9, 1970.

14. B. Green, "The Prime Minister," letter to the editor, *Globe and Mail*, January 13, 1970.

15. Munnoch, interview, August 17, 2016.

16. Bill Fox, interview by author, Toronto, July 26, 2016.

17. Heather Scoffield, "PM Ignored Objections in Buying Luxury Jets: Full Cabinet Excluded," *Globe and Mail*, April 12, 2002.

18. "$48,000 Spent on Grounded Flight Crew During PM's Caribbean Vacation," CTV News, March 18, 2016, www.ctvnews.ca/politics/48-000-spent-on-grounded-flight-crew-during-pm-s-caribbean-vacation-1.2824018.

19. Dale C. Thomson, *Louis St. Laurent: Canadian* (Toronto: Macmillan of Canada, 1967), 361.
20. Charles Ritchie, *Diplomatic Passport: More Undiplomatic Diaries, 1946–1962* (Toronto: Macmillan of Canada, 1981), 66.
21. Wilson, radio address.
22. Robert Taylor, "St. Laurent Rumpled in Crash, Woman Driver Is Praised," *Toronto Star,* May 17, 1957.

CHAPTER 4

1. Marjorie "Bunny" Pound, November 24, 1988, R1026, Vol. 2659, LAC.
2. Letter to John A. Macdonald, 1885, C-22506, C-33889, C-43252, LAC.
3. Martin F. Auger, "On the Brink of Civil War: The Canadian Government and the Suppression of the 1918 Quebec Easter Riots," *Canadian Historical Review* 89, no. 4 (2008): 503.
4. Sclanders, "How the Prime Minister Became Uncle Louis."
5. *Capital City*, directed by Fergus McDonnell (Montreal: National Film Board of Canada, 1957).
6. Van Dusen, *The Chief,* 100.
7. Edwin Bolwell, "5 Women Strip at Rally but PM Keeps Composure," *Globe and Mail*, May 28, 1962.
8. Letter to Lester B. Pearson, January 1964, RG 2, Ban 2000-01376-7, Box 81, LAC.
9. RCMP Police Report, July 13, 1964, RG 2, Ban 2000-01376-7, Box 81, LAC.
10. Alastair Fraser, interview.
11. George Bain, "The Dangers in Parliament," *Globe and Mail*, May 23, 1966.
12. Michael Gillian, "LBJ Day at the LBP Cottage and the Old Place 'Will Never Be the Same Again,'" *Globe and Mail*, May 26, 1967.
13. RCMP Memo, May 10, 1963, RG 2, Ban 2000-01376-7, Box 81, LAC.
14. "No Desire for Melodrama, but Kennedy in Mind: Police Protection for PM with Rifle on Roof," *Globe and Mail*, June 15, 1968.

15. Frank Jones, "'Horrified' Trudeau Watches RFK News," *Toronto Star*, June 5, 1968.
16. Jones.
17. Thomas Claridge, "The PM Mixes Politics and Fun," *Globe and Mail*, November 30, 1970.
18. Dave McIntosh, quotes from the report in an appendix to his interview, R1026, Vol. 2563, LAC.
19. Bain, "The Dangers in Parliament."
20. Hugh Winsor, "Intruder Arrested Quickly: RCMP Play Down Incident," *Globe and Mail*, March 4, 1996.
21. Peter Donolo, interview by author, July 27, 2016.
22. *Inside 24 Sussex: The Home of Canada's Prime Minister*, (CPAC 2015) video, 58:30, www.cpac.ca/en/programs/documentaries/episodes/39822742/.
23. Donolo, interview by author.
24. "Mounties Disciplined in Wake of Threat to PM," *Globe and Mail*, November 11, 1995.
25. Rheal Seguin, "PM Gets Rough Treatment in Quebec," *Globe and Mail*, February 17, 1996.
26. Martin, *Iron Man*, 145.
27. Seguin, "PM Gets Rough Treatment in Quebec."
28. "Embarrassing Trail of Security Lapses," *Toronto Star*, August 18, 2000.
29. Bill Curry, "Anti-Terrorist Security Urged for PM's Residences," *Globe and Mail*, March 9, 2009, www.theglobeandmail. com/news/national/anti-terrorist-security-urged-for-pms-residences/article20441726/.
30. Glen McGregor, "'He Stood His Ground": Constable Lauds PM Harper's Courage During Oct. 22 Attack," *Ottawa Citizen*, October 21, 2015, http://ottawacitizen.com/news/national/he-stood-his-ground-constable-lauds-pm-harpers-courage-during-oct-22-attack.
31. Daniel Leblanc, "Tightened Tactics Breed Dissent in Harper's Security Detail," *Globe and Mail*, June 23, 2012, www.theglobeandmail.com/news/politics/tightened-tactics-breed-dissent-in-harpers-security-detail/article4366007/.

32. Diana Mehta, "Stephen Harper Security Breach Happened Because It's 'About Democracy,' Says Ex-Mountie," *Huffington Post*, January 7, 2014, www.huffingtonpost.ca/2014/01/07/stephen-harper-security-breach-bc_n_4557502.html.

33. Jeff Sallot, "Bodyguards' Role Not Always Clear," *Globe and Mail*, August 31, 1993.

34. Robin Gill, "Security Detail Tries to Keep Up with PM Trudeau on Whistler Snowboarding Trip," *Global News*, March 1, 2016, last modified March 2, 2016, http://globalnews.ca/news/2551398/pm-justin-trudeau-keeps-security-detail-on-its-toes-and-the-slopes/.

35. Martin, interview.

36. The descriptions are based on interviews with police officers, past and present, who wished to remain anonymous but worked in VIP security.

37. Email to author from Media Relations Services, RCMP National Division, September 15, 2017.

38. "How Safe Are Our Leaders?," *Globe and Mail*, May 21, 1966.

CHAPTER 5

1. Robert Borden, October 21, 1913, MG 26, Vol. 453, LAC.

2. Robert Borden, January 2, 1916, MG 26, Vol. 450, LAC.

3. Harry W. Anderson, "Grateful to God for His Recovery, He Tells Newspapermen," *Globe*, April 17, 1935.

4. William Marchington, "Will to Return," *Globe*, April 16, 1935.

5. Allan Levine, *King: William Lyon Mackenzie King: A Life Guided by the Hand of Destiny* (Vancouver: Douglas and McIntyre, 2011), 423.

6. Fraser, interview.

7. Victor Mackie, interview, February 25, 1984, R1026, Vol. 2563, LAC.

8. Robert Bothwell, "St. Laurent, Louis-Stephen (Baptized Louis Étienne)," in *Dictionary of Canadian Biography*, vol. 20, University of Toronto/Université Laval, 2003–, accessed July 21, 2017, www.biographi.ca/en/bio/st_laurent_louis_stephen_20E.html.

9. Walter Gray, "Doctor's Report of Good Health," *Globe and Mail*, March 1, 1963.

10. "Rajput Says Diefenbaker Didn't Have Parkinson's, and Names 'Essential Tremors' After Former PM," *On Campus News*, University of Saskatchewan, August 10, 2001, https://news.usask.ca/archived_ocn/aug10-01/news14.shtml.

11. Pound, interview.

12. Pound, interview.

13. "Away 10 Days: PM Goes to Hospital for Removal of Cyst," *Globe and Mail*, June 28, 1963.

14. Beddoes, "Gentleman Jock of Parliament Hill."

15. Creighton, *Sir John A. Macdonald*, 164.

16. *The Last Days of the Life of The Right Honourable Sir John Alexander Macdonald, GCB, Prime Minister of Canada, By his attending physician Robert Wynard Powell, June 8, 1891, MD*, MG 27 I J 3 Macdonald Papers, LAC.

17. Milnes, *Canada Always*, 137.

18. Granatstein and Hillmer, *Prime Ministers*, 40.

19. P.B. Waite, "Thompson, Sir John Sparrow David," in *Dictionary of Canadian Biography*, vol. 12, University of Toronto/Université Laval, 2003–, accessed July 21, 2017, www.biographi.ca/en/bio/thompson_john_sparrow_david_12E.html.

20. Granatstein and Hillmer, *Prime Ministers*, 42.

21. FOX, interview.

CHAPTER 6

1. Donald Newman, "Praise for Trudeau from the Lennons," *Globe and Mail*, December 24, 1969.

2. Olivier Driessens, "The Celebritization of Society and Culture: Understanding the Structural Dynamics of Celebrity Culture," *International Journal of Cultural Studies* 16, no. 6 (2012): 652.

3. Marie-Danielle Smith, "'We Don't Beat the Celebrity-in-Chief with Another Celebrity-in-Chief': CPC Leadership Hopefuls Target O'Leary," *National Post*, February 5, 2017, http://

nationalpost.com/news/politics/we-dont-beat-the-celebrity-in
-chief-with-another-celebrity-in-chief-cpc-leadership-hopefuls-
target-oleary.

4. "On the Cover of the Rolling Stone," *Toronto Sun*, July 26, 2017,
    www.torontosun.com/2017/07/26/on-the-cover-of-the-rolling-
    stone.

5. "Mary Pickford Visits Home Town," AP Archive video, 0:58,
    from Movietone News on January 26, 1948, www.aparchive.
    com/metadata/youtube/c394a09399f640f9a0e3807934f140fa.

6. "Plan National Welcome for Barbara Ann Scott," *Globe and Mail*,
    February 16, 1948.

7. "Unspoiled Champion," *Globe and Mail*, February 7, 1948.

8. Peter Dempson, *Assignment Ottawa: Seventeen Years in the Press
    Gallery* (Toronto: General Publishing, 1968), 130.

9. Jayne Mansfield, "Lester Pearson's Promises Analyzed in 1963,"
    CBC Digital Archives video, 8:10, from *Inquiry*, June 10, 1963,
    www.cbc.ca/archives/entry/lester-pearsons-promises-analyzed-
    in-1963.

10. "Backstage at Ottawa," *Maclean's*, April 15, 1931.

11. MTanzer, "White Trash Prince, Justin Bieber, Wears Overalls to
    Meet the Prime Minister of Canada," *Gawker*, http://gawker.
    com/5962961/white-trash-prince-justin-bieber-wears-overalls-to-
    meet-the-prime-minister-of-canada.

12. Peter Bregg, email to author, July 19, 2016.

13. Mulroney Papers, April 25, 1985, MG 26, Vol. 11, LAC.

14. Quoted in Roy MacGregor, "Celebrities May Put the Pizzazz in
    Politics, but It Doesn't Amount to Much," *Globe and Mail*, July
    7, 2006.

CHAPTER 7

1. Gloria Galloway, "Smile Mr. Harper, You're Now on Candid
    Camera," *Globe and Mail*, January 28, 2006.

2. Geoffrey Stevens, "The PM and Privacy," *Globe and Mail*,
    December 20, 1973.

3. Michael Valpy, "Satire of PM's Daughter Despicable," *Globe and Mail*, September 11, 1991.

4. William Walker, "Livid PM Says Article Urged 'Rape' of His Daughter," *Toronto Star*, March 11, 1992.

5. "24 Sussex weekend medical call not for Harper family member: RCMP," CBC News, April 23, 2014, www.cbc.ca/news/politics/24-sussex-weekend-medical-call-not-for-harper-family-member-rcmp-1.2619343.

6. Bruce Ward, "The Women: Young and Beautiful But He Liked Them to Be Discreet," Montreal *Gazette*, March 1, 1984.

7. Quoted in George Bain, "Angry Trudeau Flays the 'Crummy Behavior' of Prying Reporters," *Globe and Mail*, January 16, 1969.

8. Ivan Head, interview, September–November 1989, R1026, Vol. 2570, LAC.

9. Bain, "Angry Trudeau Flays."

10. Charles Ritchie, *Storm Signals: More Undiplomatic Diaries, 1962–71* (Toronto: Macmillan of Canada, 1963), 124.

11. Margaret Wente, "Trudeau and His (Many) Women," *Globe and Mail*, October 28, 2009, www.theglobeandmail.com/opinion/pierre-trudeau-and-his-many-women/article791993.

12. Christopher Andersen, *Barbra: The Way She Is* (New York: HarperCollins, 2006), 191.

13. John Burns, "Trudeau Dates Streisand on Quiet New York Visit," *Globe and Mail*, November 11, 1969.

14. Andersen, *Barbra*, 191.

15. John Burns, "Trudeau Dates Barbra Streisand, Upstages Royal Winnipeg Ballet." *Globe and Mail*, January 29, 1970.

16. "Streisand Pierre's Date at Ballet in Ottawa," *Toronto Star*, January 29, 1970.

17. Andersen, *Barbra*, 193.

18. John Doig, "PM Fusses and Waves at Barbra Then Goes for a Run in the Park," *Toronto Star*, January 30, 1970.

19. John Burns, "Barbra Streisand Draws Smile from Trudeau in the Commons," *Globe and Mail*, January 30, 1970.

20. Doig, "PM Fusses and Waves."

21. Doig.
22. Andersen, *Barbra*, 193.
23. Andersen, 194.
24. Warren Caragatta, "A Very Strong Person," *Maclean's*, December 6, 1993.
25. Val Sears, "Travels with Pierre Fun Only for Luggage," *Toronto Star*, March 1, 1984.
26. Dick Beddoes, "Ship of Love on the Rocks," *Globe and Mail*, May 30, 1977.
27. Ian Urquhart, "The Media and Mrs. Trudeau: They'll Stop if She Will," *Maclean's*, April 4, 1977.
28. Quoted in, Charlotte Gray, "Where are Those Mulroney Rumours Coming From?," *Globe and Mail*, May 4, 1991.
29. Gray.
30. Levine, *King*, 18.
31. Julianne Labreche, "The Once and Future King," *Maclean's*, January 15, 1979.
32. Labreche.
33. "Pearson Warns of War Danger," *Globe and Mail*, January 22, 1969.
34. Eric Dowd, "Pearson Warns He'll Fire Anyone Deviating from High Standards," *Globe and Mail*, February 5, 1965.

CHAPTER 8

1. Robert Taylor, "St. Laurents Give Party to Open New Residence Drew Gets Special View," *Toronto Star*, May 23, 1951.
2. Maria Cook, "Château Laurier: A Place of Politics and Play," *Ottawa Citizen*, May 30, 2012, www.ottawacitizen.com/news/Chateau+Laurier+place+politics+play/6679655/story.html.
3. Christina Newman, "Authentic Canadian Style or Swank at 24 Sussex?," *Globe and Mail*, February 1, 1975.
4. Susan Delacourt, "Residents of 24 Sussex Drive Stress They're Just Ordinary Folk," *Toronto Star*, April 26, 2013, www.thestar.com/news/insight/2013/04/26/residents_of_24_sussex_drive_stress_theyre_just_ordinary_folk_delacourt.html.

5. "A gracious addition," *Globe and Mail*, November 3, 1966.

6. "A Visit with Maryon Pearson at 24 Sussex Drive," CBC Digital Archives video, 13:42, from *Take 30*, November 7, 1963, www.cbc.ca/archives/entry/a-visit-with-maryon-pearson-at-24-sussex-drive.

7. Newman, "Authentic Canadian Style."

8. Helen Worthington, "Ottawa Still Waits for Trudeau to Start the Town Swinging," *Toronto Star*, December 7, 1968.

9. Roy MacGregor, "Mulroneys, Turners, Play Musical Houses," *Toronto Star*, September 30, 1984.

10. MacGregor, "Mulroneys, Turners."

11. "Swimming Pool Gift Will Help PM Shape Up," *Globe and Mail*, December 24, 1974.

12. "Now for a Cinder Track," *Globe and Mail*, December 30, 1974.

13. "They Used to Call 24 Sussex the Sex Drive," *Toronto Star*, August 26, 1979.

14. Bonnie Brownlee, telephone interview by author, July 14, 2016.

15. Joe O'Donnell, "I'll Pay Tab for Hot Tub, PM Says," *Toronto Star*, December 1, 1984.

16. O'Donnell.

17. Brian Mulroney, April 24, 1987, MG26, Vol. 5, File 6-14, Mulroney Papers, LAC.

18. Mulroney.

19. John Geddes, "'We've Hit Our Stride,'" *Maclean's*, December 27, 2004.

20. *Report of the Auditor General to the House of Commons*, Chapter 6: Conservation of Federal Official Residences (Ottawa: Office of the Auditor General of Canada, 2008), 12, www.oag-bvg.gc.ca/internet/docs/aud_ch_oag_200805_06_e.pdf.

21. *Report of the Auditor General*.

22. Julie Smyth, "The Renovation Debate at 24 Sussex," *Maclean's*, August 20, 2013, www.macleans.ca/news/canada/this-old-house/.

23. Chrétien, interview by author.

24. Maureen McTeer, *Residences: Homes of Canada's Leaders* (Toronto: Prentice-Hall, 1982), 113.

25. Reginald Hardy, "Our Fantastic Legacy from Mackenzie King," *Maclean's*, July 15, 1951.

26. Hardy.

27. Landon Pearson, "Pearsons Up the Gatineau," *Up the Gatineau!* 38 (2012): 8.

28. Justin Trudeau, *Common Ground* (Toronto: HarperCollins Canada, 2014), 12.

29. Justin Trudeau, "A Canadian Childhood," *National Post*, July 1, 2016, http://nationalpost.com/features/canadian-childhood.

30. "Stephen Harper Wants to Retire at Harrington Lake All-Season Retreat Gatineau Park," YouTube video, 2:13, from *A Conversation with the Prime Minister* televised on CTVNews, posted by "peaceandfreedom2011," May 19, 2012, www.youtube.com/watch?v=p0qYeZPl2Ro.

31. Ian Brodie, telephone interview by author, June 28, 2016.

32. Jane Taber, "The Progeny of PMs," *Globe and Mail*, July 17, 2009, www.theglobeandmail.com/news/politics/the-progeny-of-pms/article4289137/.

CHAPTER 9

1. Mary Trueman, "King Felt His Dog Deserved Order of Merit, Diary Says," *Globe and Mail*, January 4, 1978.

2. Fraser, "Mackenzie King As I Knew Him."

3. Bruce Hutchison, "End of a Long Companionship," *Victoria Times*, July 31, 1941.

4. "Mackenzie King on His Dog, 'My Little Friend Pat,'" CBC Digital Archives audio, 3:42, from *Morningside*, March 7, 1978, radio broadcast, www.cbc.ca/archives/entry/mackenzie-king-on-his-dog-my-little-friend-pat.

5. "Mackenzie King on His Dog."

6. Trueman, "King Felt His Dog Deserved."

7. Bruce West, "A Lonely Life," *Globe and Mail*, January 9, 1978.

8. "Pat the Third Joins Mr. King," *Globe and Mail*, August 14, 1948.

9. Van Dusen, *The Chief*, 99.

10. "Happy Wasn't Happy, So He's Dead," *Globe and Mail*, August 9, 1963.

11. Kay Kritzwiser, "The Chatelaine at 24 Sussex Drive," *Globe Magazine*, March 24, 1962.

12. Kritzwiser.

13. Van Dusen, *The Chief*, 99.

14. "Toronto Owner Awarded Prize by Diefenbaker," *Globe and Mail*, May 3, 1965.

15. "Dief's Dog Killed," *Toronto Star*, November 23, 1968.

16. Landon Pearson, email to author, May 2, 2017.

17. Pearson, email to author, January 6, 2017.

18. Claire Mowat, letter to author, August 13, 2017.

19. Mowat.

20. Joe Clark, email to author, October 12, 2017.

21. Don McGillivray, "It's Oscar Time at 24 Sussex," *Ottawa Citizen*, January 13, 1986.

22. Alex Beam, "What Kind of Pet Should Donald Trump Get?," *New York Times*, April 15, 2017, www.nytimes.com/2017/04/15/opinion/sunday/what-kind-of-pet-should-donald-trump-get.html.

23. "Research Shows Personality Differences Between Cat and Dog People," University of Texas at Austin, January 13, 2010, https://news.utexas.edu/2010/01/13/personality_dogs_cats.

24. Aaron Wherry, "The Harpers' Feline Fixation," *Maclean's*, July 15, 2011.

25. Julie Smyth, "Laureen Harper in Conversation," *Maclean's*, November 11, 2013.

26. Helen Gougeon, *Weekend Picture Magazine*, January 3, 1953, St. Laurent papers, MG 26, Vol. 401–8, LAC.

27. W.P Anderson, C.M Reid, and G.L Jennings, "Pet Ownership and Risk Factors for Cardiovascular Disease," *Medical Journal of Australia* 157, no. 5 (1992): 298–301.

CHAPTER 10

1. Ben Forster, "Mackenzie, Alexander," in *Dictionary of Canadian Biography*, vol. 12, University of Toronto/Université Laval, 2003–, accessed July 21, 2017, www.biographi.ca/en/bio/mackenzie_alexander_12E.html.

2. Lawrence Martin, *The Presidents and the Prime Ministers* (Toronto: Doubleday, 1982), 167.

3. Thomson, *Louis St. Laurent*, 405.

4. William J. Clinton, "The President's News Conference with Prime Minister Jean Chrétien of Canada," April 8, 1997, *American Presidency Project*, www.presidency.ucsb.edu/ ws/?pid=53964.

5. Graham Fraser and Edward Greenspon, "On the Fairway to Foreign Policy," *Globe and Mail*, April 5, 1997.

6. Martin, *Iron Man*, 171.

7. Lawrence Martin, interview by Anna Maria Tremonti, "Golf and Politics," *The Current*, CBC Radio, June 9, 2003.

8. Roy MacGregor, email to author, June 2, 2016.

9. "Dief and Clark Among 6 Named to Angler Hall," *Globe and Mail*, August 25, 1976.

10. Geoffrey Stevens, "June Election Left in Air but Trudeau Cabinet in Merry Mood at Swearing In," *Globe and Mail*, April 22, 1968.

11. Jennifer Lewington, "Fish, Tennis on the Agenda as Mulroney Visits Bush," *Globe and Mail*, August 31, 1989.

12. Hilary Mackenzie, "A Working Holiday," *Maclean's*, September 11, 1989.

13. Michael Farber, Montreal *Gazette*, March 1, 1984.

14. Douglas Sagi, "Trudeau's Trend Is to Untraced Powder Snow on the Peaks," *Globe and Mail*, March 24, 1969.

15. Ivan Head, "He Chutes, He Scores!" *Globe and Mail*, February 16, 2002, www.theglobeandmail.com/opinion/he-chutes-hescores/article753078/.

16. Roy MacGregor, *Canoe Country* (Toronto: Random House, 2015), 77–8.

17. Declan Hill, "Here's What It's Like to Punch the Prime Minister," *Toronto Star*, March 31, 2017, www.thestar.com/news/ canada/2017/03/31/heres-what-its-like-to-punch-the-prime-minister.html.

18. Peter Broisseau, "Boxing Rebranded Justin Trudeau as Leader: U of T Study," *U of T News*, June 4, 2015, www.utoronto.ca/news/ boxing-rebranded-justin-trudeau-leader-u-t-study.

SELECT BIBLIOGRAPHY

BOOKS

Andersen, Christopher. *Barbra: The Way She Is.* New York: HarperCollins, 2006.

Auger, Martin. "On the Brink of Civil War: The Canadian Government and the Suppression of the 1918 Quebec Easter Riots." *Canadian Historical Review* 89, no. 4 (2008): 503–40.

Bélanger, Réal, and Ramsay Cook. *Canada's Prime Ministers: Macdonald to Trudeau.* Toronto: University of Toronto Press, 2007.

Biggar, E.B. *Anecdotal Life of Sir John Macdonald.* Montreal: John Lovell and Son, 1891.

Bliss, Michael. *Right Honourable Men: The Descent of Canadian Politics from Macdonald to Mulroney.* Toronto: HarperCollins, 1994.

Borden, Robert Laird. *His Memoirs.* 2 vols. London: Macmillan, 1938.

Bosc, Marc, ed. *The Broadview Book of Canadian Parliamentary Anecdotes.* Peterborough, ON: Broadview Press, 1988.

Boyko, John. *Bennett: The Rebel Who Challenged and Changed a Nation.* Toronto: Key Porter Books, 2010.

Brown, Robert Craig. *Robert Laird: A Biography.* Vol. 2, *1914–1937.* Toronto: Macmillan, 1980.

Brunt, Stephen. *100 Grey Cups: This Is Our Game.* Toronto: McClelland and Stewart, 2012.

Bryson, Bill. *One Summer: America, 1927.* Toronto: Anchor Canada, 2014.

Campbell, Kim. *Time and Chance: The Political Memoirs of Canada's First Woman Prime Minister.* New York: Doubleday, 1996.

Chrétien, Jean. *My Years as Prime Minister.* Toronto: Knopf Canada, 2007.

———. *Straight From the Heart.* Toronto: Key Porter Books, 1995.

Cook, Tim. *Vimy: The Battle and the Legend.* Toronto: Allen Lane, 2017.

———. *Warlords: Borden, Mackenzie King, and Canada's World Wars.* Toronto: Allen Lane, 2012.

Cowley, Michael. *Sex and the Single Prime Minister: A Study in Liberal Lovemaking.* Toronto: Greywood, 1968.

Creighton, Donald. *John A. Macdonald: The Old Chieftain.* Toronto: Macmillan, 1955.

Davidson, Mark. "Preparing for the Bomb: The Development of Civil Defence Policy in Canada, 1948–1963." *Canadian Military History* 16, no. 3 (2012): 29–42.

Dempson, Peter. *Assignment Ottawa: Seventeen Years in the Press Gallery.* Toronto: General Publishing, 1968.

Diefenbaker, John. *One Canada: Memoirs of the Right Honourable John G. Diefenbaker: The Tumultuous Years, 1962–1967.* Toronto: Macmillan of Canada, 1977.

Donaldson, Gordon. *Eighteen Men: The Prime Ministers of Canada.* Toronto: Doubleday Canada, 1985.

Dummitt, Christopher. *Unbuttoned: A History of Mackenzie King's Secret Life.* Montreal and Kingston: McGill-Queen's University Press, 2017.

Dutil, Patrice. *Prime Ministerial Power in Canada: Its Origins Under Macdonald, Laurier, and Borden.* Vancouver: UBC Press, 2017.

Dutil, Patrice, and Roger Hall. *Macdonald at 200: New Reflections and Legacies.* Toronto: Dundurn Press, 2015.

Dutil, Patrice, and David Mackenzie. *Canada 1911: The Decisive*

Election That Shaped the Country. Toronto: Dundurn Press, 2011.

English, John. *Just Watch Me: The Life of Pierre Elliott Trudeau: 1968–2000.* Toronto: Vintage Canada, 2009.

———. *Shadow of Heaven: The Life of Lester B. Pearson.* Vol. 1, *1897–1948.* Toronto: Lester Orpen Dennys, 1989.

———. *The Worldly Years: The Life of Lester Pearson.* Vol. 2, *1949–1972.* Toronto: Vintage Canada, 1992.

Eyman, Scott. *Mary Pickford: From Here to Hollywood.* Toronto: HarperCollins, 1990.

Goldenberg, Eddie. *The Way It Works: Inside Ottawa.* Toronto: McClelland and Stewart, 2006.

Graham, Roger. *Arthur Meighen.* Vol. 2, *And Fortune Fled.* Toronto: Clarke, Irwin, 1963.

Granatstein, J.L., and Norman Hillmer. *Prime Ministers: Ranking Canada's Leaders.* Toronto: HarperCollins, 1999.

Gratton, Michel. *Still the Boss: A Candid Look at Brian Mulroney.* New Jersey: Prentice-Hall, 1990.

Grayson, L.M., and Michael Bliss. *The Wretched of Canada: Letters to R.B. Bennett, 1930–1935.* Toronto: University of Toronto Press, 1971.

Gwyn, Richard. *John A: The Man Who Made Us: The Life and Times of Sir John A. Macdonald.* Vol. 1, *1815–1867.* Toronto: Random House, 2009.

———. *Nation Maker: Sir John A. Macdonald; His Life, Our Times.* Vol. 2, *1867–1891.* Toronto: Random House, 2011.

Hutchison, Bruce. *Mr. Prime Minister: 1867–1964.* London: Longmans, 1965.

Ibbitson, John. *Stephen Harper.* Toronto: McClelland and Stewart, 2015.

Iglauer, Edith. *The Strangers Next Door.* Madeira Park, B.C.: Harbour Publishing, 1991.

Levine, Allan. *King: William Lyon Mackenzie King: A Life Guided By the Hand of Destiny.* Vancouver and Toronto: Douglas and MacIntyre, 2011.

———. *Scrum Wars: The Prime Ministers and the Media.* Toronto: Dundurn Press, 1993.

MacGregor, Roy. *Canoe Country: The Making of Canada.* Toronto: Random House, 2015.

Mallory, J.W. *The Structure of Canadian Government,* rev. ed. Toronto: Gage, 1984.

Martin, Lawrence. *Iron Man: The Defiant Reign of Jean Chrétien.* Toronto: Viking, 2003.

———. *The Presidents and the Prime Ministers.* Toronto: Doubleday Canada, 1982.

Martin, Paul. *Hell or Highwater: My Life In and Out of Politics.* Toronto: McClelland and Stewart, 2008.

McDonell, Fergus. *Capital City.* Video. Directed by Fergus McDonell. Montreal: National Film Board, 1957. www.nfb.ca /film/capital_city/

McIlroy, Thad, ed. *Personal Letters of a Public Man: The Family Letters of John G. Diefenbaker.* Toronto: Doubleday Canada, 1985.

McTeer, Maureen. *Residences: Homes of Canada's Leaders.* Toronto: Prentice-Hall. 1982.

Milnes, Arthur, ed. *Canada Always: The Defining Speeches of Sir Wilfrid Laurier.* Toronto: McClelland and Stewart, 2016.

Mulroney, Brian. *Memoirs: 1939–1993.* Toronto: McClelland and Stewart, 2007.

Neatby, H. Blair. *William Lyon Mackenzie King, 1924–1932: The Lonely Heights.* Toronto: University of Toronto Press, 1963.

———. *William Lyon Mackenzie King, 1932–1939: The Prism of Unity.* Toronto: University of Toronto Press, 1976.

Newman, Peter C. *Renegade In Power: The Diefenbaker Years.* Toronto: McClelland and Stewart, 1963.

———. *The Secret Mulroney Tapes: Unguarded Confessions of a Prime Minister.* Toronto: Random House, 2006.

O'Leary, Grattan. *Recollections of People, Press and Politics.* Toronto: Macmillan of Canada, 1977.

Oliver, Craig. *Oliver's Twist: The Life and Times of an Unapologetic Newshound.* Toronto: Viking, 2011.

O'Sullivan, Sean, and Rod McQueen. *Both My Houses: From Politics to Priesthood.* Toronto: Key Porter Books, 1986.

Pearson, Lester B. *Mike: The Memoirs of the Right Honourable Lester B. Pearson.* Vol. 1, *1897–1948.* Toronto: University of Toronto Press, 1972.

———. *Mike: The Memoirs of the Right Honourable Lester B. Pearson.* Vol. 3, *1957–1968.* Toronto: University of Toronto Press, 1976.

Phenix, Patricia. *Private Demons: The Tragic Personal Life of John A. Macdonald.* Toronto: McClelland and Stewart, 2006.

Pickersgill, J.W. *The Mackenzie King Record.* Vol. 1, *1939–1944.* Toronto: University of Toronto Press, 1960.

———. *My Years with Louis St. Laurent: A Political Memoir.* Toronto: University of Toronto Press, 1975.

Pickersgill, J.W., and D.F. Forster. *The Mackenzie King Record.* Vol. 2, *1944–1945.* Toronto: University of Toronto Press, 1968.

———. *The Mackenzie King Record.* Vol. 4, *1947–1948.* Toronto: University of Toronto Press, 1970.

Pope, Maurice, ed. *Public Servant: The Memoirs of Sir Joseph Pope.* Toronto: Oxford University Press, 1960.

Power, Chubby. *A Party Politician: The Memoirs of Chubby Power.* Toronto: Macmillan, 1966.

Pratte, André. *Extraordinary Canadians: Wilfrid Laurier.* Toronto: Penguin, 2011.

Punnett, R.M. *The Prime Minister in Canadian Government and Politics.* Toronto: Macmillan of Canada, 1977.

Radwanski, George. *Trudeau.* Toronto: Macmillan, 1978.

Ritchie, Charles. *Diplomatic Passport: More Undiplomatic Diaries, 1946–1962.* Toronto: Macmillan of Canada, 1981.

———. *Storm Signals: More Undiplomatic Diaries, 1962–1971.* Toronto: Macmillan of Canada, 1983.

Robertson, Gordon. *Memoirs of a Very Civil Servant: Mackenzie King to Pierre Trudeau.* Toronto: University of Toronto Press, 2000.

Robertson, Heather. *More Than A Rose: Prime Ministers, Wives, and Other Women.* Toronto: Seal Books, 1991.

Savoie, Donald J. *Governing from the Centre: The Concentration of Power in Canadian Politics.* Toronto: University of Toronto Press, 1999.

Schull, Joseph. *Laurier: The First Canadian.* Toronto: Macmillan of Canada, 1965.

Smith, Denis. *Rogue Tory: The Life and Legend of John G. Diefenbaker.* Toronto: Macfarlane Walter and Ross, 1995.

Southam, Nancy, ed. *Pierre: Colleagues and Friends Talk About the Trudeau They Knew*. Toronto: McClelland and Stewart, 2005.

Stacey, C.P. *A Very Double Life: The Private World of Mackenzie King*. Toronto: Macmillan of Canada, 1976.

Stevens, Geoffrey. *The Player: The Life and Times of Dalton Camp*. Toronto: Key Porter, 2003.

Thomson, Dale C. *Louis St. Laurent: Canadian*. Toronto: Macmillan of Canada, 1967.

Trudeau, Justin. *Common Ground*. Toronto: HarperCollins, 2014.

Trudeau, Margaret. *Beyond Reason*. New York: Paddington Press, 1979.

Trudeau, Pierre. *Memoirs*. Toronto: McClelland and Stewart, 1993.

Van Dusen, Thomas. *The Chief*. Toronto: McGraw Hill, 1968.

Walker, John, dir. *Playing a Dangerous Game*. Toronto: Bell Media, 2012.

Wells, Paul. *The Longer I'm Prime Minister: Stephen Harper and Canada, 2006–*. Toronto: Random House Canada, 2013.

Wright, Robert. *Trudeaumania: The Rise to Power of Pierre Elliott Trudeau*. Toronto: HarperCollins, 2016.

IMAGE CREDITS

176   Library and Archives Canada/C-029451

189   Courtesy the Rt. Hon. Brian Mulroney, Brian Mulroney
       Collection, Library and Archives Canada

200   Chuck Mitchell, Canadian Press

239   Courtesy the Rt. Hon. Brian Mulroney, Brian Mulroney
(top)   Collection, Library and Archives Canada

239   Courtesy the Rt. Hon. Brian Mulroney, Brian Mulroney
(bottom) Collection, Library and Archives Canada

240   Bruce Amos/Shutterstock.com

248   Library and Archives Canada C-024304

256   University of Saskatchewan, University Archives & Special
       Collections, John G. Diefenbaker fonds MG 411, JGD
       2024 XB

267   Library and Archives Canada/PA-117658

277   University of Saskatchewan, University Archives & Special
(top)   Collections, John G. Diefenbaker fonds MG 411, JGD
       2024 XB

277   University of Saskatchewan, University Archives & Special
(bottom) Collections, John G. Diefenbaker fonds MG 411, JGD
       2024 XB

INDEX

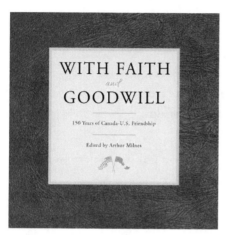

**With Faith and Goodwill:
150 Years of Canada-U.S.
Friendship**
Edited by Arthur Milnes

**For 150 years Canada and the United States
have shared something truly unique.**

The countries may have the world's longest unmilitarized border and the most prosperous free-trade arrangement in history, but what most distinguishes the Canada-U.S. relationship is neither geographic nor commercial — it's personal. Our special relationship is the product of shared values, countless cross-border connections, and generations of combined experience. Our two countries have grown into more than just friends. We are family.

On the occasion of Canada's 150th anniversary, *With Faith and Goodwill* celebrates the ups and downs, the vigour and variety of that family history by showcasing the words and images of prime ministers, presidents, and other dignitaries. From Sir John A. Macdonald to Donald J. Trump and including everyone from Tommy Douglas to Hillary Clinton, this beautifully designed collection of speeches and rarely seen photographs offers a privileged peek into the power politics of Canada-U.S. relations.

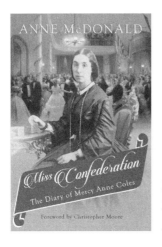

**Miss Confederation: The Diary of
Mercy Anne Coles**
Anne Mcdonald

History without the stiffness and polish time creates.

Canada's journey to Confederation kicked off with a bang — or rather,
a circus, a civil war (the American one), a small fortune's worth of
champagne, and a lot of making love — in the old-fashioned sense.
Miss Confederation offers a rare look back, through a woman's eyes, at
the men and events at the centre of this pivotal time in Canada's history.

Mercy Anne Coles, the daughter of P.E.I. delegate George Coles,
kept a diary of the social happenings and political manoeuvrings as
they affected her and her desires. A unique historical document, her
diary is now being published for the first time, offering a window into
the events that led to Canada's creation, from a point of view that has
long been neglected.

**Is Canada Even Real? How a
Nation Built on Hobos, Beavers,
Weirdos, and Hip Hop Convinced
the World to Beliebe**
J.C. Villamere

This quirky ode to a quirky land is a humorous nostalgia trip and
a fun Canadian history lesson couched in a hipster quiz book.

If you've ever wondered

- Why is the inuksuk more revered than Wheelchair Jimmy?
- Does the iconic beaver really represent us better than *The
  Littlest Hobo*?
- Is everyone going canoeing without me or is canoeing way
  less of a thing than it's made out to be?

then this book is for you.

Is Canada even real? It's a question that's being asked more and
more, thanks to our waterproof, see-through, supposedly maple-
scented currency and our improbably hot prime minister's assertion
that Santa lives here.

In the age of Google Maps and #factcheck, how could the
existence of Canada be questioned? And yet how could a nation that's
the home of toboggans, Drake, and KD exist in the same realm as,
say, Belgium or Niger?

Is Canada Even Real? examines the cultural factors behind the
twenty-first-century monolithic myth of Canada, a nation that is
lovable and real — if only in your imagination.

BOOK CREDITS

Acquiring Editor: Carrie Gleason
Editor: Dominic Farrell
Project Editor: Elena Radic
Proofreader: Ashley Hisson

Designer: Laura Boyle
E-Book Designer: Carmen Giraudy

Publicists: Kendra Martin and Michelle Melski

DUNDURN

Publisher: Kirk Howard
Acquisitions: Scott Fraser
Managing Editor: Kathryn Lane
Director of Design and Production: Jennifer Gallinger
Marketing Manager: Kate Condon-Moriarty
Sales Manager: Synora Van Drine

Editorial: Allison Hirst, Dominic Farrell, Jenny McWha, Rachel Spence, Elena Radic
Design and Production: Laura Boyle, Carmen Giraudy, Lorena Gonzalez Guillen
Marketing and Publicity: Andre Bovée-Begun, Michelle Melski, Kendra Martin

dundurn.com   dundurnpress
@dundurnpress   dundurnpress
dundurnpress   info@dundurn.com

FIND US ON NETGALLEY & GOODREADS TOO!

DUNDURN